# Therapeutics, evidence and decision-making

## Professor Sir Michael Rawlins

**Michael D Rawlins** MD FRCP FMedSci
Chairman, National Institute for Health and Clinical Excellence, London

Emeritus Professor, University of Newcastle

Honorary Professor, London School of Hygiene and Tropical Medicine

**Foreword by Professor Parveen J Kumar, President, Royal Society of Medicine**

**RSM**
*Books*

**HODDER**
ARNOLD
AN HACHETTE UK COMPANY

First published in Great Britain in 2011 by
Hodder Arnold, an imprint of Hodder Education, a division of Hachette UK
338 Euston Road, London NW1 3BH

**http://www.hodderarnold.com**

Hachette UK's policy is to use papers that are natural, renewable and recyclable products and made from wood grown in sustainable forests. The logging and manufacturing processes are expected to conform to the environmental regulations of the country of origin.

Whilst the advice and information in this book are believed to be true and accurate at the date of going to press, neither the author nor the publisher can accept any legal responsibility or liability for any errors or omissions that may be made. In particular, (but without limiting the generality of the preceding disclaimer) every effort has been made to check drug dosages; however it is still possible that errors have been missed. Furthermore, dosage schedules are constantly being revised and new side-effects recognized. For these reasons the reader is strongly urged to consult the drug companies' printed instructions, and their websites, before administering any of the drugs recommended in this book.

*British Library Cataloguing in Publication Data*
A catalogue record for this book is available from the British Library

*Library of Congress Cataloging-in-Publication Data*
A catalog record for this book is available from the Library of Congress

ISBN-13        978 1 853 15947 3

1 2 3 4 5 6 7 8 9 10

| | |
|---|---|
| Commissioning Editor: | Caroline Makepeace |
| Project Editor: | Francesca Naish |
| Production Controller: | Kate Harris |
| Cover Design: | Helen Townson |

Cover image © iQoncept – Fotolia.com

The logo of the Royal Society of Medicine is a registered trade mark, which it has licensed to Hodder Arnold.

Typeset in 10/12 pt Minion by Phoenix Photosetting, Chatham, Kent
Printed and bound in the UK by CPI Antony Rowe

What do you think about this book? Or any other Hodder Arnold title?
Please visit our website: www.hodderarnold.com

# Contents

For:

Jack and Daphne; Vicky, Lucy and Suzannah; Laura and Annabel; Emily, Lotte and Tilly; Alfie, Daisy and Sam; and she who must be obeyed.

# Foreword

We live in an uncertain climate of ever increasing healthcare costs. The demands on the health service inevitably increase with an ageing population, a changing pattern of disease and the ever rising expectations of patients and the public. Modern technology has provided huge benefits for both diagnosis and treatment and the advent of new drugs, with innovative modes of action, have all added to the costs of modern healthcare provision. Diseases are being redefined within the context of the advances made in genomic medicine and one can envisage a future of personalised medicine. But this will not be an answer for all diseases or, indeed, be any cheaper. In an attempt to try and control these costs, clinical and cost effective measures, based on carefully designed guidelines and a strong evidence base, have been rolled out across countries.

Nevertheless, much of the medicine that we practise as clinicians in our daily lives lacks a rigorous evidence base. The evidence that is available is often based on hierarchical levels with randomized control trials being the accepted, possibly undisputed, 'norm'. We are all mesmerised by statistics with a slavish following of the 'statistical value' but with little thought about how these values are derived and what they actually mean. So where does a book like 'Therapeutics, evidence and decision-making' fit in? Another stats book to read and digest unpalatable facts and figures? Or could it be an understandable rendition on what statistics can do and also where they can go wrong.

On reading the book, I was pleasantly surprised by the refreshing and questioning attitude of the author. The book teases out the nature of the evidence available with a critical analysis of probability, bias and confounding factors. It discusses the usual systematic reviews, randomized control trials, observational studies and qualitative research but with the critical approach of a coach reviewing his players on the football field; each one having its own advantages and disadvantages. The author peppers the book with actual examples from everyday medical challenges and also from peer reviewed papers, to support or refute the analyses. It is a sobering thought that, by changing certain assumptions made in a methodology, the conclusions of a paper could be changed or even be reversed. Clearly this is a matter of great concern, and can be extremely costly, if decisions are made to change conventional practice across a population based on these results.

There is no doubt that this book will be a continual source of information for all decision makers. It does not assume that all those who read it will be research workers well versed and steeped in statistics. It is very approachable and well written. It gives a background of the historical derivations of some of what we use in our daily analysis of facts and figures. There are useful hints for the individual, health economists, healthcare advisers as well as doctors working on the ground. This book is certainly a must for all students and doctors, as well as for those who have to make difficult decisions that will impact on the lives of patients and the finances for any health service.

Professor Parveen J Kumar
President, Royal Society of Medicine

# Preface

This book is intended to help decision-makers use, assess and appraise the evidence that underpins decisions about the use of therapeutic interventions. Decisions about the appropriate use of therapeutic interventions are made at various levels. Practising clinicians make decisions about when, and whether, particular treatments should be recommended for individual patients. Formulary committees in hospitals decide which products should be available at their institutions. Health insurers make the coverage decisions about the interventions that they offer to their clients. Clinical guideline developers make recommendations about the treatments they incorporate in their advice. And decisions are also made about the extent to which interventions can be considered to be safe and effective – as well as cost effective – for entire healthcare systems.

In reaching such decisions, whether for individuals or populations, decision-makers need to base their conclusions on the available evidence. The evidence base, however, is usually complex and multidimensional but rarely complete. Decision-makers must therefore assimilate, assess and appraise the available evidence; and then form a judgement about the appropriate use of the particular intervention. Some believe that such evidence can be placed in methodological 'hierarchies' but this approach is at best illusory and at worst dangerous. Although conventional randomized controlled tests have substantial merits, they also have defects. Other – observational – techniques can also be of value in the assessment of efficacy, effectiveness and safety.

This book is not intended for those who undertake primary or secondary research. Rather it is hoped that it will inform decision-makers about the nature of evidence, the strengths and weaknesses of the available approaches, and how these can be most effectively distilled for the purpose of reaching reliable conclusions. It aims to encourage decision makers to base their judgements about the use of therapeutic interventions on an informed appraisal of the totality of the evidence base. Is it reliable? Is it generalizable beyond the context of the environment in which the primary research has been conducted? Do the intervention's benefits outweigh its harms? Is it cost effective as well as clinically effective? Is it, indeed, 'fit-for-purpose'?

In writing this book I have assumed that readers possess only a modest knowledge of research methodology and especially of statistics and economics. Readers will, on reading the book, note that I am critical of some of the assumptions and prejudices that pervade the literature on the evaluation and appraisal of therapeutic interventions; and I have deliberately tried to expose those that irk me most.

Some readers, particularly those who depend on hierarchies of evidence, distrust judgements whether they are individual or collective. After a professional life-time spent in assessing, appraising, making and defending decisions about the use of therapeutic interventions – at all levels – I have little sympathy with this view. Good judgement, ultimately, is at the heart of decision-making in therapeutics.

Michael D. Rawlins
London

# Acknowledgements

This book was originally conceived while I was preparing to deliver the Harveian Oration, at the Royal College of Physicians of London, in October 2008[1]. I did not think, though, that the accompanying short monograph (which is traditionally given to the audience as they leave the lecture) did justice to a full discussion of nature of the evidence that should underpin the use of therapeutic interventions. This book is an attempt to remedy matters.

In preparing both my Harveian Oration, and now this book, many friends and colleagues have been extraordinarily generous with their time in reading, and commenting on, various drafts. Although I take sole responsibility for any and all the errors of omission and commission, my helpers include Jeffrey Aronson (University of Oxford), Deborah Ashby (Imperial College, London), David Barnett (University of Leicester), Kalipso Chalkidou (National Institute for Health and Clinical Excellence, London), Iain Chalmers (James Lind Library), Mary Docherty (National Institute for Health and Clinical Excellence, London), Stephen Evans (London School of Hygiene and Tropical Medicine, London), Robin Ferner (University of Birmingham), Alastair Fischer (National Institute for Health and Clinical Excellence, London), Sarah Garner (National Institute for Health and Clinical Excellence, London), Kent Johnson (University of Newcastle, New South Wales, Australia), David Jones (University of Leicester), Stephen Pearson (Institute for Clinical and Economic Review, Massachusetts General Hospital and Harvard Medical School, USA), Nancy Wexler (Columbia University and the Hereditary Disease Foundation, USA) and Alice Wexler (University of California, Los Angeles and the Hereditary Disease Foundation, USA).

I am also extremely grateful to the staff at Hodder including Caroline Makepeace and Francesca Naish, Aileen Castell at Naughton Project Management and Colette Holden who copyedited the text. They have been assiduous in their attention to detail; and generous with their patience.

Finally, this book would never have appeared without the help of the ground staff at London Heathrow, John F Kennedy and Los Angeles airports. I left my computer – containing various draft chapters – at each of them on different occasions. Undisciplined as I am, to backing up my work, I was weeks in arrears at saving hundreds of hours of writing. Thank you so much for your help in retrieving my laptop!

---

1   Rawlins MD. De Testimonio: *On the evidence for decisions about the use of therapeutic interventions*. London: Royal College of Physicians, 2008.

# SECTION 1
# Introduction

# CHAPTER 1.1
## THE NATURE OF EVIDENCE

*It is base to receive instructions from others' comments without examination of the objects themselves, especially as the book of nature lies so open and is so easy of consultation.* William Harvey[1]

William Harvey (1576–1657) was the first, and one of the greatest, clinician–scientists. He studied medicine at Cambridge and Padua before establishing a flourishing medical practice in London, where his patients included two kings (James I and Charles I) and the Lord Chancellor of England (Francis Bacon). At the same time he pursued a parallel career as a clinical scientist. Among many discoveries, he showed that the blood circulated around the body, rather than ebbing and flowing along the arteries and veins, and that the heart acted as a pump rather than a sucking device. In doing so he changed beliefs that had existed for more than 1000 years.

Harvey was thus one of a group of natural philosophers – as scientists were then called – who were no longer prepared to accept the authority of Aristotle, Plato and Galen as a reliable basis for understanding the natural world. But although seventeenth-century natural philosophers were united in their quest to examine Harvey's *The Book of Nature* for themselves, they were divided about how it should be done. Some such as Galileo Galilei (1564–1642), Robert Boyle (1627–91) and Robert Hooke (1635–1703) believed *The Book of Nature* could be understood only by experimentation. Others, including Francis Bacon (1561–1626), René Descartes (1596–1650) and Thomas Hobbs (1588–1679), considered observation to be the most appropriate approach.

This dispute about the nature of scientific method, and the proper basis for scientific inference, still persists.[2] The relative merits of deduction and induction, as the cornerstones of scientific reasoning, have been interminably discussed. The debate may seem arcane, but it has had very profound consequences; and none more so in assessing the nature of the evidence that should support the use of therapeutic interventions.

## Deduction and induction

Philosophers of science have, for several centuries, made a distinction between deductive and inductive forms of reasoning.

*Deductive inference* involves inferring, from a premise or a hypothesis, a prediction that can then be tested by empirical study. It has been described, in shorthand, as 'reasoning from the general to the particular'. An example of deductive reasoning, about the treatment of myxoedema, would be as follows. Myxoedema is caused by atrophy of the thyroid gland. This is the 'premise'. Since the thyroid gland normally produces thyroxine, the administration of thyroxine will cure myxoedema. This is the 'prediction'.

An extreme form of deductive inference – deductive falsification – was proposed by Karl Popper (1902–95). He suggested that the fundamental feature of science and of scientific inference was that a scientific premise should be falsifiable by experimentation or observation.[3] If a prediction arising from the premise was wrong, then the premise too was wrong. In Popper's view, science was concerned exclusively with postulating premises and undertaking studies that might falsify them. Popper's views were very influential during much of the twentieth century and have left a legacy – the 'null hypothesis' – that continues to dominate much thinking about the evidential nature of therapeutics.

*Inductive inference* is the reverse of deduction and involves constructing a premise on the basis of one or more observations. It has been described, again in shorthand, as involving 'reasoning from the particular to the general'. An example of inductive reasoning, about the teratogenicity of thalidomide, would be as follows. William McBride observed an unexpectedly large number of babies born with *phocomelia* in his obstetric practice.[4] He also noted that in all instances, the babies' mothers had received thalidomide during pregnancy. This observation represents the 'particular'. He concluded that thalidomide causes phocomelia if the fetus is exposed during the first trimester of pregnancy. This is the 'premise'.

The relative merits of deductive and inductive inference, as the basis for drawing scientific inferences, have been the subject of intense debate for centuries. The Scottish philosopher David Hume (1711–76) posed what has become known as 'the problem of induction'. He raised the fundamental question as to how we can ever be justified in making inferences that carry us beyond our past and present observations. Indeed, in expressing inductive reasoning in terms of probability, Hume stated: 'Probability is founded on the presumption of a resemblance betwixt those objects, of which we have had experience, and those, of which we have had none; and therefore 'tis impossible this presumption can arise from probability.'[5]

The claim that science is concerned solely with making deductive inferences is contradicted by disciplines that are generally regarded as 'scientific' but that are largely (if not entirely) based on induction. They include subjects such as astronomy, geology, evolutionary biology and meteorology as well as much of epidemiology and modern genetics. In genetics, for example, the universal acceptance that Down's syndrome is due to trisomy 21 is based entirely on induction.[6] Similarly, the premise that Huntington's disease is caused by an expanded repeat of the base pairs coding for glutamine in the first exon of a gene on the short arm of chromosome 4 is also based on inductive inference.[7] Most philosophers of science indeed now accept the role of pluralism in the development of scientific inferences. Nor does Popper's principle of deductive falsification dominate modern thought as it did in the past. Scientists seek not only to falsify hypotheses but also to devise experiments that will verify them; and in order to do so, they often resort to inductive reasoning.

# Hierarchies of evidence

The dispute about the nature of evidence, and misconceptions about the place of induction and deduction in drawing scientific inferences are partly responsible for the emergence of what are variously known as 'hierarchies', 'levels' and 'rules' of evidence in therapeutic research. A typical example is shown in Table 1.1.1.[8]

The first hierarchy of evidence was published in 1970.[9] Such hierarchies place randomized controlled trials at their summit, with various forms of observational studies in the foothills. They are used, as a form of shorthand, to provide some intimation of the strength of the underlying evidence. Many people in the evidence-based medicine and

**Table 1.1.1** Typical hierarchy of evidence

| Level | Criteria |
|-------|----------|
| 1++ | High-quality meta-analyses, systematic reviews of RCTs, or RCTs with a very low risk of bias |
| 1+ | Well-conducted meta-analyses, systematic reviews of RCTs, or RCTs with a low risk of bias |
| 1– | Meta-analyses, systematic reviews of RCTs, or RCTs with a high risk of bias |
| 2++ | High-quality systematic reviews of case–control studies or cohort studies; or high-quality case–control or cohort studies with a very low risk of confounding, bias or chance |
| 2+ | Well-conducted case–control or cohort studies with a low risk of confounding, bias or chance |
| 2– | Case–control or cohort studies with a high risk of confounding, bias or chance |
| 3 | Non-analytical studies (e.g. case reports, case studies) |
| 4 | Expert opinion |

RCT, randomized controlled trial.

health technology assessment movements have adopted them. They have also been used by many developers of clinical guidelines in order to grade their recommendations on the basis of the perceived strength of the evidence.

These hierarchies are of little value to decision-makers. A reasonable decision-maker, for example, will have as much confidence in the benefits of penicillin in the treatment of lobar pneumonia (level 2– or 2+ evidence in Table 1.1.1) as in the value of low-dose aspirin for the secondary prevention of myocardial infarction (level 1++ evidence in Table 1.1.1). As Austin Bradford Hill (1897–1991), the architect of the randomized trial, stated so cogently: 'Any belief that the controlled trial is the only way would mean not that the pendulum had swung too far but that it had come right off the hook'.[10]

Hierarchies cannot, moreover, accommodate evidence that relies on combining the results from randomized controlled trials with those based on observational studies. Such combinations of evidence, from a range of study designs, are a central feature of economic modelling (see Chapter 5.1), which lies at the heart of contemporary cost-effectiveness and cost–utility analysis. Economic modellers may integrate evidence from such disparate sources as randomized controlled trials, case registries, public health statistics, preference surveys and (at least in the USA) insurance claims.

The sheer number of these hierarchies, as well as the lack of consistency between them, demonstrates their unsatisfactory nature. A survey in 2002 identified 40 such grading systems and noted marked disparities between them:[11] a study two years later uncovered a further 20 grading systems.[12] The inconsistencies between hierarchies include the variable prominence given to meta-analyses, with some people positioning these above high-quality randomized controlled trials but with others ignoring them altogether.[13–16] There are also substantial inconsistencies between hierarchies in their positioning of observational studies. The hierarchy shown in Table 1.1.1 gives equal ranking to case–control and cohort studies. Other hierarchies give superiority to one or another form of observational study design. And none incorporates qualitative evidence except in relation to 'expert opinion', which is almost invariably given the lowliest place.

## Discussion

One of the most influential contributions to the philosophy of science, in the twentieth century, was made by Thomas Kuhn (1922–96). Based on his knowledge of the history of science,[17] he rejected the idea that there was some algorithm, based on the 'principles of scientific method', that scientists use in choosing between one theory over another.

Hierarchies of evidence are such algorithms. They attempt to replace judgement with an oversimplistic, pseudo-quantitative assessment of the quality of the available evidence. Moreover, they necessarily incorporate implicit judgements about what constitutes 'high-quality' or 'well-conducted' studies. Decision-makers have to incorporate explicit judgements in their appraisal of the evidence and in reaching their conclusions.[18] Such judgements relate to the extent to which each of the components of the evidence base is 'fit for purpose'.[19] Is it reliable? Does it appear to be generalizable? Do the intervention's benefits outweigh its *harms* and costs? Those who develop and use hierarchies of evidence are attempting to replace judgements with what, in their eyes, is a more reliable and robust approach to assessing evidence. Kuhn's analysis of how science develops shows they are wrong. It is scientific judgement – conditioned, of course, by the totality of the available evidence – that is at the heart of making decisions about the benefits, harms and costs of therapeutic interventions.

This book attempts to provide decision-makers with the tools to make judgements about the *utility* of therapeutic interventions. All the available approaches have their strengths and weaknesses, and decision-makers must, ultimately, make up their own minds.

# References

1.  Shapin S. *The Scientific Revolution*. Chicago, London: University of Chicago Press, 1996.
2.  Gower B. *Scientific Method: An Historical and Philosophical Introduction*. London, New York: Routledge, 1997.
3.  Popper K. *Conjectures and Refutations*. London: Routledge, 1963.
4.  McBride WG. Thalidomide and congenital abnormalities. *Lancet* 1961;**ii**:1358.
5.  Ayer AJ. *Hume: A Very Short Introduction*. Oxford: Oxford University Press, 2000.
6.  Osaka S. *Philosophy of Science: A Very Short Introduction*. Oxford: Oxford University Press, 2002.
7.  Huntington's Disease Collaborative Research Group. A novel gene containing a trinucleotide repeat that is expanded and unstable on Huntington's disease chromosomes. *Cell* 1993;**72**:971–83.
8.  Harbour R, Miller J. A new system for grading recommendations in evidence based guidelines. *BMJ* 2001;**323**:334–6.
9.  Canadian Task Force on the Periodic Health Examination. The periodic health examination. *Canadian Medical Association Journal* 1979;**121**:1193–154.
10. Hill AB. Heberden Oration 1965: reflections on the controlled trial. *Annals of Rheumatic Disease* 1966;**25**:107–13.
11. Agency for Healthcare Research and Quality. Systems to rate the strength of scientific evidence. AHRQ report no. 02-E015. Rockville, MD: Agency for Healthcare Research and Quality, 2002.
12. Schünemann HJ, Fretheim A, Oxman AD. Improving the use of research evidence in guideline development: 9. Grading evidence and recommendations. *Health Research Policy and Systems* 2006;**4**:21.
13. US Preventive Services Task Force. *The Guide to Clinical Preventive Services*, 2nd edn. Washington, DC: US Preventive Services Task Force, 1996.
14. Guyatt GH, Haynes RB, Jaeschke RZ, *et al*. Users' guides to the medical literature: XXV. Evidence-based medicine: principles for applying the users' guides to patient care. *Journal of the American Medical Association* 2000; **284**:1290–96.

15. Ebell MH, Siwek J, Weiss BD, *et al*. A strength of recommendation taxonomy (SORT): a patient-centered approach to grading evidence in the medical literature. *Journal of the American Board of Family Practitioners* 2004;**17**:59–67.
16. GRADE Working Group. Grading quality of evidence and strength of recommendations. *BMJ* 2004;**328**:1482–90.
17. Kuhn TS. *The Structure of Scientific Revolutions*, 3rd edn. Chicago, London: University of Chicago Press, 1996.
18. Rawlins MD, Culyer AJ. National Institute for Clinical Excellence and its value judgments. *BMJ* 2004;**329**:224–7.
19. Rawlins MD. *De Testimonio: On the Evidence for Decisions about the Use of Therapeutic Interventions*. London: Royal College of Physicians, 2008.

# CHAPTER 1.2
## PROBABILITY

*Like fire, the χ² test is an excellent servant and a bad master.* Austin Bradford Hill[1]

Probability theory plays an important role in interpreting the results of studies of the effects of interventions. Despite the long usage of the term 'probability' it is remarkable that there is still no universally agreed definition. In everyday language, however, the term is used to denote the chance or likelihood of a particular event occurring at some future date.

## Background

Interest in the theory of probability dates back to the seventeenth century. Gamblers seeking better ways to win at games of chance aroused the interest of some of the greatest mathematicians, such as Pierre Fermat (1601–65) and Blaise Pascal (1623–62). Pierre-Simon Laplace (1749–1827) appears to have been the first to advocate the use of probability theory in therapeutic research, even though nothing came of his suggestion for 120 years:[2]

> To determine the best of treatments used in the cure of a disease it suffices to test each of them on an equal number of patients, while keeping all circumstances perfectly comparable. The superiority of the most advantageous treatment will become increasingly manifest as the number increases; and the calculus will determine the probability corresponding to the observed advantage.

The notion of hypothesis testing was introduced by Ronald Fisher (1890–1962). He proposed that, at the outset of a trial, the hypothesis under investigation should be one of no difference between treatments. This, the null hypothesis, is redolent of the deductive falsificationist approach to scientific inference introduced by Karl Popper (see Chapter 1.1). Fisher proposed that the null hypothesis should be tested 'by estimating the probability of observing a result as extreme or more extreme than the one observed given that the null hypothesis is true'. Fisher's interpretation of an extreme *P*-value was that either the null hypothesis was false or a very rare event had occurred.

Fisher's ideas were developed jointly by the émigré Polish mathematician Jerzy Neyman (1894–1981) and Egon Pearson (1895–1980). They added two additional elements. First, if the null hypothesis is rejected, then the alternative hypothesis should be accepted and one treatment should be regarded as superior to the other. Second, they introduced the notion of *errors of the first kind* involving rejection of the null hypothesis when it is true (known as a *type I error*); and *errors of the second kind* where the null hypothesis is accepted when it is false (known as a *type II error*). These are, respectively, false negative and false positive results, but the terminology of type I and type II errors is entrenched in the statistical literature.

When Neyman and Pearson published their notions of an alternative hypothesis, and of type I and II errors, they were hotly (and viciously) disputed by Fisher. The differences of opinion, though, were due more to a personality clash (and Ronald Fisher could be notoriously caustic) than to immutable disagreements about probability. In reality, most clinical trials today are designed from a Neyman–Pearson standpoint but analysed using a Fisherian approach.[3]

The Fisherian Neyman–Pearson approach to hypothesis testing is concerned with the probability that a particular set of data (such as the results of a clinical trial) is improbable given that the null hypothesis is true. This is often known as 'the frequentist approach'. There is, however, a different – inverse – approach involving the probability of a particular hypothesis or premise given a specific set of data. It is the inductive, as opposed to the deductive, approach to scientific inference (see Chapter 1.1).

This inverse approach to probability is used in the formulation of Bayes' theorem. Thomas Bayes (1701–61) was a Nonconformist minister in Tunbridge Wells, Kent, whose essay on probability was not published until after his death. In its simplest expression, Bayes' theorem relates the probabilities with what is known or can be assumed before (a priori) an experiment is undertaken, to the probabilities recalculated after (a posteriori) the experiment. The link between the prior and posterior probabilities is the result of the experiment itself. The posterior probability is an estimate of the probability of a hypothesis conditional on the observed data but taking account of what was already known (the prior) before the experiment was performed. The application of Bayesian statistics to the design and analysis of clinical trials is discussed more fully in Chapter 2.2.

## Probabilities and odds

In analysing the results of studies of the *effectiveness* of interventions, investigators sometimes report the *odds*. Odds were introduced and are still used for gambling. When a six-sided die is thrown, the probability of throwing one particular number – say, a six – is 1/6 ($P = 0.167$). The probability of *not* throwing a number – say, a one – is 5/6 ($P = 0.833$). The odds of throwing a one, in gambling parlance, is therefore expressed as 'five to one against', thus indicating that there are five failures for every one success. (For the inquisitive, 'five to one on' indicates five successes to one failure.) In formal terms, the relation between probability of success – $P$(success) – and odds on success is:

$$\text{Odds (success)} = \frac{P(\text{success})}{1 - P(\text{success})} = \frac{P(\text{success})}{P(\text{failure})}$$

For those unfamiliar with gambling, odds are not intuitively obvious in their interpretation. In statistics, however, odds – and particularly the ratio between two odds (the *odds ratio*) – have special properties that are important in various analyses, especially after logarithmic transformation (log-odds ratios). Odds ratios are discussed more fully in Chapter 1.4.

## Types of probability

As described earlier in this chapter there are two, very different, approaches to probability – frequentist and subjective.

### Frequentist probability
If a die is tossed 600 times, a one (on average) ought to turn up 100 times; a two (on average) should also turn up 100 times, a three (on average) 100 times, and so on. The probability that, on average, each number will be rolled is $P = 0.167$. After just six

throws, however, the play of chance makes it very unlikely (the probability is 0.015) that each of the six numbers will appear just once. If the die is rolled 6000 times or 60 000 times, it becomes ever more likely that the empirical probability, for each number on the die, will approach 0.167. A frequentist analysis thus estimates the proportion of times a particular event will occur in a long-running series of repeated – and identical – situations; and it forms the basis for the Fisherian Neyman–Pearson approach to empirical probability.

By convention the probability required to avoid rejecting the null hypothesis when it is true (a type I error) – often abbreviated to $\alpha$ – is when the $P$-value is less than 0.05. The probability of accepting the null hypothesis when it is false – often abbreviated to $\beta$ – is usually set at 0.20 (sometimes 0.1). The term 'extreme' – in relation to the circumstances when the null hypothesis can be rejected – is therefore defined mathematically as data with a probability of less than 1 in 20 when the null hypothesis is true. Although this might appear to be a useful rule of thumb, it is fraught with difficulties.

The $P$-value that separates a significant from a non-significant finding is often said to be arbitrary but it is essentially pragmatic. If the critical $P$-value for $\alpha$ were set at 0.1 or 0.2, there would be a greater likelihood, in a clinical trial, of obtaining a false positive result. If the critical $P$-value for $\beta$ were set at 0.95 rather than 0.80, the number of participants would need to be increased by a factor of 1.7 (e.g. from 1000 to 1700).

This pragmatic approach to setting $P$-values is neatly exemplified by the significance levels used by the US Food and Drug Administration (FDA) in interpreting the results of long-term animal carcinogenicity studies. Because a threshold of $P < 0.05$ for $\alpha$ would result in too many false positives, the FDA has adopted rules (sometimes referred to as the 'Fairweather rules') that use $P < 0.005$ as the significance level for common tumours and $P < 0.025$ for rarer ones. Even then there is an overall false positive rate of about 10 per cent.[4] This approach, in the context of a frequentist analysis, is reasonable but emphasizes how $P$-values are malleable and that they can be, and are, changed to suit particular circumstances.

Just because the results of a clinical trial provide a $P$-value of less than 0.05, it does not necessarily mean that one intervention is more effective than the other. It may merely mean – paraphrasing Fisher – that a very rare event has occurred due to the play of chance. Similarly, just because $P > 0.05$, it does not mean that the intervention is ineffective.

Table 1.2.1 demonstrates the frailty of an overreliance on $P$-values. In this hypothetical study,[5] the participants received both treatment A and treatment B and were asked to express their preference. The trial could, for example, be a comparison of two analgesics in the treatment of people with osteoarthritis.

**Table 1.2.1** Results of four hypothetical studies comparing patients' preferences for two treatments (A and B)[5]

| Study | Number of patients | Patients preferring treatment A to treatment B | Two-sided $P$-value |
|---|---|---|---|
| I | 20 | 15 : 5 | 0.041 |
| II | 200 | 115 : 86 | 0.041 |
| III | 2000 | 1046 : 954 | 0.041 |
| IV | 2 000 000 | 1 001 445 : 998 555 | 0.041 |

A decision-maker would be entitled to reject the results of Study I on the grounds that although the results are interesting, the number of participants ($n = 20$) is too small to allow reliable conclusions to be drawn. On the other hand, a decision-maker would be equally entitled to conclude from the results of Study IV that the two treatments are equivalent in their *effectiveness*. Yet both studies yield a P-value of 0.041.

The P-value provides no indication of the clinical importance of an observed difference. A large trial may give rise to a small P-value (as in Study IV in Table 1.2.1) but with such a small effect size that it is unlikely to have any impact on clinical practice or patient wellbeing. A decision-maker would therefore be entitled to ignore the evidence unless, in an active comparator trial, the intervention was less harmful or less costly.

Reports of randomized controlled trials and observational studies often include a large number of analyses, each with their own test of statistical significance. These may be difficult to interpret because if enough tests are done, something significant is likely to turn up with a P-value less than 0.05 and give rise to false positive conclusions. This is known as the problem of *multiplicity*.

If $d$ is the number of independent comparisons, then the chance that one will be found to be significant (at a P-value of < 0.05) is equivalent to 1 minus the probability that $d$ subsets conform to the null hypothesis. That is:

$$1 - (1 - 0.05)^d$$

Where ten separate assumptions are tested, the probability that one of them will be statistically significant, with a P-value of 0.05, is 40 per cent. This increases to 64 per cent if 20 analyses are undertaken; and to 87 per cent if 40 are performed. The problem of multiplicity in randomized controlled trials is very real and stirs heated debate amongst statisticians and epidemiologists.

Various approaches to resolving the problem of multiplicity have been advocated. Most of these involve reducing the P-value as the number of tests is increased. The most well known is the Bonferroni correction, which divides the conventional P-value (usually 0.05) by the number of additional analyses. Thus, if the original P-value is 0.05, and five subanalyses are undertaken, the significant P-value becomes 0.01 (i.e. 0.05/5). The Bonferroni correction, however, is regarded by some as too conservative, with, as a consequence, the risk of false negative findings.[6] The issues are discussed further in Chapters 2.2, 2.3 and 2.4.

Rather than adherence to hypothesis testing, and the difficulties associated with P-values, the use of confidence intervals has become increasingly common.[7] Confidence intervals provide a range of values around the mean that are plausible values for the true effect size in the population studied. If, for example, the same trial were to be repeated on 20 occasions, and the 95 per cent confidence interval effect size were calculated for each, then on average 19 out of 20 would contain the true effect size; one in 20 (five per cent) would not.

Where the confidence intervals of two populations are separate, as might be the case in the analysis of the results of a randomized controlled trial, a P-value for the difference in means will be less than 0.05. Where the confidence intervals for the two populations overlap substantially, the P-value for the difference in means will fail to reach statistical significance. A modest overlap may, however, be consistent with the difference between means being significant at the five per cent level. The great value for decision-makers, with the reporting of means and their associated confidence intervals, is that they provide a far better indication of the effect size of an intervention together with some notion of the range of possible (likely) variation.

## Subjective probability

As discussed earlier, the frequentist approach to probability is concerned with the extent to which some particular data refute a specific hypothesis (often the null hypothesis). Subjective probability – sometimes described as Bayesian or inverse probability – is the reverse. It is the likelihood of a hypothesis, given specific data, and is allied to the inductive approach to scientific inference (see Chapter 1.1).

Subjective probability underpins many, if not most, decisions made in both private and public life. They include mundane decisions based on judgements about distance and speed, and about when (and whether) to cross the street in the face of oncoming traffic. They also include decisions by the UK's Monitory Policy Committee about when (and whether) to raise or lower interest rates. The subjective view of probability is not a recent innovation: Jacob Bernoulli (1645–1705) introduced the notion that 'probability is uncertain and varies with individuals' knowledge'.[8]

Subjective probabilities are often depicted as probability density curves (see Figure 1.2.1). In this hypothetical example, the horizontal axis is the effect size shown as the percentage reduction in mortality (on a logarithmic scale) compared with, say, placebo. The vertical axis represents the probability of the reduction in mortality. The area under the probability distribution curve is 1 because it covers the entire range of possible probabilities. The curve shows the probabilities for all values of the reduction in mortality compared. As can be seen, the probability curve is at a maximum when the reduction in mortality is around 25 per cent, and it falls away to zero when the reduction in mortality is either –55 per cent or +10 per cent. This figure also shows the 95 per cent credible intervals that describe the 95 per cent boundaries of the probability density curve.

Probability curves allow a decision-maker to decide – without reference to any P-value – whether the data appear to be sufficiently convincing to recommend the adoption of a particular intervention. In Figure 1.2.1 a decision-maker, on this evidence, might conclude that patients would be likely to be better off using rather than not using the intervention. Probability distributions can also be constructed with data from a frequentist analysis but are more commonly used in reporting the results of Bayesian ones (see Chapter 2.1).

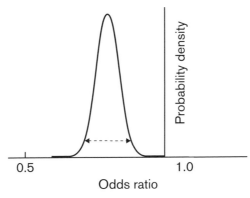

**Figure 1.2.1** Typical probability distribution curve. The dotted horizontal line shows the 95 per cent credible interval.

Therapeutics, evidence and decision-making

# Discussion

Much has been written about the inherent weaknesses of conventional approaches to the use – and misuse – of probability, as expressed by *P*-values, in the analysis of the evidence underpinning the acceptance and rejection of therapeutic interventions. Yet *P*-values retain a powerful hold on decision-makers. The comfortable, but illusory, security of a clear definition of what constitutes an extreme or rare event, based on a *P*-value, appears to provide an intellectual crutch, and many people use *P*-values in a binary way to distinguish truth from falsehood. The use of mean differences, with estimates of their confidence intervals, provides decision-makers with a better frame of reference; but problems remain. Of these, the most daunting is the problem of multiplicity, which is discussed at length in various chapters in Section 2.

A growing number of statisticians believe that the solution to many of the difficulties inherent in the frequentist approach to the design, analysis and interpretation of clinical trials is the greater use of Bayesian statistics.[9,10] These are used widely outside medicine. Alan Turing and his cryptographic colleagues at Bletchley Park used Bayesian statistical methods to help decode signals from German and Japanese submarines during the Second World War. Spam filters in email systems use Bayesian probabilities to try to distinguish genuine from unwanted messages; and bookmakers have been instinctive Bayesians for generations. (And bookmakers expect to make a ten per cent return on their turnover at each race meeting.) The use of Bayesian statistics in the design and analysis of randomized controlled trials is discussed further in Chapter 2.1.

In using or interpreting results expressed in terms of probabilities, decision-makers should take the following issues into account when forming their judgements and reaching conclusions:

- *P*-values should not be ignored, but decisions on evidence using a frequentist approach should be based on mean differences and their confidence intervals.
- Where the *P*-value is less than 0.05, it should not necessarily be concluded that the null hypothesis can be rejected.
- Where the *P*-value is greater than 0.05, it should not necessarily be concluded that the alternative hypothesis can be rejected. Indeed, there may be occasions when the alternative hypothesis can be accepted even in the absence of conventional levels of statistical significance. Figure 1.2.1 is an example of an instance when a decision-maker might reasonably conclude that – on average – patients are likely to be better off using an intervention than not using it.
- Encourage those responsible for developing and analysing the evidence to display results more often as probability densities.
- Look kindly, though not uncritically, on Bayesian analyses.

Most importantly, decision-makers should always avoid the trap of interpreting frequentist *P*-values as distinguishing proof, from falsification, of the null hypothesis.

# References

1. Hill AB. The environment and disease: association or causation? *Proceedings of the Royal Society of Medicine* 1965;**58**:295–300.
2. Hill G, Forbes W, Kozak J, MacNeill IM. Likelihood and clinical trials. *Journal of Clinical Epidemiology* 2000;**53**:223–7.

3. Sen S. *Statistical Issues in Drug Development.* Chichester: John Wiley & Sons, 1997.

4. Lin KK, Rahman MA. Overall false positive rates in tests for linear trend in tumor incidence in animal carcinogenicity studies of new drugs. *Journal of Biopharmaceutical Statistics* 1998;**8**:1–15, discussion 17–22.

5. Freeman P. The role of *p*-values in analysing trial results. *Statistics in Medicine* 1993;**12**:1443–52.

6. Perneger TV. What's wrong with the Bonferroni adjustments. *BMJ* 1998;**316**:1236–8.

7. Gardner MJ, Altman DG. Confidence intervals rather than *P* values: estimation rather than hypothesis testing. *BMJ* 1986;**292**:746–50.

8. Fienberg S. A brief history of statistics in three and one-half chapters: a review essay. *Statistical Science* 1992;**7**:208–25.

9. Ashby D. Bayesian statistics in medicine: a 25 year review. *Statistics in Medicine* 2006;**25**:3589–363.

10. Spiegelhalter DJ, Myles JP, Jones DR, Abrams KR. Bayesian methods in health technology assessment: a review. *Health Technology Assessment* 2000;**4**:1–130.

# CLINICAL ENDPOINTS OF BENEFITS AND HARMS

Clinical outcomes (clinical endpoints) fall into two broad types. *Final outcomes* are those that represent the ultimate goal of treatment; for example, survival or death from a potentially fatal condition, and success or failure in the relief of a symptom such as pain. *Intermediate outcomes* are *biomarkers* that reflect some biological action of an intervention but that may not necessarily reflect a therapeutic effect. Biomarkers that are known to predict final outcomes are *surrogate outcomes* (or surrogate markers).

## Final outcomes

Final (or ultimate) outcomes may be dichotomous or continuous.

### Dichotomous outcome measures

Dichotomous (binary) outcomes are measures for which there are only two possible alternatives. Examples include alive versus dead, and recovered versus not recovered. Dichotomous outcomes such as these are commonly used because of their relative simplicity for data collection, their veracity (leaving aside the potential for diagnostic *bias*, which is discussed in Chapter 1.5), and their advantages in relation to statistical analysis. Dichotomous outcomes are also widely used in assessing *harms* and benefits.

### ■ Composite outcomes

Dichotomous outcomes for benefits are sometimes reported as composite measures that combine two or more binary outcomes. They have been especially common in trials of cardiovascular agents. For example, in investigating the benefits of an antihypertensive agent on coronary artery disease, the outcome may be the sum of people dying from acute myocardial infarction and people surviving an acute infarction during the course of the study. More complicated composite outcomes might include summating all those participants experiencing 'any cardiovascular event'; this could include both death and survival from acute myocardial infarction and death and survival from thrombotic stroke.

There are two advantages to using composite outcomes. First, in instances such as the prevention of myocardial infarction and stroke with antihypertensive agents, there is some logic to summating people who have events related directly to the overall anticipated benefits of treatment. Second, the use of a composite outcome may substantially reduce the size, duration and cost of a study because of the increase in the total number of events and the associated increase in statistical power.

There has, however, been some disagreement over the value of composite outcomes. Despite their attractions, there are sometimes difficulties in the interpretation of the findings. Ferreira-Gonzalez and colleagues undertook a systematic review of randomized controlled trials published during 2002 and 2003 that used composite endpoints of interventions to treat cardiovascular disease.[1] They claimed that in almost half of these studies the component endpoints were of variable importance to patients; and that endpoints of least importance to patients typically contributed most of the events. A more recent review made similar criticisms of the choice of the individual endpoints that were used to make up composite endpoints.[2]

The idea that all the components of a composite endpoint should, however, be of similar important has been challenged.[3] Mortality is not the only *adverse event* worth considering as the endpoint in a clinical trial. In heart failure trials, for instance, it is common for the primary endpoint to combine mortality rates together with admission rates to hospital with clinical deterioration. In such circumstances, merely using mortality as the outcome measure would consign patients who had deteriorated and had been admitted to hospital to the same group as patients who remained clinically stable and minimally symptomatic.[4]

## Continuous outcome measures

Continuous outcome measures may be ordinal or interval. Rating scales, which tend to incorporate a number of individual items, are considered separately. All of these approaches can be used to detect both harms and benefits.

### ■ Ordinal outcomes

These use labels for response categories such as – in the assessment of an analgesic – 'no pain', 'mild pain', 'moderate pain' or 'severe pain'. Participants are invited to respond at appropriate intervals by describing their experience in this format.

The technique is simple but is associated with two difficulties.[5] First, participants will almost inevitably differ in what they regard as 'mild', 'moderate' or 'severe' because people use adjectives in different ways. This is, perhaps, less important in crossover studies than in studies with parallel group designs because in the former type of design there is an assumption that the participants' responses will be consistent on each occasion. The second difficulty is that the intervals between each category hold no intrinsic numerical meaning. The increment in the severity of pain between 'moderate' and 'severe' is not necessarily the same as the increment between 'mild' and 'moderate'.

The inability to necessarily assume linearity in the use and interpretation of ordinal measures thus poses particular difficulties when the adjectives are translated into numerical values. In the analgesic example, 'no pain' might equal 0, 'mild pain' 1, 'moderate pain' 2, and 'severe pain' 3. Nevertheless, pragmatists claim that the errors are relatively minor.[5]

### ■ Interval outcomes

These are numerical measures so that a unit change in the scale value represents a constant change across its range. Weight loss with an intervention to treat obesity, reduction in blood pressure with an antihypertensive agent, and a child's gain in height with growth hormone are typical examples. With such interval outcomes, changes in scores, with their means and confidence intervals, are usually relatively straightforward to interpret.

### ■ Rating scales

Rating scales have been developed, particularly in neurology and psychiatry, to assess the severity of disease and the response to therapeutic interventions. Such rating scales usually include a number of individual items and tend to incorporate dichotomous, ordinal and interval scales. Though not invariably the case, these may then be combined to yield a single response measure. Although some rating scales rely on participants' responses to questions, many also include scoring investigators' assessments. These may be subjective (such as an investigator's assessment of a participant's mood); but they may also be semi-objective (such as an investigator's judgements about the degree of muscle strength or the normality of gait).

In evaluating trials where rating scales make a major contribution to the reported outcomes, decision-makers have to satisfy themselves that they are appropriate for the purpose.[6,7] The key elements comprise:

- validity (i.e. it measures what it is intended to measure);
- reliability (i.e. it yields reproducible and consistent results);
- sensitivity (i.e. it is capable of detecting differences between groups);
- responsiveness (i.e. it responds to relevant changes in the participants' condition).

The development and evaluation of rating scales is a sophisticated and complex endeavour.[5] Their robustness is important both to enhance the quality of the report and to assist in comparisons with similar studies.[8] In a review of 149 randomized controlled trials of the treatment of schizophrenia,[9] the authors noted that 196 different rating scales had been used. Moreover, the authors noted that reports using unpublished scales were almost twice as likely to claim treatment superiority than those using published scales.

Measures of *health-related quality of life* are a special form of rating scale that attempt to capture the overall impact of interventions on patients' lives. The concept usually includes:

- physical functioning (i.e. ability to carry out activities of daily living such as self-care and mobility);
- psychological functioning (i.e. emotional and mental wellbeing);
- social functioning (i.e. relationships with others and the ability to take part in social activities);
- perceptions of health status;
- presence of pain;
- overall satisfaction with life.

Two broad varieties of health-related quality-of-life instrument are used. Some assess the overall health-related quality of life in a specific condition such as a particular form of malignant disease. Others, such as the EuroQol-5D (EQ-5D) and the short-form health survey (SF-36), try to assess generic health-related quality of life so that the degree of improvement for one intervention for one condition can be compared with other interventions for other conditions. Generic health-related quality-of-life measures are of special relevance in the economic evaluation of interventions and are discussed in greater detail in Chapter 5.2.

# Intermediate outcomes

Ideally, the outcomes (or endpoints) assessed in a clinical trial will provide direct evidence of the benefits and harms of an intervention that will be relevant to patients in the future. It may, however, take months or even years for such ultimate outcomes to become apparent. Consequently there is particular interest in using intermediate – shorter-term – outcomes on which to adduce evidence of the benefits and harms of an intervention. The use of biomarkers and surrogate outcomes in the application of interventions to treat malignant disease is considered separately.

## Biomarkers

The term 'biomarker' has been used in a variety of contexts and with a multiplicity of meanings. In this discussion the term is restricted to those parameters that are used to assess whether an intervention appears to possess biological activity. Whether a biomarker is a harbinger of therapeutic benefit (or harm) may be less clear. In general, it is a parameter that can be used to characterize a disease, measure its progress or monitor the effects of treatment. The parameter can be chemical, physical or biological; or it may be one based on imaging techniques such as X-rays, ultrasonography or magnetic resonance imaging.

Biomarkers, even if not established as valid surrogate outcomes, play an important role in the development of new pharmaceutical products. They are important in establishing during phase 1 studies whether a new intervention's pharmacological properties are as apparent in humans as they were in animals. They are also used widely during early phase 2 studies to identify appropriate dose schedules in respect of both putative benefits and harms.

## Surrogate outcomes

Surrogate outcomes are biomarkers that are reliable substitutes for a clinically relevant final endpoint that measures directly how a patient feels, functions or survives. Justification for the use of a surrogate outcome therefore requires that changes predict the effect of an intervention on the final clinical outcome. Typical surrogate outcomes include:

- pharmacokinetic studies to compare one formulation of a product with another (such as a generic product with its branded counterpart);
- routine liver function tests to assess whether a product is showing hepatotoxicity;
- immunological responses (such as anti-haemagglutinin titres) to influenza vaccines;
- reduction in the viral load (in plasma) with anti-human immunodeficiency virus (HIV) products;
- reduction in blood pressure or low-density lipoprotein (LDL) cholesterol in the prevention of coronary artery disease.

Apart from these special instances, surrogate outcomes are not widely accepted. In particular, the validation of whether a biomarker is indeed a surrogate outcome can be established only once it has been shown to be predictive of the final outcome. In the examples shown above, such relationships have been demonstrated formally, although controversy exists as to the extent to which quantitative comparisons can be made. For example, in the case of statins, there is still controversy. Do the differences between them in reducing LDL-cholesterol levels reflect differences in their ability to reduce the *incidence* of coronary artery disease?

## Endpoints in malignant disease

The use of biomarkers and presumed (or assumed) surrogate outcomes play an important – albeit controversial – role in the development of interventions used to treat malignant disease. Four outcome measures have been particularly widely used:[10]

- overall survival;
- objective response rates;
- progression-free survival;
- disease-free survival.

## ■ Overall survival

Overall survival is the time between randomization and death from any cause.[11] It is regarded as the most dependable endpoint in cancer trials because of the relative freedom from bias and because of its value in balancing benefits and harms. Studies with overall survival as the endpoint, however, usually require larger numbers of participants and longer periods of follow-up compared with studies using objective response rates or progression-free survival as endpoints. As an endpoint the use of overall survival can be impossibly compromised if participants are transferred to alternative treatments when their tumours progress. This may, of course, be in the best interests of the participants; but attributing an increase in longevity to the investigational treatment is fraught with difficulty.

## ■ Objective response rates

Evidence of a positive response in patients with advanced malignancies has been inferred using a variety of methods. These include regression of the size of solid tumours as shown by the use of imaging techniques, reductions in leucocyte counts in leukaemias, and falls in plasma levels of carcinoembryonic antigen in colorectal cancer. Indeed, in the past such outcomes were often accepted by drug regulatory agencies as appropriate evidence of *efficacy*.[10]

Objective response rates can provide some indication that a new agent may have therapeutic activity and can be used in non-randomized (single-arm) studies. However, there is only a weak relationship with improved survival rates or patients' quality of life.[11] Where objective response rates are around 10–20 per cent, it is unlikely that significant increases in survival will be observed. Where objective response rates are of the order of 80–90 per cent, it is likely (in the absence of substantial harms) that the product will produce positive clinical outcomes. Even then, no reliable quantitative estimates of an increase in survival can be reliably made. Changes in observed response rates can be useful in a drug's early clinical development, but decision-makers should beware of drawing conclusions based on such findings alone.

## ■ Progression-free survival

Progression-free survival is the time between randomization and evidence of either objective tumour progression or death. A very similar measure, time to progression, censors deaths that occur before progression. The use of both progression-free survival and time to progression is based on the presumption that such an increase in such time intervals will predict either an increase in overall survival or an enhanced quality of life, or both. There is evidence for the most common solid tumours (non-small-cell lung, colorectal and breast) that progression-free survival correlates positively with increased overall survival. Whether an increase in progression-free survival is followed by an increase in post-progression-free survival remains unclear.

## ■ Disease-free survival

Disease-free survival is the time from randomization to tumour recurrence or death from any cause. It is used in trials of adjuvant therapy when survival is expected to be long and thus rendering overall survival an impractical endpoint. Disease-free survival may provide direct evidence for clinical benefit in some disease settings, depending on the magnitude of the effect and the balance between the benefits and harms of treatment. In patients with colorectal cancer undergoing adjuvant chemotherapy, there is evidence that disease-free survival after 3 years' follow-up predicts overall survival at five years.[12]

# Discussion

Confidence in the reliability and relevance of the outcomes used in studies of the *effectiveness* of interventions is obviously a critical element for decision-makers. In assessing both benefits and harms, decision-makers will inevitably prefer to base their conclusions on final, rather than intermediate, outcomes. In reality, however, intermediate outcomes are sometimes – for very practical reasons – the only available measures.

Dichotomous final outcomes are, usually, relatively simple to interpret. Difficulties can arise, however, in the assessment of composite endpoints. Interpreting of the results of such studies requires care, but decision-makers should not dismiss them out of hand. The results of studies with composite endpoints can be interpreted most confidently when the individual components are of similar relevance and importance to patients, and where there are similar *relative risk* reductions across each. Where the component endpoints are of variable importance to patients, or where there are marked variations in treatment effects between components, more careful scrutiny is needed.

The interpretation of the results of studies using continuous outcome measures depends on the nature of the outcome measure. With interval measures that are related directly to a parameter of direct relevance to health (such as weight or height), then assessment is usually straightforward. Similarly, where a favourable change in a parameter that is well established as a surrogate (such as a reduction in blood pressure or LDL cholesterol), evaluation is relatively simple. There are also well-validated rating scales to assess the benefits of interventions used in the treatment of pain and conditions such as depression.

Difficulties arise where an intermediate outcome has not been fully validated. This is particularly problematic in the assessment of interventions where no effective treatment is available. As a consequence, complete validation of a particular endpoint is impossible. For example, there are no effective interventions that will attenuate the progression of neurodegenerative conditions such as Alzheimer's disease, Parkinson's disease and Huntington's disease. No intermediate endpoint is therefore available to enable the criteria of sensitivity and responsiveness to be met. Decision-makers have to exercise judgement in assessing the extent to which a particular biomarker – such as serial magnetic resonance imaging in the case of these progressive neurodegenerative diseases – is likely to predict a desirable final outcome.

In the evaluation of interventions to treat malignant conditions, the use of overall survival is the preferred approach. This, however, is often neither practical nor ethical. Consequently the use of intermediate outcomes (such as objective response rates, progression-free survival and disease-free survival) have become commonplace. Despite their widespread use in the past, there is now broad agreement that objective response rates are poor correlates with overall survival. Progression-free survival and disease-free survival appear to have greater merit. Whether they are sufficiently sensitive to detect extensions to life of only a few weeks remains unclear.

The European[13] and US[14] drug regulatory authorities have expressed an increasing interest in what are known as 'patient-reported outcome measures' (PROMs). This resurgence of interest is, in some respects, surprising because the use of PROMs is not a recent innovation. As already discussed, the clinical *utility* of many interventions – including analgesics, hypnotics, antidepressants and anxiolytics – has relied solely on patient-reported outcomes using appropriate rating scales. In reality, the interest by these regulatory authorities in patient-reported outcomes relates to the desire of some pharmaceutical manufacturers to make claims about the benefits of their products to patients' health-related quality of life. The pronouncements by these regulatory authorities are thus more limited in scope than the term PROM might appear to encapsulate. To confuse matters further, the same term (PROMs) is also used to describe a management tool that is used in the British National Health Service to survey patients' experiences with the UK's healthcare system.

# References

1. Ferreira-Gonzalez I, Busse JW, Heels-Ansdell D, *et al.* Problems with use of composite endpoints in cardiovascular trials: systematic review of randomized controlled trials. *BMJ* 2007;**334**:786.
2. Cordoba G, Schwartz L, Woloshin S, Bae H, Gøtzsche PC. Definition, reporting, and interpretation of composite outcomes in clinical trials: systematic review. *BMJ* 2010;**341**:c3920.
3. Freemantle N. Interpreting composite outcomes in trials. *BMJ* 2010;**341**:c3529.
4. Packer M. Proposal for a new clinical endpoint to evaluate the clinical efficacy of drug and devices in the treatment of chronic heart failure. *Journal of Cardiac Failure* 2001;**7**:176–82.
5. McDowell I. *Measuring Health: A Guide to Rating Scales and Questionnaires*. Oxford: Oxford University Press, 2006.
6. Staquet MJ, Hays RD, Fayers PM (eds). *Quality of Life Assessment in Clinical Trials*. Oxford: Oxford University Press, 1998.
7. Fayers PM, Machin D. *Quality of Life Assessment, Analysis and Interpretation*. Chichester: John Wiley & Sons, 2000.
8. Moher D, Hopewell S, Schulz KF, *et al.* CONSORT 2010 explanation and elaboration: updated guidelines for reporting parallel group randomised controlled trials. *BMJ* 2010;**340**:c869.
9. Marshall M, Lockwood A, Bradley C, *et al.* Unpublished rating scales: a major source of bias in randomised controlled trials of treatments for schizophrenia. *British Journal of Psychiatry* 2000;**176**:249–52.
10. US Department of Health and Human Services. Guidance for industry: clinical trial endpoints for the approval of cancer drugs and bilogics. Rockville, MD: Food and Drug Administration, 2007.
11. McKee AE, Farrell AT, Pazdur R, Woodcock J. The role of the US Food and Drug Administration review process: clinical trial endpoints in oncology. *Oncologist* 2010;**15**(Suppl. 1):13–18.
12. Sargent DJ, Wieand HS, Haller DG, *et al.* Disease-free survival versus overall survival as a primary endpoint for adjuvant colon cancer studies: individual patient data from 20,898 patients on 18 randomized trials. *Journal of Clinical Oncology* 2005;**23**:8664–70.
13. Committee for Medicinal Products for Human Use. Reflection paper on the regulatory guidance for the use of health-related quality of life (HRQL) measures in the evaluation of medicinal products. London: European Medicines Agency, 2005.
14. US Department of Health and Human Services Food and Drug Administration. Guidance for industry: patient-reported outcome measures – use in medical product development to support labelling claims. Rockville, MD: Food and Drug Administration, 2009.

# CHAPTER 1.4

## STATISTICAL EXPRESSIONS OF BENEFIT AND HARM

The results of studies examining the benefits and *harms* of interventions can be expressed statistically in a variety of ways. Many are not entirely helpful to decision-makers, and some are unquestionably confusing. The expressions used depend largely on the types of outcome that have been measured. These, broadly, fall into the following three groups:

- Studies where the outcome is binary (dichotomous), such as alive versus dead, or responders versus non-responders.
- Studies in which individuals are observed over a long(ish) period of time, and where it is unreasonable (or crroneous) to assume that event rates are constant. In these instances, techniques of *survival analysis* are generally used.
- Studies in which the results are expressed as quantitative changes in measured outcomes such as a fall in blood pressure or a rise in haemoglobin concentrations. Included in this category of continuous outcomes are numerical changes in rating scales measuring, for example, depressive symptoms or the *health-related quality of life*.

Because studies tend to include several different outcomes, reports of most clinical trials use more than one approach in examining and analysing the data.

## Binary (dichotomous) outcomes

### Counts and rates

Many studies report, at least as part of the analysis, results as counts or rates. Such counts or rates may be expressions of benefit or harms.

For binary outcomes, the counts at a particular time can be usefully summarized in a $2 \times 2$ contingency table (Table 1.4.1).

**Table 1.4.1** $2 \times 2$ table for estimating relative risks and odds ratios of death

|  | Dead | Alive | Total |
|---|---|---|---|
| Experimental group | $a$ | $b$ | $a + b$ |
| Control group | $c$ | $d$ | $c + d$ |

The mortality rates (*risk rates*) in the two groups would be:

Mortality rate (experimental group) = $a/(a + b)$
Mortality rate (control group) = $c/(c + d)$

The differences between them can be subjected to conventional tests of statistical significance such as a $\chi^2$ test or Fisher's exact test.

The results of the Scandinavian Simvastatin Survival Study (see Case study 1.4.1) provide typical binary data from the analysis of a randomized controlled trial.[1] In this study, patients with a history of ischaemic heart disease were allocated to long-term treatment with either placebo or simvastatin. After a median of 5.4 years' follow-up, the all-cause mortality rates in the placebo and simvastatin groups were 256/2223 (12 per cent) and 182/2221 (8 per cent), respectively. The difference was highly ($P$-value < 0.001) statistically significant. This study also showed that there was a significant reduction in coronary death rates (8.5 per cent versus 5.0 per cent).

---

**Case study 1.4.1** The Scandinavian Simvastatin Survival Study[1]

| | |
|---|---|
| **Background** | At the time this study was instigated, in 1987, it was known that statins such as simvastatin reduced low-density lipoprotein (LDL) cholesterol. There was uncertainty, however, as to whether this translated into improved survival when used to treat patients with coronary heart disease. This study was designed to test this hypothesis. Secondary endpoints included the effects of simvastatin on the incidence of non-fatal coronary events and its long-term safety, but these are not considered here. |
| **Methods** | A total of 4444 patients aged 35–70 years with angina or previous myocardial infarction and a serum cholesterol level of 5.5–8.0 mmol/L despite a lipid-lowering diet were randomized to double-blind treatment with simvastatin or placebo. The study was planned to have 95 per cent power to detect a 30 per cent reduction in mortality. |
| **Results** | After a median follow-up period of 5.4 years, mortality was as follows: |

Overall mortality

> Placebo = 256/2223 (12 per cent)
> Simvastatin = 182/2221 (8 per cent)
> Relative risk = 0.70 (95% CI 0.58 to 0.85)

Coronary deaths

> Placebo = 189/2223 (8.5 per cent)
> Simvastatin = 111/2221 (5.0 per cent)
> Relative risk = 0.58 (95% CI 0.46 to 0.73)

Non-cardiovascular deaths

> Cancer = 35 placebo, 33 simvastatin
> Suicide = 4 placebo, 5 simvastatin
> Trauma = 3 placebo, 1 simvastatin
> Other = 7 placebo, 7 simvastatin

Overall 6-year probability of survival

> Placebo = 87.7 per cent
> Simvastatin = 91.3 per cent

| | |
|---|---|
| **Conclusions** | The study provided definitive evidence that long-term treatment with simvastatin in patients with coronary heart disease improved survival. |

## Relative risk (risk ratio)

A frequent approach to expressing the benefits or harms of an intervention is to estimate the ratio of the two risk rates (see Table 1.4.1). This – the *relative risk* or the *risk ratio* – is calculated thus:

$$\text{Relative risk (of death)} = \frac{[a/(a + b)]}{[c/(c + d)]}$$

A relative risk of 1 indicates that the intervention is neither beneficial nor harmful. A relative risk of less than 1 suggests that the outcome is less likely to occur in the intervention group and usually denotes potential benefit. A relative risk of greater than 1 suggests the outcome is more likely to occur in the experimental group and that it is harmful in comparison with the control group. Sometimes, and very confusingly, relative risks are expressed inverted, so that a relative risk of greater than 1 indicates benefit and a relative risk of less than 1 suggests harm.

Relative risks are usually reported with their 95 per cent confidence intervals (CI). A relative risk of 0.50 (95% CI 0.40 to 0.60) suggests that the particular intervention is associated with a 50 per cent reduction in the outcome of interest. A relative risk of 1.00 (95% CI 0.92 to 1.08) suggests neither a beneficial nor a harmful effect. A relative risk of 3.00 (95% CI 2.75 to 3.25) indicates that the intervention is associated with around a threefold increase in harmfulness. The relative risks of simvastatin on overall and coronary deaths in the Scandinavian Simvastatin Survival Study are shown in Case study 1.4.1. The reduction in the relative risks, with their reasonably narrow 95 per cent confidence intervals, indicates a striking reduction in mortality associated with the long-term use of simvastatin in the circumstances of the trial.

The *rate ratio* is based on the ratio of events per person-time (such as per 100 person-years). It is very similar to the relative risk (or risk ratio) and the interpretation is the same.

## Risk difference (attributable risk and absolute risk reduction)

The *risk difference* – also known as the attributable risk or *absolute risk reduction* – is the difference between the two risk ratios (see Table 1.4.1) and is calculated as follows:

$$\text{Risk difference} = [a(a + b)] - [c/c + d)]$$

Risk differences are usually reported together with their 95 per cent confidence intervals. Although it was not reported in Case study 1.4.1, the risk difference can be calculated as –0.034 (i.e. 3.4 fewer deaths per 100 patients treated). This indicates that despite the very significant effect of simvastatin on reducing mortality at a population level, this is not quite as dramatic as it might seem from the estimates of the relative risk as a measure of *effectiveness*.

## Vaccine efficacy

*Efficacy* of a treatment or intervention can be measured by the proportion of cases it prevents and can be estimated thus:

$$\text{Efficacy} = 1 - \text{relative risk}$$

It is usually expressed as a percentage (with its associated 95 per cent confidence intervals). In general it has only modest advantages over the relative risk and is not used widely, except in assessing the protective effects of vaccines.[2] Full protection from a vaccine would provide 100 per cent efficacy. An example from the results from a randomized trial of influenza vaccine[3] is shown in Case study 1.4.2.

| Case study 1.4.2 | Effectiveness of influenza vaccine in healthcare professionals[3] | | |
|---|---|---|---|
| **Background** | Although the effectiveness of influenza vaccine in reducing mortality and morbidity in children and elderly people is well-documented, there is no clear evidence for its effectiveness in healthcare professionals. This study was designed to explore the utility of influenza vaccination in this specific group. | | |
| **Methods** | A total of 264 hospital-based healthcare professionals (mean age 28.4 years) were recruited over three consecutive years and randomly assigned to receive either an influenza vaccine or placebo. Active weekly surveillance for illness was conducted during each influenza epidemic period. | | |
| **Results** | There were 4746 person-weeks of illness surveillance with 100 per cent follow-up. In total, 24 of 179 controls (13.4 per cent) and 3 of 180 vaccine recipients (1.7 per cent) developed serological evidence of influenza type A or B infection: | | |

| | **Influenza type A** | **Influenza type B** |
|---|---|---|
| Vaccine efficacy (%) | 88 | 89 |
| 95% CI | 47% to 97% | 14% to 99% |

| | | | |
|---|---|---|---|
| **Conclusions** | Influenza vaccination is effective at preventing influenza infection by both influenza A and B. | | |

## Number needed to treat (or harm)

The *number needed to treat* is the reciprocal of the risk difference:

Number needed to treat = 1/risk difference

It describes the number of patients who must be treated in order to achieve one desirable outcome. A number needed to treat of 1 suggests that every recipient will benefit. A totally ineffective intervention would have a number needed to treat of infinity. In the case of the Scandinavian Simvastatin Survival Study (see Case study 1.4.1), although not reported, the number needed to treat is 30. In other words, 30 patients have to be treated with simvastatin in order to avoid 1 death.

The same approach can be used to estimate the *number needed to harm*. This describes the number of recipients that will need to be treated to cause one to develop a particular undesirable outcome. It is sometimes helpful to compare, for a particular intervention, the number needed to treat with the number needed to harm.

## Odds ratio

The *odds ratio* is the ratio of the *odds* (see Chapter 1.2) rather than the risks. In the $2 \times 2$ contingency table (see Table 1.4.1), the odds of death in patients receiving the active treatment is $a/b$; and the odds of death in the controls is $c/d$. The ratio of the odds of death is therefore:

$$\text{Odds ratio (of death)} = \frac{(a/b)}{(c/d)}$$

Odds ratios, like relative risks, are usually reported with their 95 per cent confidence intervals. Like relative risks, an odds ratio of 1 indicates no effect of the intervention; less than 1 suggests benefit; and more than 1 is indicative of harm. Here, though, the similarity ends because the odds ratio is not numerically equivalent to the relative risk. Where the outcome is relatively rare, the odds ratio and relative risk will be approximately equal (see Chapter 1.2). In the Scandinavian Simvastatin Survival Study (see Case study 1.4.1), in which the mortality events were uncommon, the odds ratio and relative risk for overall mortality are 0.69 and 0.70, respectively. But where the outcome is relatively frequent, the odds ratio will differ numerically from the relative risk. Moreover, in such circumstances the relative risk is constrained and odds ratios therefore retain considerable value in the analysis of binary outcomes, even though they are less easy to interpret.[2] And odds ratios are the statistic of choice for the analysis of case–control studies (see Chapter 3.5).

## Survival analysis (time-to-event analysis)

In some clinical trials the outcome of most interest is the time to a particular event, such as death. Such 'survival curves' may involve non-lethal events such as the time to tumour progression or the time to hospital discharge rather than death. For this reason, some people prefer to use the term 'time-to-event'. Figure 1.4.1 shows the survival curves for all-cause mortality in patients treated in the Scandinavian Simvastatin Survival Study.

With survival data, generally the particular event will not have occurred in all patients by the end of the follow-up period. In Figure 1.4.1, for example, over 90 per cent of all patients were alive after 5 years. Moreover, in most studies, patients are recruited over a

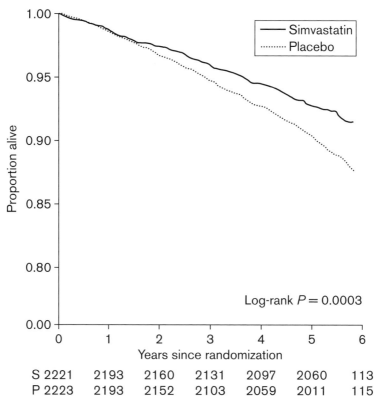

*Therapeutics, evidence and decision-making*

**Figure 1.4.1** Survival curves from the Scandinavian Simvastatin Survival Study.[1]

period of time: those entering the study later on will therefore be studied for a shorter period of time. It is therefore customary to 'censor' the data for those patients in whom the observation period was cut off before the event occurred. Censoring may include not only later entrants into the trial but also patients lost to follow-up during the study. Furthermore, patients with so-called 'competing events' may also be censored. This, for example, would occur when the event of interest is cardiac death: patients dying from other causes would consequently be censored.

Survival analyses of the results of clinical trials usually adopt the Kaplan–Meier method. This makes three important assumptions.[4] First, it assumes that the survival prospects of censored patients are the same as for those who continue to be followed up; this is not easily tested. Second, it assumes that the survival probabilities are the same for those patients recruited earlier rather than later; in other words, the analysis is based on the presumption that the case-mix of patients has not changed and changes in ancillary treatments have not influenced survival. These assumptions can be tested, if necessary, by appropriate subgroup analyses. Third, it assumes that the particular event occurs at the specified time. This is reasonable when the event is death. It is less reasonable when, as is the case with studies of oncology drugs, the event is tumour progression, which will occur at some time between two successive examinations. The frequency of visits and the intensity of monitoring at each visit will be important considerations in assessing the reliability of the data.

Testing hypotheses about the survival of two (or more groups) involves formal analytical approaches, of which the log-rank and the more complex Cox regression methods are the most commonly used.

## Log-rank test

The log-rank test is one that tests the hypothesis of no difference between two populations in the time-specific probability of a particular event. It is based on the principles of the $\chi^2$ test and is usually reported as a *P*-value. (Its rather obscure name comes from an alternative derivation of the underlying mathematics.) In the case of the Scandinavian Simvastatin Survival Study (see Figure 1.4.1), the log-rank test provides a *P*-value of 0.0003, indicating that there is a highly significant difference between the two survival curves.

## Hazard ratio

It is now more common in the analysis of survival curves comparing two (or more) treatments to estimate the *hazard ratio* using Cox's proportional hazards model. The hazard ratio is the ratio of the hazard rates of the two groups and is usually reported with its 95 per cent confidence intervals. The hazard rate is the probability that if an event in question has not already occurred, then it will happen in the next (short) time interval. The time intervals are made very short so that, in effect, the hazard rate is instantaneous. The Cox model makes the fundamental assumption that the hazard ratio is constant over time. In a clinical trial such as the Scandinavian Simvastatin Survival Study, the hazard ratio (if it had been reported) would indicate the relative likelihood of death in the treated group compared with the placebo group at any given time point.

The interpretation of the hazards ratio is, in some respects, similar to that of the relative risk. A hazard ratio of 1 suggests no difference between the groups. A hazard ratio of less than 1 indicates (assuming that the upper 95 per cent confidence interval is also less than 1) that the active treatment is superior to the control (i.e. it is beneficial). A hazard ratio of greater than 1 (assuming that the lower 95 per cent confidence interval is greater than 1) suggests that the active treatment is more harmful than placebo.

The numerical value of a hazards ratio, however, is different from that for a relative risk. A relative risk of 0.5 suggests that the endpoint (such as death) occurs 50 per cent less in the treatment group compared with the control at a specific point in time. A hazard ratio of 0.5, however, indicates that patients in the treated group have a 50 per cent chance of remaining alive at the next point in time compared with patients in the control group.

## Continuous variables

In some studies (see Chapter 1.3) the relevant outcome is a change in a continuous measure such as blood pressure, body weight or haemoglobin concentration. Outcomes assessed using rating scales are usually summarized in numerical terms as a score and are handled in a similar manner as those derived from truly continuous measures.

In all such studies, measurements are typically made at the start (baseline) and at the end of the study. They may also be made at predetermined intervals during the course of the study. These approaches are particularly useful in trials of chronic diseases, where relevant outcomes may, for example, be reduction in pain, anxiety or blood pressure, or improvements in the quality of life.

The results of a study in which the results are expressed using a continuous variable are shown in Case study 1.4.3.[5] This study was designed primarily to investigate the effects of tetrabenazine on the chorea associated with Huntington's disease. The measure used provides a quantitative estimate of the severity of the abnormal choreiform movements that are characteristic of the condition. Although the investigators also reported the effects of tetrabenazine on other outcomes, these have not been included in this case study.

## Discussion

The results of studies using binary outcome measures tend to be more helpful to decision-makers if they also include estimates of the attributable risk or the number needed to treat (or harm). This is because expressions such as relative risks and odds ratios – in describing either benefits or harms – are not necessarily intuitively obvious. A relative risk of 3, for example, might indicate that the *incidence* of a specific harm due to an intervention could reflect an increase of 1 in 100 to 3 in 100; but equally, the same relative risk of 3 would be calculated if the incidence increased from 10 in 100 to 30 in 100. Similarly, a relative risk of 0.5 might represent a reduction in mortality of 2 per cent to 1 per cent but equally a change from 50 per cent to 25 per cent.

The use of relative risks and odds ratios, however, enables statistical adjustments to be made to take account of baseline imbalances. For example, in a randomized controlled trial the treatment groups are all samples from the same population. Nevertheless, important prognostic factors may – purely by chance – be distributed unequally between the groups. The usual approach to the analysis of binary data, to take account of such baseline imbalances, is to use logistic regression analysis.[6,7] Logistic regression analysis also provides a better estimate of the effect size. For statistical reasons,[2] this technique is generally based on odds ratios and results in an adjustment of the crude values to take account of one or more of such baseline imbalances. The technique may also be used to take account of potential *confounding* factors in observational studies. Regression analysis can also be performed using relative risks but, when the outcome is common,

*Therapeutics, evidence and decision-making*

**Case study 1.4.3** Tetrabenazine in the treatment of Huntington's disease[5]

| | | |
|---|---|---|
| **Background** | Huntington's disease is an autosomal dominant condition that usually develops in mid-life but can present at any age. It is a neurodegenerative disorder characterized by abnormal involuntary movements (chorea) and progressive cognitive impairment. There is currently no treatment that prevents the inexorable decline in function. | |

Tetrabenazine is a drug that has the effect of reducing dopamine transmission in the caudate nucleus and might therefore be expected to improve the chorea associated with Huntington's disease.

**Design**   A total of 84 patients with Huntington's disease and significant chorea were randomly allocated to treatment with tetrabenazine ($n = 54$) or placebo ($n = 30$) for 12 weeks. A prior power calculation indicated that this approximate 2:1 randomization would provide a more than 80 per cent chance of a significant effect.

The primary endpoint was the change in the total maximum chorea score domain of the United Huntington Disease Rating Scale (UHDRS). This was estimated from the sum (0 to 4) of each of the maximal chorea scores for facial, buccal-oral-lingual, truncal and each limb. The maximum score is therefore 28 and the minimum 0. Patients were required to have a chorea score of more than 10 as a condition for entry.

**Results**   The total maximum chorea scores at baseline and after 12 weeks' treatment were as follows:

| | Placebo ($n = 30$) | Tetrabenazine ($n = 54$) |
|---|---|---|
| Baseline score | 15.2 (SD 4.4) | 14.7 (SD 3.8) |
| Change at 12 weeks | −1.5 (SD 0.7) | −5.0 (SD 0.5) |
| SD, standard deviation. | | |

Treatment effect:

UHDRS chorea scale units: −3.5* (95% CI −1.9 to −5.2)
Percentage change in baseline score: −24 per cent (95% CI −8 per cent to −35 per cent)

* Analysis of covariance $P < 0.0001$.

**Conclusions** The results indicate that tetrabenazine effectively reduces chorea in patients with Huntington's disease by around 25 per cent from baseline.

modelling may become difficult or impossible. This is why there is continuing widespread – and appropriate – use of logistic regression based on odds ratios. Analogous methods are also available to take account of baseline imbalances for survival curves.

Expressions of the results of studies using continuous outcomes are often easier to interpret in an intuitive manner. When the effects are described in terms that have a close relationship to participants' experiences (such as a reduction in pain or the relief of depression), using validated instruments, the effect of an intervention can be assessed directly. For example, tetrabenazine (see Case study 1.4.3) reduces, on average, the chorea associated with Huntington's disease by 25 per cent.[5] Nevertheless, correcting for baseline imbalances is no less important for continuous outcomes than it is for the analysis with binary outcomes.

There are two ways in which the results of studies with continuous outcomes may be analyzed. The first is to make a simple comparison of the end-of-treatment measurements between the two groups. Depending on the direction of the difference, however, such simple comparisons at the end of treatment may either overestimate or underestimate the true difference if there are significant baseline imbalances. The second is to estimate the change between baseline and end-of-treatment measurements for each group, and then to compare the two mean change scores. This, sometimes called 'change score', has sometimes been used – erroneously – in an attempt to take account of these imbalances, but in practice it fails to do so[8,9] because of the phenomenon of regression to the mean. (Regression to the mean describes the phenomenon whereby a variable (such as blood pressure) that is extreme on its first measurement will tend to be closer to the centre of the distribution (i.e. lower) on a later measurement. The concept was first introduced by Galton (who called it 'regression to mediocrity') after observing that the average height of children was closer to the mean of all children than to the average (mid-parent) height of their parents.)

In the analysis of continuous outcomes, the correct approach to examining the data is to compare the difference between scores at the end of treatment using analysis of covariance.[9] This technique adjusts the treatment differences in a way that takes baseline covariates into account. Potential covariates can be confined to a single prognostic factor or can include multiple factors. The tetrabenazine trial (see Case study 1.4.3) provides an example of the use of analysis of covariance using only one covariate (the baseline chorea score). In this particular study, analysis of covariance made little difference because the mean baseline chorea scores were similar in the two randomized groups.

In evaluating the results of both randomized controlled trials and observational studies, decision-makers should be especially vigilant about three particular issues:

- The interpretation of relative risks and odds ratios requires considerable care. As already discussed, understanding the implications of the numerical values of these measures of an intervention's effects – whether beneficial or harmful – requires knowledge of their associated attributable risks.
- In assessing the effect of potential confounding factors in observational studies, decision-makers should carefully examine the extent of the changes that occur as a result of any statistical modelling. Where the adjusted result (such as an odds ratio) is substantially different from the unadjusted result – as might occur when a crude odds ratio of 5.0 reduces to 2.0 after adjustment for confounders – confidence in the overall findings may be diminished. This is because such large changes may herald the existence of other, unknown baseline imbalances or confounding factors.
- As already discussed, results expressed in terms of relative risks or odds ratios may sometimes be inverted. Under such circumstances relative risks (or odds ratios) greater than 1 will be indicative of benefit and those less than 1 will suggest harms. A particularly egregious example of this was contained in an early report comparing the upper gastrointestinal toxicity of rofecoxib and naproxen in patients with rheumatoid arthritis.[10] In this study the relative risk of the gastrointestinal toxicity of rofecoxib compared with naproxen was estimated as 0.5 (95% CI 0.3 to 0.6). This indicated that there was a significant advantage of rofecoxib over naproxen in relation to an important adverse effect that is characteristically associated with conventional non-steroidal anti-inflammatory drugs. The report, however, also described the relative

risk of myocardial infarction between the two products as being 0.2 (95% CI 0.1 to 0.7). A superficial reading of this might have suggested that rofecoxib reduced the risk of myocardial infarction. In fact, this relative risk was inverted and reflected the risk of myocardial infarction with naproxen compared with rofecoxib. If the relative risk of myocardial infarction with rofecoxib compared with naproxen had been estimated appropriately, it would have been 4.0 (95% CI 2.4 to 5.6). The adverse cardiovascular effects of rofecoxib were subsequently confirmed in other studies, and the product was withdrawn from the market.[11]

In cases of doubt, wise decision-makers will seek expert advice before basing far-reaching conclusions on the results of (what may appear to be) impenetrable statistical modelling.

# References

1. Scandinavian Simvastatin Survival Study Group. Randomized trial of cholesterol lowering in 4444 patients with coronary heart disease: the Scandinavian Simvastatin Survival Study (4S). *Lancet* 1994;**344**:1383–9.

2. Kirkwood BR, Stone JAC. *Medical Statistics*. Oxford: Blackwell, 2003.

3. Wilde JA, McMillan JA, Serwint J, *et al*. Effectiveness of influenza vaccine in health care professionals. *JAMA* 1999;**281**:908–13.

4. Bland JM, Altman DG. Survival probabilities (the Kaplan–Meier method). *BMJ* 1998;**317**:468–9.

5. Huntington Study Group. Tetrabenazine as antichorea therapy in Huntington disease: a randomised controlled trial. *Neurology* 2006;**66**:366–72.

6. Armitage P, Berry G, Matthews JNS. *Statistical Methods in Medical Research*. Oxford: Blackwell, 2002.

7. Matthews JNS. *Introduction to Randomized Controlled Trials*, 2nd edn. London: Chapman & Hall, 2006.

8. Senn S. *Statistical Issues in Drug Development*. Chichester: John Wiley & Sons, 1997.

9. Vickers AJ, Altman DG. Analysing controlled trials with baseline and follow up measures. *BMJ* 2001;**323**:1123.

10. Bombardier C, Laine L, Reicin A, *et al*. Comparison of upper gastrointestinal toxicity of rofecoxib and naproxen in patients with rheumatoid arthritis. *New England Journal of Medicine* 2000;**343**:1520–28.

11. Rawlins MD. *De Testimonium: On the Evidence for Decisions about the Use of Therapeutic Interventions*. London: Royal College of Physicians, 2008.

# BIAS AND CONFOUNDING

Research into the effects of therapeutic interventions is bedevilled by the dual problems of bias and confounding. *Bias* refers to any systematic error in the design, conduct, analysis, publication or review of a study leading to conclusions that are systematically different from the truth. *Confounding* literally means confusion of effects. It occurs when there are other differences between two (or more) groups that influence the apparent outcomes of an intervention and are independent of the effects of the intervention itself. These other factors are known as 'confounders' or 'confounding factors'. For a factor to be a confounder it must differ between the comparison groups and be a predictor of the outcome of interest.

Bias and confounding are not synonymous.[1] Nevertheless, the terminology is often observed in the breach, with selection bias and confounding by indication, in particular, often being used interchangeably. Bias arises from flawed information or subject selection, so that an incorrect association is observed. Confounding produces relationships that are factually correct but that cannot be interpreted as causally related. Both may occur in randomized controlled trials and in observational studies, but they are particularly awkward in the design and interpretation of the latter types of investigation.

## Bias

Biases may lead to an underestimate or overestimate of the apparent size of an intervention's effects. Because there is usually more interest in showing that an intervention is effective rather than ineffective, biases are generally believed to exaggerate the magnitude or importance of an outcome.[2] Bias is rarely the result of a conscious or malicious attempt to manipulate the results or interpretation of data. The term, in the context of studies of the *effectiveness* of interventions, does not imply – as in common parlance – deliberate prejudice. Bias is often unintentional and is sometimes appreciated by investigators themselves.

A variety of potential biases have been described in the literature. Broadly, they fall into three types:[2]

- bias as a result of the way a study has been designed or conducted;
- bias that occur during the analysis of a study;
- bias as a consequence of the manner in which a study has been (or is not) reported and assessed by third parties.

### Biases in the design and conduct of a study

A variety of biases can arise from the manner in which studies are designed and conducted.

#### ■ Selection bias
#### Randomized controlled trials

Selection bias (sometimes described as allocative bias) occurs in trials where there is a mismatch in some relevant respect between the subjects exposed to an intervention and the control (whether a placebo or an active comparator).

Selection bias may occur if eligible subjects are excluded from taking part because an investigator knows in advance the intervention to which a particular participant will be assigned, or if – perhaps on compassionate grounds – an investigator tries to ensure that participants with more (or less) severe disease states are allocated (or not allocated) to a new treatment. Bias can also occur if an investigator is knowingly able to allocate subjects to a particular treatment group. Selection bias can be reduced in well-conducted trials of an appropriate size if interventions are truly allocated – at random – to the participants. Randomization ensures that each participant will have an equal chance of receiving each intervention.

There are many ways in which investigators can subvert allocation in randomized controlled trials.[3] Even allocation codes kept in opaque sealed envelopes have been sabotaged by the use of powerful lights; by steaming open and then resealing envelopes; and by other devious means.[4] There is empirical evidence to show that the effect size of an intervention can be exaggerated by as much as 40 per cent if the randomization sequence is not concealed from the investigator,[3] and by 30 per cent where it is unclear from the published report whether allocation has, or has not, been adequately concealed.

Surveys suggest that 44–93 per cent of publications of randomized controlled trials fail to provide a clear account of the method of allocation concealment.[5] This does not appear to be merely a matter of poor description in the relevant publication. A comparison of published reports with their original protocols, and with a liberal interpretation of the descriptions in the protocols, indicated that 81 per cent of a sample of trials had unclear methods of allocation concealment.[6]

**Observational studies**

Selection bias can be even more problematic in observational studies.[7] In such investigations the allocation of interventions will not have been randomized; consequently, the underlying reason why some participants have been treated with one intervention rather than another may have an influence on the outcomes.

In observational studies selection bias may be subtle. For example, cases that are incident rather than prevalent are to be preferred. This is because patients whose illnesses are of a short duration (either because of early cure or early death) may be underrepresented – particularly if the study is hospital-based – as a result of their unavailability at the time when they might have been studied. This use of prevalent, rather than incident, data can result in so-called 'survival bias' and can lead to distortions of the results. Moreover, even though patients have been recruited appropriately, they may decline to participate. This, too, can lead to selection bias.

The appropriate selection of controls in observational studies is often equally crucial. In hospital-based studies, the most appropriate catchment population from whom controls should be drawn is other in-patients who would have been admitted if they had developed the condition of interest. But using other in-patients with other conditions as controls poses two difficulties.[7] First, the catchment populations for different specialties in the same hospital may not necessarily coincide. Second, in-patients with other conditions cannot be assumed to be representative of the general population of people without the disease of interest. To obviate this difficulty, investigators sometimes select, for each case, both an in-patient and a community control and compare the results. If they are similar, then there will greater confidence in the findings. If they are different, then an appropriate explanation will be required before drawing conclusions.

Selection bias in observational studies can sometimes be reduced by a nested design. In this, the study base (both cases and controls) consists of a documented and closely traced cohort. Matching cases with controls in one or more important respects can also reduce selection bias. Age, a common suspected source of bias in observational studies, can, for example, be offset by matching cases and controls to within (say) ±5 years.

Selection bias can particularly distort the results of historical controlled trials. If the control group differs from the active treatment group in a way that is independent of the intervention itself but that changes its underlying prognosis, a false impression of therapeutic benefit may occur. This important form of bias is discussed further in Chapter 3.2.

### ■ Ascertainment bias

Ascertainment bias occurs when the results of a study are distorted by knowledge about which treatment participants have received.

#### Randomized controlled trials

In clinical trials ascertainment bias may be due to the investigator who administers the intervention, to the subject receiving it, or to the analyst assessing the outcomes. It is especially problematic where outcomes are subjective, such as the effects of interventions on pain, depression or cognition.[8] Ascertainment bias may, however, still be problematic when the outcome is objective. For example, in studies of treatments with potential beneficial effects on cardiovascular mortality, assessors will often be asked to assign deaths to 'cardiovascular' or 'non-cardiovascular' causes. In the absence of data from autopsies (and sometimes even with the benefit of a post mortem report), the attribution may depend largely on the judgement of those making such assignments and, consequently, it can be sensitive to conscious or unconscious bias.

In order to minimize ascertainment bias in clinical trials, investigators and/or participants are often 'blind' to the treatment group to which they have been allocated. (Although the term 'blinding' may be inappropriate in the context of ophthalmological research,[9] for which the term 'masking' has been advocated, its continued use in other contexts has been stoutly defended on historical grounds spanning at least 200 years.[10]) Studies are described as 'single blind' if either the investigators or the participants are blinded; and as 'double blind' if both the investigators and the participants are ignorant of treatment allocations. Blinding of assessors, in determining the cause of death in trials where the endpoint is a specific mortality rate, is now common practice. Similarly, blinding of radiologists to treatment allocations in trials where outcomes are measured by using imaging techniques is also common. In instances where it is virtually impossible to 'blind' the investigator, such as in some surgical trials, a third party who is unaware of the treatment to which patients have been allocated may be used to assess outcomes.

In a desire to undertake an unbiased assessment of the effects of a therapeutic intervention investigators may, however, sometimes be tempted to go too far. In order to study the effectiveness of implanted human fetal nigrostriatal neurons into the caudate nuclei of patients with Parkinson's disease, suitable patients were recruited into a randomized controlled trial.[11] Those allocated to the placebo arm underwent sham surgery involving general anaesthesia followed by the introduction of bilateral partial burr holes. Patients in the placebo group also received low-dose ciclosporin for 6 months. After 24 months' follow-up no real benefit was observed in those undergoing implantation of fetal neurons.

The trial investigators argued vehemently that a fully placebo-controlled randomized controlled trial was essential if the benefits of nigrostriatal transplantation were to be

*Therapeutics, evidence and decision-making*

properly assessed.[12] There were also suggestions that growth factors might be stimulated by surgery, and that even ciclosporin itself could be therapeutic. One of America's most distinguished bioethicists concluded, however: 'The placebo controlled trial may well be the gold standard of research design, but unlike pure gold, it can be tarnished by unethical applications'.[13] Put another way, the interests of patients must always take precedence over the interests of clinical research.

**Observational studies**

Ascertainment bias can, equally, be a significant issue in observational studies. One form, *information bias*, arises when there is misclassification between study groups of the exposure to an intervention under assessment. In case–control studies, for example, subjects with the condition of interest (often a potential adverse reaction) may remember their drug histories more reliably than controls lacking the condition; and field workers may unconsciously interrogate cases and controls differently.

Obtaining participants' medical records can minimize information bias with respect to their medication histories. These records will provide accurate information about prescribed medicines but they will be of little value in ascertaining use of over-the-counter and complementary remedies. As a further measure to minimize information bias, attempts have sometimes been made to ensure that field workers are unaware as to whether subjects are cases or controls. Occasionally, they have even been blinded as to the nature of the study hypothesis itself. Such measures, however, pose considerable logistic problems. More commonly, field workers undergo specific training before a study is started and may be provided with a checklist or script with which to interview participants.

A further form of ascertainment bias, *diagnostic bias*, occurs in observational studies when exposure to a suspected cause – such as a particular pharmaceutical product – leads to preferential investigation. Patients on oral contraceptives, for example, may be more readily investigated by their physicians for suspected venous thromboembolic disorders than patients not taking such products. One approach to assessing the possibility of diagnostic bias, especially in case–control studies, is to undertake an independent review of the strength of the particular diagnosis without knowledge of the patient's exposure status.

Diagnostic bias may also occur in observational studies if cases, but not controls, undergo more frequent medical surveillance (*surveillance bias*). As a consequence, intercurrent symptoms may be reported less frequently by controls drawn from the general population. In an observational study of patients receiving the early $H_2$ receptor antagonist cimetidine, it was noted that an excess of patients on the drug had been referred to hospital with suspected cataracts compared with age-matched controls drawn from the general population.[14] The numbers eventually undergoing cataract surgery, however, were similar in the two groups. It seemed highly likely that surveillance bias rather than a causal explanation was responsible for the difference in referral rates.

### ■ Population bias

**Randomized controlled trials**

The choice of the population studied in clinical trials can seriously influence its generalizability. Typical exclusions include women (*gender bias*), children and elderly people (*age bias*) and people from ethnic minorities (*racial bias*). The population may also exclude people with mild or severe forms of a condition (*severity of illness bias*) or people with other concurrent disorders (*comorbidity bias*). Population bias may also reduce the *generalizability* of a study if participants are recruited from among hospital patients with interventions intended for wider use. This includes, for example, interventions for conditions such as hypertension or moderate depression that are usually managed in the community. Participants attending hospital may have more severe forms of the disorder and therefore be unrepresentative of a general population.

Population bias can be lessened by undertaking 'pragmatic' trials (see Chapter 2.1). These are designed to recruit participants who are more likely to be representative of the wider population. Pragmatic trials, however, have their own problems, and population bias remains a substantial issue in the interpretation of the results of studies of the effectiveness of interventions.

**Observational studies**

Population bias in observational studies might be expected to be less problematic than in randomized controlled trials, because such designs mainly investigate the effects of interventions under normal conditions of use. This, indeed, is one of their strengths (see Chapter 3.1). Nevertheless, population bias in observational studies (as discussed earlier) may not only limit their veracity but also adversely influence their generalizability.

### ■ Comparator bias
**Randomized controlled trials**

A placebo-controlled trial will show whether an intervention has any beneficial (or adverse) effects. It will not show whether the intervention is likely to be worse than, as good as or better than other active treatments for the same indication. In conditions for which effective treatments are available, an active comparator is therefore to be preferred.

Clinical trials with an active comparator should reflect current medical practice in the choice of the intervention used in the control arm. An obvious way to make an intervention appear to be more effective than it really is would be to choose an ineffective or outdated active comparator. The active comparator should therefore have been shown previously to be effective for the condition under investigation and should reflect the current standard of clinical care. There may, however, be differing therapeutic traditions between countries, and between experts within countries, that complicate the choice of suitable comparators.

To complicate matters further, in a rapidly moving field such as oncology, best current clinical practice at the time a trial was started may have changed by the time the results are reported. Moreover, some drug regulatory authorities prefer to base their licensing decisions on placebo-controlled rather than active comparator-controlled trials. As a consequence, there is much current interest in the use of *indirect comparisons* of effectiveness. These involve attempts to compare the effectiveness of two interventions when each has been studied only in placebo-controlled trials. This approach is discussed in greater detail in Chapter 1.6.

**Observational studies**

Comparator bias is not generally an issue in observational studies, provided that these are based on contemporaneously treated patients. It may, however, be significant in interpreting the results of historical controlled trials (see Chapter 3.2).

## Analytical bias
### ■ Withdrawal bias
**Randomized controlled trials**

In almost all clinical trials some participants will invariably fail to complete the study or will fail to adhere precisely to the study protocol. Indeed, 'dropouts' are virtually ubiquitous. Subjects may find the assessments too burdensome; they may move away; their underlying condition may deteriorate to an extent that further treatment becomes inappropriate (a special problem of trials in advanced cancer); or they may develop an intercurrent condition that stops them from participating further. In addition, some patients may be withdrawn because of suspected or established adverse effects to one of the interventions.

Excluding some of the participants from the analysis of a trial can seriously distort the results. In a survey of 167 trials, only 39 (23 per cent) included all the patients in the final analysis.[15] This study also noted that the effect sizes of interventions in trials with exclusions tended to be greater than those without exclusions, although neither the direction nor the extent was predictable.

A widely used approach to handling withdrawals and patients who complete the study but do not fully adhere to the protocol is to undertake the analysis by *intention-to-treat*. In this technique all randomized patients are included in the final analysis. The clinical status of those participants who fail to complete the study is based on their condition at the time of the last observation (known as the *last observation carried forward*, often abbreviated to LOCF). It has been claimed that an intention-to-treat analysis is a conservative one because it assumes that dropouts gain no further benefit.[16]

The use of the last observation carried forward is not, however, without its flaws. In trials of interventions for neurodegenerative disorders such as Huntington's disease and Alzheimer's disease, the use of the last observation carried forward in patients failing to complete the study would assume that there was no further decline in cognitive function.[17] If the intervention reduced or arrested the neurodegenerative process, then this might be acceptable. If, however, the intervention's effects are solely symptomatic, then the use of the last observation carried forward would overestimate its benefits because it would assume no further deterioration had occurred.

To overcome this limitation, in a last observation carried forward analysis, a worst-case *sensitivity analysis* can be undertaken. In this, the analysis is repeated, assigning the worst possible outcomes to the missing patients in the best-performing group, and assigning the best-performing outcomes to the missing patients in the worst-performing group. If the results from the two analyses are similar, then the findings from the overall intention-to-treat analysis are more likely to be reliable. If they differ to any substantial extent, then the results should be treated with greater scepticism.

A *per protocol* analysis excludes patients who have withdrawn from a study or who have completed the trial but deviated from the protocol. It may sometimes be undertaken as an exploratory analysis, but it is an unreliable basis for determining the effectiveness of an intervention in a real-world population. It may also mask *safety* signals and thereby minimize the recognition of adverse effects.

### ■ Selective reporting bias
There is sometimes a tendency to underreport or underplay the unexpected or undesirable results of a study. Alternatively, although reported, authors may attribute them to measurement error or the play of chance, or offer some other explanation.

**Randomized controlled trials**
Incomplete reporting of the outcomes of clinical trials appears to be a common failing. In their survey of 519 published studies, Chan and Altman observed that, on average, over 20 per cent of the outcomes in randomized parallel group trials were incompletely

reported.[18] Furthermore, within a trial, they found that unreported outcomes had a greater chance of being non-significant than fully reported ones.

**Observational studies**

Selective reporting of the results of observational studies would be as potentially damaging as the selective reporting of the results of randomized controlled trials. There is, however, little evidence of this.

### ■ Fraud

Two forms of fraud (often called *misconduct*) in clinical research are recognized: *data fabrication* refers to making up data, and *data falsification* describes changing or eliminating data values.

The extent to which fraud occurs in randomized trials is difficult to estimate,[19] although it is probably unusual.[20] National drug regulatory authorities have mechanisms in place to detect or prevent fraud in clinical trials undertaken for regulatory purposes. These involve making monitoring visits to clinical trial centres, but these are labour-intensive and costly and have not been invariably successful.[21]

If fraud has been detected it is essential to quantify its impact on the outcome of the trial. Although morally reprehensible, many instances of fraud probably have a negligible impact on the trial's scientific conclusions and are unlikely to affect the results if any of the following conditions are met:[20]

- The fraud is limited to a few investigators or a few data items.
- The fraud bears on secondary variables that have little or no impact on the primary endpoint of a trial.
- The fraud affects all treatment groups equally and thus generates 'noise' but no 'bias'.

A trial where fraud has been detected should not, therefore, be necessarily rejected in its totality. Obviously, the results from the fraudulent centre should be excluded from the final analysis, but it is not necessarily the case that the study as a whole should be abandoned or ignored.

## Assessment bias

### ■ Publication bias

There is a tendency for negative studies of the effects of interventions to remain unpublished. Indeed, empirical evidence shows that the failure to publish the results of studies is strongly influenced by the direction and strength of the findings, and that study reports with statistically significant positive results are more likely to be published than those with negative findings.[22] *Language bias* is a form of publication bias. There is a tendency for positive reports to be published in English-language journals and for negative reports to be published in other languages.[23]

Publication bias occurs for many reasons. Disappointed investigators may fail to write up the results of negative findings (the so-called 'file drawer problem'), and journal editors may decline to publish articles with negative findings. Publication bias can also result from the failure of pharmaceutical manufacturers to report unfavourable findings with their products, or where they believe publication would damage their commercial interests. Of the 164 *efficacy* trials submitted to the US Food and Drug Administration (FDA) in 2001 and 2002 for drugs subsequently approved for marketing, 22 per cent remained unpublished five years later.[24] Published reports were more likely than unpublished reports to have favourable outcomes. Moreover, 41 outcomes submitted in reports to the FDA were omitted from the published articles; of the outcomes that did not favour the product, 20 were not included in the published reports.

An example of publication bias is shown in Case study 1.5.1, which describes the failure of several pharmaceutical companies to make negative findings publicly available. The authors of this study were developing a clinical guideline on the management of depression in children and adolescents.[25] If they had relied solely on the published literature, it is very likely that they would have recommended the use of ineffective and unsafe treatments.

---

**Case study 1.5.1** Selective serotonin reuptake inhibitors in childhood depression: systematic review of published versus unpublished data[25]

**Background** It is estimated that 2–6 per cent of children and adolescents have depression; and suicide is the third most common cause of death in 10- to 19-year-olds. The National Institute for Health and Clinical Excellence (NICE) therefore commissioned the National Collaborating Centre for Mental Health to develop a guideline on the management of depression in this age group. As part of the guideline development process, a systematic review of the safety and efficacy of selective serotonin reuptake inhibitors (SSRIs) was undertaken.

**Methods** The authors searched four electronic databases and the Cochrane Library for published randomized placebo-controlled trials in which participants aged 5–18 years with depression were treated with an antidepressant. Only five studies fulfilled the selection criteria.

The authors also contacted the manufacturers of all marketed antidepressants requesting unpublished data. No data were forthcoming.

Fortuitously, at the same time, the UK's Committee on Safety of Medicines undertook a review of the safety and efficacy of SSRIs in children and published its findings on its website. This identified a further six randomized controlled trials (RCTs).

**Results** The authors compared the results of published and unpublished RCTs as well as their conclusions about the overall risk/benefit profiles of each SSRI based on the combined data.

| SSRI | Published RCTs | Unpublished RCTs | Overall risk/benefit assessment |
|---|---|---|---|
| Fluoxetine | 2 (*n* = 315) | 0* | Favourable |
| Paroxetine | 1 (*n* = 180) | 2 (*n* = 478) | Unfavourable |
| Sertraline | 2 (*n* = 376) | 0* | Unfavourable |
| Citalopram | 0 | 2 (*n* = 422) | Unfavourable |
| Venlafaxine | 1 (*n* = 40) | 2 (*n* = 334) | Unfavourable |

*N* = total number of enrolled patients.
*Additional unpublished efficacy and/or safety data.

**Conclusions** It is striking that more patients were included in the unpublished data (*n* = 1234) than in the published data (*n* = 911). The unpublished studies failed to show any significant clinical benefit. In addition, many of these demonstrated serious adverse reactions (increased suicide attempts and suicidal ideation). Only fluoxetine was recommended for use in the guideline.

A number of attempts have been made to remedy the problem of publication bias. Those undertaking systematic reviews (see Chapter 1.6) are encouraged to try to identify unpublished studies by enquiry of those with a known interest in the subject, and to interrogate non-English-language as well as English-language journals. Neither approach is foolproof. Attempts to discover unpublished manuscripts are likely to be fruitless if the original investigators never drafted one; and scrutiny of the non-English literature can be extremely time-consuming and expensive if professional translations are required.

The International Committee of Medical Journal Editors now requires that trials be registered prospectively if they are to be considered for publication;[26] and a number of online databases have been created for this purpose.[27] Many funding bodies now require prospective registration as a condition of grant awards. The International Federation of Pharmaceutical Manufacturers and Associations has committed its members, who include all the major pharmaceutical companies, to register their exploratory and confirmatory trials with appropriate Internet-based registries.[28] Prospective registration of trials means that in the future, it should be possible to cross-check reports of trial results in the public domain with those that have been previously registered.

■ **Prejudicial bias**
Bias is not confined to trial investigators. The readers, interpreters, commentators and assessors of studies of interventions may have prejudicial biases. These include biases against studies sponsored by the pharmaceutical industry (*pharmaceutical industry bias*) and biases against certain methods (usually an antipathy towards observational studies) resulting in *methodological bias*. Prejudicial bias may be directed in favour of *esteemed authors*, *prestigious journals* and publications in the *peer-reviewed* literature. A further variety, *systematic reviewer bias*, is bias in which reviewers dismiss studies that contain any flaws, however minor, in design, analysis or interpretation.

Avoiding prejudicial bias requires readers, evaluators and appraisers of original reports to be alert to its possibility and for them to be honest with themselves in distinguishing between their critical and prejudicial faculties.

# Confounding

It is possible that in any study of a particular intervention there is an important influence on the outcome(s) that differs systematically between the groups. Any apparent effect of the intervention may then be due to these differences rather than to the intervention itself, and a comparison between the groups is said to be confounded.[29] *Confounding* may occur in randomized controlled trials but is a particular problem in the design and interpretation of observational studies.

To be a confounder, a factor must satisfy two conditions:[7]

■ It must be a risk factor for the disease under study.
■ It must be associated with an intervention but not a consequence of its use.

## Randomized controlled trials

In clinical trials there is a presumption that, because treatment allocations are random, confounding factors will be distributed equally between the groups. As discussed in the context of baseline imbalances (see Chapter 1.4), if by chance known confounders are distributed unequally, then techniques such as logistic regression and analysis of covariance can be used to take them into account. There is a general assumption that

*Therapeutics, evidence and decision-making*

unknown confounders will be distributed equally between the groups, although this is impossible to confirm or refute.

## Observational studies

Confounding may seriously compromise the findings and conclusions of observational studies. Case study 1.5.2 is an example.[30] The authors of this systematic review concluded, from an analysis of this series of observational studies, that 'postmenopausal oestrogen therapy can substantially reduce the risk for coronary heart disease'. As a result of this and other similar reports hormone replacement therapy became used widely during the 1990s in the USA and the UK, supposedly to reduce the risk of coronary heart disease. This was despite the fact that drug regulatory authorities in both countries did not permit claims for this indication to be made by any of the manufacturers of these interventions. It is now known from the results of a number of well-conducted randomized controlled trials that hormone replacement therapy has no beneficial effect in preventing coronary heart disease.[31]

---

**Case study 1.5.2** Hormone replacement therapy and coronary heart disease[30]

**Background** A variety of individual observational studies had claimed to show that hormonal replacement therapy in postmenopausal women reduced the risk of ischaemic heart disease. This quantitative overview was designed to assess the strength of this claim.

**Methods** Through computer searches and review of references, the authors sought to collect all articles with quantitative data of the effect of hormone replacement therapy on coronary heart disease.

**Results** The literature revealed 31 individual studies with several different designs and conducted across various patient populations. The summary (weighted) relative risks for each type are shown here:

| Population (number studies) | Design | Relative risk (95% CI) |
|---|---|---|
| Hospital-based ($n = 6$) | Case–control | 1.33 (0.93 to 1.91) |
| Community-based ($n = 7$) | Case–control | 0.76 (0.61 to 0.94) |
| Community-based ($n = 16$) | Prospective cohort | 0.58 (0.48 to 0.69) |
| Coronary angiography ($n = 3$) | Case–control | 0.41 (0.34 to 0.50) |
| CI, confidence interval. | | |

Across all studies, the summary (weighted) estimate of the pooled relative risk was 0.56 (95% CI 0.50 to 0.61).

**Discussion** The authors considered whether the results might be confounded and that users of hormone replacement therapy might, anyway, have a reduced risk of coronary heart disease. In so far as was possible, from the available data, they rejected this explanation and concluded that the preponderance of the evidence from epidemiological studies strongly supported the view that postmenopausal oestrogen therapy substantially reduces the risk of coronary heart disease.

---

The reason for the discrepancies between the results of these observational and experimental studies was due, in large part,[32] to a failure to take into account, in the majority of the observational studies, the well-established relationship between coronary health disease and socioeconomic status. Socioeconomic status was a confounding factor because women taking hormone replacement therapy tended to belong to a higher socioeconomic group with a lower risk of coronary heart disease. Indeed, in the relatively few observational studies that adjusted the results for socioeconomic status, the summary *relative risk* for coronary heart disease was 0.97 (95% confidence interval (CI) 0.82 to 1.16). By contrast, in those studies that did not control for this, the summary relative risk was 0.71 (95% CI 0.64 to 0.78).

There are various techniques that can be used to adjust for confounding. They include matching cases and controls, stratification, multivariate analysis[7] and propensity scoring.[33] Observational studies usually report the crude (unadjusted) and the adjusted *odds ratios*. If the crude and adjusted odds ratios are similar, then the influence of the known potential confounders is probably slight. If they are substantiality different, then the degree of confounding will have been considerable. The problem, however, is that only known confounders can be accounted for in the analysis; unknown confounders may still account for an apparent association.

## Discussion

It is impossible to eliminate entirely all possible sources of bias and confounding in the design, conduct or analysis of randomized controlled trials or observational studies. Over the past 15 years, however, substantial steps have attempted to improve the minimization of them.

Biases arising from the design, conduct and analysis of clinical trials have been reduced by adherence to the principles of the CONSORT (consolidated standards of reporting trials) statement. Since its publication in 1996,[34] and subsequent revisions,[35,36] this guideline has been adopted by over 400 of the world's leading major medical journals and has probably had a significant impact on the quality of clinical trials. Although the CONSORT statement and its extensions (which include cluster trials, equivalence trials and the consideration of *harms*) are intended to provide the authors of randomized controlled trials, and journal editors, with a framework for reporting trial results, it has had a very positive impact on the quality of clinical trials themselves.

Publication bias, whether complete or partial, may be very damaging to patients. As shown in Case study 1.5.1, it can prejudice patient welfare by failing to place data demonstrating both inefficacy and harms in the public domain. Moreover, selective publication of the results of negative studies, even where a product has been licensed for the particular indication, may lead to an exaggeration of its benefits. This is of special importance if the evidence for effectiveness is to be used in any form of economic evaluation because any overestimate of an intervention's health gains will lead to overestimates of its cost-effectiveness.

The commitment by the global pharmaceutical industry[28] to make the results of exploratory and confirmatory studies available not more than a year after a product has been licensed in one country is encouraging. This, together with the agreement to register prospectively all studies sponsored by the industry, provide some optimism that publication bias and selective reporting will become less pervasive. There are, however, two caveats to this seemingly beneficial development. First, the commitment extends only to confirmatory trials for products licensed since July 2005; and, for exploratory trials, only those licensed since September 2009. There are many trials published before these dates that are likely to remain unavailable for wider scrutiny. One company,[37] however, has made summaries of the results of all the clinical trials of its marketed products available online. Second, the commitment by the industry as a whole applies only to products that are granted a marketing licence; the results of studies for products (or indications) that fail or are never submitted for, licensure may remain undisclosed. The use of selective serotonin reuptake inhibitors for the treatment of depression in adults and children (see Case study 1.5.1) is a case in point, although at least the existence – if not the results – of such studies will, in the future, appear in trial registries.

The success of CONSORT has encouraged the development of comparable advice – STROBE (strengthening the reporting of observational studies in epidemiology) – on the reporting of observational studies.[38] More recently, a group including statisticians, surgeons and others with a special interest in evidence-based medicine has proposed novel approaches – IDEAL (innovation, development, exploration, assessment, long-term) – to surgical innovation and evaluation.[39] Taken together, these measures provide further hope for the future.

Bias in the design and analysis in clinical trials of the benefits and harms of interventions is not confined to studies in humans. There is a growing literature showing that similar problems (including the failure of randomization and blinding of observers) occurs in animal studies of potential therapeutic interventions.[40] Moreover, such failings have the same consequences in animals as in humans, with a strong tendency for an exaggeration of effect sizes.[41] Failures in conforming to sound principles in the design and analysis of interventional studies in animals are almost as important as they are in humans. New products proceed to trials in patients only if positive results have been observed in animal models. False positive results in animal studies will lead to true negative results in patients, with attendant and unnecessary risks to the participants. As a result, the animal equivalent of the CONSORT statement – ARRIVE (animals in research: reporting *in vivo* experiments) – has been published.[42]

The problems of bias and confounding are perhaps the most challenging aspects of the design and interpretation of clinical studies of therapeutic interventions. Ultimately, it is a matter of judgement in determining the extent to which possible biases may have over- or underestimated the effectiveness of an intervention in both human and animal studies.

# References

1. Vandenbroucke JP, von Elm E, Altman DG, *et al.* Strengthening the reporting of observational studies in epidemiology (STROBE): explanation and elaboration. *PLoS Medicine* 2007;**4**:e297.

2. Jadad AR, Enkin MW. *Randomized Controlled Trials: Questions, Answers and Musings*, 2nd edn. London: Blackwell, 2007.

3. Schultz KF, Chalmers I, Hayes RJ, Altman DG. Empirical evidence of bias: dimensions of methodological quality associated with estimates of treament effects in controlled trials. *Journal of the American Medical Association* 1995;**273**:408–12.

4. Peto R. Failure of randomisation by 'sealed' envelope. *BMJ* 1999;**354**:73.

5. Altman DG, Schulz KF, Moher D, *et al.* The revised CONSORT statement for reporting randomized trials: explanation, and elaboration. *Annals of Internal Medicine* 2001;**134**:663–94.

6. Pildal J, Chen A-W, Hrobjartson A, *et al.* Comparisons of descriptions of allocation concealment in trial protocols and the published reports: cohort study. *BMJ* 2005;**330**:1049.

7. Schlesselman JJ. *Case–Control Studies: Design, Conduct, Analysis*. Oxford: Oxford University Press, 1983.
8. Wood L, Egger M, Gluud LL, *et al*. Empirical evidence of bias in treatment effect estimates in controlled trials with different interventions and outcomes: meta-epidemiological study. *BMJ* 2008;**336**:601–5.
9. Morris D, Fraser S, Wormald R. Masking is better than blinding. *BMJ* 2007;**334**:799.
10. Schulz KF, Altman DG, Moher D. Blinding is better than masking. *BMJ* 2007;**334**:918.
11. Olanow CW, Goetz CG, Kowdower JH, *et al*. A double-blind controlled trial of fetal nigral transplantation in Parkinson's disease. *Annals of Neurology* 2003;**54**:403–14.
12. Freeman TB, Vawter DE, Leaverton PE, *et al*. Use of placebo surgery in controlled trials of a cellular-based therapy for Parkinson's disease. *New England Journal of Medicine* 1999;**341**:988–92.
13. Macklin R. The ethical problems with sham surgery in clinical research. *New England Journal of Medicine* 1999;**341**:992–6.
14. Colin-Jones DG, Langman MJS, Lawson DH, Vessey MP. Postmarketing surveillance of the safety of cimetidine. *QJM* 1985;**54**:253–68.
15. Nüesch E, Trelle S, Reichenbach S, *et* al. The effects of excluding patients from the analysis in randomised controlled trials: meta-epidemiological study. *BMJ* 2009;**339**:b3244.
16. Lavouri PW. Clinical trials in psychiatry: should protocol deviation censor patient data? *Neuropharmacology* 1992;**6**:39–48.
17. Mackinnon A. Statistical treatment of withdrawals in trials of anti-dementia drugs. *Lancet* 2008;**372**:1382–3.
18. Chan A-W, Altman DG. Identifying outcome reporting bias in randomised trials on PubMed: review of publications and survey of authors. *BMJ* 2005;**330**:753.
19. Van den Dungen H. Monitoring medical research: better to prevent than to cure? In: Wells F, Farthing M (eds). *Fraud and Misconduct in Medical Research*, 4th edn. London: Royal Society of Medicine Press, 2008.
20. Buyse M, George SL, Evans S, *et al*. The role of biostatistics in the prevention, detection and treatment of fraud in clinical trials. *Statistics in Medicine* 1999;**18**:3435–51.
21. Ross DB. The FDA and the case of Ketek. *New England Journal of Medicine* 2007;**356**:1601–4.
22. Dickersin K. How important is publication bias? A synthesis of available data. *AIDS Education Prevention* 1997;**9**(Suppl. A):15–21.
23. Moher D, Pham B, Lawson ML, Klassen TP. The inclusion of reports of randomised trials published in languages other than English in systematic reviews. *Health Technology Assessment* 2003;**7**:1–90.
24. Rising K, Bacchetti P, Bero L. Reporting bias in drug trials submitted to the Food and Drug Administration: review of publication and presentation. *PLoS Medicine* 2008;**5**:e217.
25. Whittington CJ, Kendall T, Fonagy P, *et al*. Selective serotonin reuptake inhibitors in childhood depression: systematic review of published versus unpublished data. *Lancet* 2004;**363**:1341–5.
26. De Angelis CD, Drazen JM, Frizelle FA, *et al*. Is this clinical trial fully registered? A statement for the International Committee of Medical Journal Editors. *Annals of Internal Medicine* 2005;**143**:146–8.
27. Current Controlled Trials. Metaregister of randomised controlled trials. www.controlled-trials.com/mrct/.
28. International Federation of Pharmaceutical Manufacturers and Associations. Joint position on the disclosure of clinical trial information via clinical trial registries and

databases: updated November 2008. www.ifpma.org/clinicaltrials/fileadmin/files/pdfs/EN/Revised_Joint_Industry_Position_Nov_2008.pdf.

29. Clayton D, Hills M. *Statistical Models in Epidemiology*. Oxford: Oxford University Press, 1993.

30. Stampfer MJ, Colditz GA. Estrogen replacement therapy and coronary heart disease: a quantitative assessment of the epidemiological evidence. *Preventive Medicine* 1991;**20**:47–63.

31. Beral V, Banks E, Reeves G. Evidence for randomised trials on the long-term effects of hormone replacement therapy. *Lancet* 2002;**360**:942–4.

32. Pettiti DB, Freedman DA. How far can epidemiologists get with statistical adjustments? *American Journal of Epidemiology* 2005;**162**:415–18.

33. Glynn RJ, Schneeweiss S, Sturmer T. Indications for propensity scores and review of their use in pharmacoepidemiology. *Basic Clinical Pharmacology and Toxicology* 2006;**98**:253–9.

34. Begg CB, Cho MK, Eastwood S, *et al*. Improving the quality of reporting of randomized controlled trials. *JAMA* 1996;**276**:637–9.

35. Moher D, Schulz KJ, Altman D. The CONSORT statement: revised recommendations for improving the quality of reports of parallel group randomized trials. *JAMA* 2001;**285**:1987–91.

36. Schulz KF, Altman DG, Moher D. CONSORT 2010 statement: updated guidelines for reporting parallel group randomised trials. *BMJ* 2010;**340**:c332.

37. Rockhold FW, Krall RL. Trial summaries on results databases and journal publication. *Lancet* 2006;**367**:1635–6.

38. Von Elm E, Altman DG, Egger M, *et al*. The strengthening the reporting of observational studies in epidemiology (STROBE) statement: guidelines for reporting observational studies. *Lancet* 2007;**370**:1453–7.

39. McCulloch P, Altman DG, Campbell WB, *et al*. No surgical innovation without evaluation: the IDEAL recommendations. *Lancet* 2009;**374**:1105–12.

40. Kilkenny C, Parsons N, Kadyszewski E, *et al*. Survey of the quality of experimental design, statistical analysis and reporting of research using animals. *PLoS One* 2009;**4**:e7824.

41. Bebarta V, Luyten D, Heard K. Emergency medicine animal research: does use of randomization and blinding affect the results? *Academic Emergency Medicine* 2003;**10**:684–7.

42. Kilkenny C, Browne WJ, Emerson M, Altman DG. Improved bioscience research reporting: the ARRIVE guidelines for reporting animal research. *PLoS Biology* 2010;**8**:e1000412.

# SYSTEMATIC REVIEWS

Until about 20 years ago reviews of the biomedical literature were generally *ad hoc* activities. A reviewer would typically search out a few of the relevant articles (often from a personal collection of reprints), supplement these articles with some of those quoted in the reference list of the published papers, and produce a review. It was invariably idiosyncratic and incomplete; and it was an unreliable basis for drawing general conclusions. It is therefore hardly surprising that an analysis of 40 reviews published in the mid-1980s found major deficiencies.[1] Only one described the methods for identifying, selecting and validating the information included in the review; and just three of them attempted a quantitative synthesis (*meta-analysis*) of the results.

Since that time a systematic approach to the reviewing of evidence, particularly about the use of interventions in healthcare, has become an important and sophisticated scientific endeavour. The burgeoning (and now almost unmanageable) medical literature, coupled with a general acceptance that clinical practice should be based on evidence rather than anecdote or expert opinion, has stimulated the emergence of the systematic review as an important aid to the evaluation of healthcare interventions. The approach has been most rigorously developed for assessing the benefits of therapeutic interventions. It is less mature for the analysis of adverse effects (*harms*), although this is being given greater attention. Methods are also emerging for systematic reviews of techniques for screening, diagnosis, prognosis and the monitoring of treatment.

This chapter outlines the strengths and weaknesses of systematic reviews of the benefits and harms of interventions. Systematic reviews of economic assessments are discussed in Chapter 5.1. Fuller descriptions of the methods underpinning systematic reviews can be found elsewhere.[2,3]

A systematic review – sometimes described as secondary research or research synthesis – has been defined as:

> *... an attempt to collate all empirical evidence that fits pre-specified eligibility criteria in order to answer a specific research question. It uses explicit, systematic methods that are selected with a view to minimizing bias, thus providing more reliable findings from which conclusions can be drawn and decisions made.*[2]

The rationale for systematic reviews is grounded on several premises:[4]

- They reduce large amounts of data to manageable quantities.
- They are quicker and less costly than starting a new study. At the same time, they can prevent investigators from pursuing well-explored paths, and they can highlight areas where further primary research is required.
- They are capable of examining the consistency of an effect among studies of the same intervention and therefore provide a context that is usually unavailable from a single study.
- When they include meta-analyses, they increase the statistical power underpinning the use of a particular intervention. This is especially relevant where there are low event rates or when modest benefits are being assessed.

- As a corollary, meta-analyses can also increase the precision of the estimates of *effectiveness*. This not only allows decision-makers to have a better understanding of the magnitude of an intervention's benefits but is also crucial for any subsequent estimates of cost-effectiveness.

# Systematic reviews for benefits

The reporting of systematic reviews evaluating the benefits of healthcare interventions generally follows the PRISMA (preferred reporting items for systematic reviews and meta-analyses) guidelines.[5,6]

## Introduction

This section provides the rationale for the review and whether it is new or an update of a previous one. It should include an explicit statement as to the purpose of the review (sometimes known as 'the review question' or 'the decision problem').

## Methods

This section outlines how the critical elements of the review have been undertaken, with particular regard to eligibility criteria, search strategies, study selection, summary outcome measures and an evaluation of the risk of bias.

There are two components to the *eligibility criteria*. *Study eligibility* refers to the populations, interventions, comparators, outcomes (including the length of follow-up) and study designs that have been included. This section should also specify the features of those studies that have been excluded. Almost all conventional systematic reviews of an intervention's benefits confine their study designs to randomized controlled trials. The *reporting eligibility* criteria indicate whether there have been language restrictions (such as English-language publications only) and whether both unpublished data and results published only as abstracts will be included if they meet the study eligibility criteria.

The *search strategy* is one of the most critical elements of a systematic review. It usually includes, as a minimum, scrutiny of the electronic databases MEDLINE, EMBASE and CENTRAL (Cochrane Central Register of Controlled Trials). It may, when appropriate, encompass other, more specialized electronic databases. Potential supplementary search techniques include checking reference lists of included studies (citation searching), interrogating clinical trial registries, searching the websites of regulatory agencies and making enquiries of manufacturers. The so-called *grey literature* (which comprises written material produced by governments, academics and businesses that is not accessible through conventional electronic databases) may sometimes provide useful information. The grey literature is, however, much more difficult to access, even though some electronic databases are now available.[2] Systematic reviewers have sometimes hand-searched relevant journals, but this is now unusual. Reviewers may also contact the authors of research findings to seek missing information.

There is no agreed standard process for *study selection*. Reviewers usually start with a large number of identified records and exclude those that fail to meet the predetermined selection criteria. The process includes an element of subjectivity, and two assessors acting independently are often used to check study reports. This reduces the possibility of excluding relevant studies and also reduces bias.

The most common *summary outcome measures* for binary (dichotomous) outcomes are the *relative risks*, *odds ratios* and *risk differences*. Relative effects are more consistent **47** than absolute effects across studies, although absolute differences are important for interpreting the findings. With time-to-event outcomes the *hazard ratio* is commonly used as a summary measure. (See Chapter 1.4.)

For continuous outcomes, the appropriate measure is the mean difference between the treatment groups at the completion of the study (see Chapter 1.4). This is straightforward when all studies use the same outcome measures (such as a reduction in blood pressure). When studies use different outcome measures – such as trials of antidepressant agents that have used different rating scales – the standardized mean difference is used. This expresses the size of an intervention's effect in each study relative to the variability in that study. However, it does not readily translate into an easily comprehensible measure of the effect size because it is an abstract unit of the standard deviation rather than any particular scale.

Systematic reviewers are exquisitely sensitive to the possibility that studies are, in one or more ways, biased. Reviews therefore invariably explore *study quality* or *risk of bias* (as it is now often called). The simple and widely used Jadad scale[7] scores the likelihood of bias from a total of 0 (high) to 5 (low) (see Table 1.6.1). Attempts to score quality, however, have been subjected to some criticism.[8] The Cochrane Collaboration has introduced its own qualitative *risk of bias* instrument,[2] but whether this offers a better approach remains uncertain.[9] It is certainly more cumbersome to undertake and, like the Jadad scale, still requires considerable judgement for completion.

**Table 1.6.1** Jadad score[7] calculation*

| Item | Score |
|---|---|
| Was the study described as randomized? | 0 or 1 |
| Was the method of randomization described and appropriate? | 0 or 1 |
| Was the study described as double blind? | 0 or 1 |
| Was the method of double blinding described and appropriate? | 0 or 1 |
| Was there a description of withdrawals and dropouts? | 0 or 1 |
| Deduct 1 point if the method of randomization was described and was inappropriate | 0 or −1 |
| Deduct 1 point if the study was described as double blind but the method of blinding was described and inappropriate | 0 or −1 |

* For each of the first five items the answer 'no' scores 0 and the answer 'yes' scores 1 point. For each of the last two items, a point is deducted from the total score of the first five items if the answer is 'yes'.

## Results

Although the ordering may differ, the results of systematic reviews usually incorporate sections dealing with study selection, study characteristics and study findings (including an examination of the risk of bias within and between studies). Systematic reviews usually (but not invariably) include a quantitative synthesis (meta-analysis) of the results. If quantitative analyses are not possible, reviews will generally include a qualitative description of the results (as in a purely narrative review).

### ■ Study selection

This describes, sometimes with a flowchart, the numbers of records screened. It should enumerate those reports that have been included and those excluded (with reasons) in the final analysis. The most common reason for excluding studies is that, on close examination, they fail to meet the predetermined inclusion criteria, but there may be other reasons, such as duplicate publications. It is particularly helpful if reviewers report the sources of the included studies: literature identified primarily from reference lists or experts, for example, may be susceptible to publication bias.

### ■ Study characteristics

Reports of the results of systematic reviews are usually presented in the form of an evidence table. This comprises a line listing for each included study, which, typically, summarizes the data for each of the following:

- bibliographic reference;
- study type (e.g. randomized controlled trial, case–control study);
- study quality (e.g. Jadad score);
- number of patients in each arm;
- patient characteristics (e.g. age, sex);
- study setting (e.g. hospital in-patients, general practice surgeries);
- intervention(s), including dose(s) and route(s) of administration;
- comparator(s);
- length of follow-up;
- outcome measure(s) and effect size(s);
- additional comments.

### ■ Synthesis of the results

The results (outcomes) can be synthesized qualitatively (*narrative synthesis*) or quantitatively (*meta-analysis*).

Almost all systematic reviews include an element of narrative synthesis outlining or expanding on aspects of the included studies, even if the term is not used explicitly. Narrative syntheses become a more significant component in systematic reviews of *complex interventions* and in assessing qualitative studies. The defining characteristic of a formal narrative synthesis is the use of a textual approach that provides an analysis of the relationships within and between studies, and an overall assessment of the robustness of the evidence. It is a more subjective process than meta-analysis and, when used, needs to be rigorous and transparent to reduce the potential for bias.

In a quantitative synthesis the results are commonly displayed and reported as 'forest plots'. (The name allegedly originates from the idea that a typical plot appears as a forest of lines.) An example is shown in Figure 1.6.1. This summarizes the results of five randomized controlled trials, each designed to assess the effect of anticoagulation with warfarin on the frequency of ischaemic stroke in patients with non-valvular atrial fibrillation.[10] In a typical forest plot, the point estimate of each study is shown as a square, and the horizontal line running through the square is the 95 per cent confidence interval (CI). The area of each square is in proportion to the number of patients in the study

Systematic reviews commonly combine the results of each study so as to obtain a more reliable estimate of the intervention's effect. In such a meta-analysis the contribution of each individual study is weighted; larger studies therefore contribute to a greater extent than smaller ones in the pooled estimate of the effect size.

The pooled estimate in the forest plot shown in Figure 1.6.1 was undertaken using a so-called 'fixed effects' model. This assumes that each study is an estimate of the same outcome of interest; that the 'true' effect is the same in all studies; and that any differences are due to chance. The fixed effects model therefore answers the question 'What is the best estimate of an intervention's effect?' An alternative approach, the so-called 'random

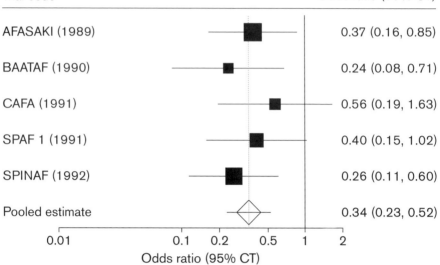

| Trial code | | Odds ratio (95% CT) |
|---|---|---|
| AFASAKI (1989) | | 0.37 (0.16, 0.85) |
| BAATAF (1990) | | 0.24 (0.08, 0.71) |
| CAFA (1991) | | 0.56 (0.19, 1.63) |
| SPAF 1 (1991) | | 0.40 (0.15, 1.02) |
| SPINAF (1992) | | 0.26 (0.11, 0.60) |
| Pooled estimate | | 0.34 (0.23, 0.52) |

0.01    0.1   0.2    0.5   1    2
Odds ratio (95% CT)

**Figure 1.6.1** Forest plot of the effects of anticoagulation on the prevention of ischaemic stroke in patients with non-valvular atrial fibrillation.[10]

CI, confidence interval.

effects' model, assumes that the effects are not identical across all the included studies but follow some distribution. It answers the question 'What is the average intervention effect?' The pooled estimate and confidence intervals from a random effects meta-analysis refer to the distribution of intervention effects but do not describe their width. Nevertheless, some consider a random effects approach to be a more natural choice than a fixed effects approach for decision-making.

The studies that are pooled in a meta-analysis will inevitably differ in some respects. The variability between studies – heterogeneity – has two components: *clinical diversity* arises from differences between the populations and outcomes studied, and *methodological diversity* is due to differences in factors such as study design and study quality. The simplest approach to examining heterogeneity is to look at the forest plot(s). If there is substantial overlap of the 95 per cent confidence intervals of the included studies, as in Figure 1.6.1, it suggests there is likely to be little statistical heterogeneity: poor overlap generally indicates statistical heterogeneity.

In systematic reviews, a formal approach to examining heterogeneity is to undertake a $\chi^2$ test (often described as the Q-statistic). The $\chi^2$ test, however, has low power and a larger P-value is often used to decide on its statistical significance. For the meta-analysis in Figure 1.6.1, the $\chi^2$ test is 1.81 ($P = 0.77$), which is reassuring. In many meta-analyses the related statistic the $I^2$ (inconsistency) test is used to estimate the percentage of the variability that is due to heterogeneity rather than sampling error: the higher the percentage, the greater the apparent degree of inconsistency. For the meta-analysis in Figure 1.6.1 the $I^2$ test is 0 per cent (95% CI 0 per cent to 64 per cent), indicating little inconsistency between the studies.

If significant heterogeneity has been identified in a meta-analysis there are various options for investigating it. These include checking that the data have been transcribed correctly; performing a random effects analysis if the original one used a fixed effects model; ignoring the heterogeneity; excluding one or two outlying studies; undertaking subgroup analyses; and abandoning a meta-analysis altogether. The choice should be carefully argued.

### ■ Risk of bias across studies

Good systematic reviews will explore the possibility of bias across studies and, in particular, publication bias. This can sometimes be detected with a funnel plot (see Figure 1.6.2). This is a simple scatter plot of the effect sizes of each of the studies (along the horizontal axis) against estimates of their precision (on the vertical axis). The effect size is often expressed as an odds ratio and an estimate of its precision as its standard error. In a funnel plot the effect estimates from smaller studies will scatter more widely across the bottom and the spread will narrow, with larger studies at the top.

In the absence of publication bias the funnel plot will be symmetrical. Asymmetry, which can be detected by visual inspection or formal tests,[11] will occur if smaller studies (without statistically significant effects) are unpublished. In this case the meta-analysis will overestimate the benefits of an intervention. Funnel plot asymmetry may occur, however, for reasons other than publication bias. These include poor methodological quality, true heterogeneity and chance. However, funnel plots are unreliable for detecting bias if fewer than ten studies are involved in their construction.

### ■ Additional analyses

Systematic reviews may incorporate additional analyses:

- subgroup analyses;
- comparisons of the effectiveness of competing interventions;
- sensitivity analyses.

*Subgroup analyses* may be undertaken for subsets of participants (e.g. men versus women), for exploring dose–response relationships and for subsets of studies (e.g. hospital-based versus community-based studies). Subgroup analyses can form part of an investigation into study heterogeneity between studies, or they may attempt to answer important clinical questions. However, the extent to which it is possible to undertake subgroup analyses is often limited by the information provided in the original study reports.

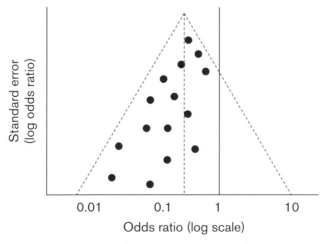

**Figure 1.6.2** Hypothetical funnel plot. (See text for explanation.)

Findings from multiple subgroup analyses can be misleading. As with subgroup analyses of the results of randomized controlled trials (see Chapters 1.2 and 2.3), if a sufficient number are performed, the chance of one or more false positive results increases with the number of comparisons. Ideally, therefore, only a small number of prespecified subgroup analyses should be undertaken.

In some systematic reviews, particularly those that will be used by decision-makers to determine priorities, the review question may not be whether two active interventions are each effective for the same indication when each is compared with placebo, but whether one is more or less effective than another. Such comparisons are, in principle, best approached with head-to-head studies (*direct comparisons*). Where two interventions have both been studied in placebo-controlled trials but not against each other, it is still possible to make an *indirect comparison* based on the placebo-controlled trials with each.

With indirect comparisons the so-called 'naive approach' to comparing competing interventions involves pooling findings from the active treatment arms of the original controlled trials and then making a comparison between them.[12] This ignores the potential benefits of randomization and has been shown to be very unpredictable, with a high frequency of statistically significant discrepancies when compared with direct comparisons. Consequently, it should never be used. In the alternative 'adjusted approach' the analysis is based on the differences between each of the treatment effects.[13] These are then combined using a random effects model. It is assumed in such adjusted indirect comparisons that the relative efficacy is consistent across the trials and is generalizable. Interpretation, however, is a matter of judgement. Nevertheless, in a study of 44 comparisons in which it was possible to compare the results of direct and adjusted indirect estimates, only three showed significant discrepancies.[12]

In some instances a systematic review may combine the results of both direct and indirect comparisons. In these circumstances both study designs are incorporated into a *mixed treatment* comparison,[14] which can accommodate three or more competing interventions. The question as to whether, and when, mixed treatment comparisons should be made is controversial. On the one hand, because of the possibility of bias and confounding, some believe that direct and indirect comparisons should be considered separately and that direct comparisons should take precedence. Others point out, however, that the precepts of systematic reviewing demand that all the available evidence be used to increase precision and examine generalizability,[14] and that anyway the issues of bias and confounding have been overemphasized. In considering evidence based on indirect and mixed treatment comparisons, decision-makers need to apply common sense.[14]

Systematic reviews involve a series of decisions in both their design and their conduct. Some are objective but others may be arbitrary. Should, for example, studies with less than a specific number of participants be excluded? Should studies in which either randomization or blinding is unclear also be excluded? Should a fixed effects or random effects model be used in the final analysis? These questions can be explored by a series of *sensitivity analyses*. When sensitivity analyses indicate that the overall results are not affected by decisions made during the review process, the findings can be regarded with a greater degree of certainty. When sensitivity analyses demonstrate vulnerability to particular decisions or uncertainties, the findings will need to be interpreted more cautiously.

## Conclusions and implications

The conclusions in systematic reviews should encompass advice on the implications for clinical practice as well as for future research.[15]

If, overall, a good systematic review shows that an intervention appears to be ineffective or dangerous, then its use in clinical practice would be regarded as inappropriate. There are, however, caveats. First, 'no evidence of an effect' should not be confused with 'evidence of no effect'. Second, if the confidence interval overlaps with the null value, it is still possible that the intervention is beneficial or harmful.

If the review indicates that an intervention is beneficial under the circumstances of the included studies, then any inference as to its place in routine care requires additional information that may not have been captured. Good systematic reviews of the benefits of interventions should incorporate an adequate assessment of harms. Yet only a minority do so.[16] Those that do include harms as well as benefits generally limit their analyses to rates of withdrawals and sometimes adverse event rates in the included studies. This information is rarely sufficient to allow the balance between benefit and harm – both in comparison with competing interventions and the nature and severity of the underlying condition – to be made with any degree of confidence.

# Systematic reviews of harms

Systematic reviews of harms are in principle no different from those of benefit, but there are some important differences.

## Introduction

The review question is critical. Is it 'hypothesis generating' and seeking to identify new, previously undiscovered harms? Or is it 'hypothesis testing' and limited to confirming the existence, and enumerating the frequency, of harms that have been identified as signals?

A broad, hypothesis-generating review question may have the potential to identify new harms and to consolidate knowledge about existing harms. The resources needed to undertake such a review, in proportion to its yield of novel data, rarely makes it appropriate.[17] A narrow, hypothesis-testing review limits the scope to a small number (and sometimes only one or two) of the most serious harms and is easier to undertake. However, its value may be limited since it will be confined largely to harms that are already known. Nevertheless, there are circumstances in which such narrow reviews provide very important information about clinically significant susceptibility factors.

## Methods
### ■ Search strategies
Randomized controlled trials are, by themselves, usually insufficient for assessing harms, especially if these are relatively uncommon or have a long latency (see Chapter 2.5). Observational studies, including controlled or uncontrolled cohort studies, case–control studies and large case series, are likely to provide more participants, longer periods of follow-up and more generalizable data. It has been pointed out, for example, that a meta-analysis of randomized controlled trials identified only 340 cardiovascular events related to cyclooxygenase 2 (COX-2) inhibitors;[18] but, by contrast, a review of observational studies identified 60 251 cardiovascular events in nine case–control studies.

No optimal search strategy for identifying reports of harms using conventional electronic databases has been established.[18] The indexing terms used in databases are currently so diverse and inconsistent that there is little confidence that publications in which adverse effects are described will be consistently retrieved from the range of observational studies and randomized trials that are available. Various approaches have been proposed but can be resource-intensive. An attempt to identify adverse effects of newer antiepileptic agents using MEDLINE and EMBASE noted a very low yield (2.8 per cent) of studies that met the inclusion criteria.[19]

The search might also include standard texts on adverse effects (such as *Meyler's Side Effects of Drugs*[20]) and the papers they summarize, together with the relevant grey literature such as safety alerts issued by national drug regulatory authorities and national adverse drug reaction registers.[21] There is no consensus, however, as to whether and how these data should be incorporated into systematic reviews, and the potential for bias is anyway considerable.

### ■ Study selection
Studies should include not only the results of randomized controlled trials but also, as a minimum, the results of controlled observational studies, supplemented perhaps by case series and case reports.[22]

## Results
### ■ Study characteristics
As with reports of systematic reviews of effectiveness, systematic reviews of harms are also presented as 'evidence tables'. These usually comprise line listings for each included study:

- bibliographic reference;
- study type (e.g. randomized controlled trial, case–control study);
- number of participants;
- intervention(s) (including dose and route of administration);
- results;
- additional comments.

These tables provide a qualitative overview of the nature of extent of an intervention's harmfulness.

### ■ Synthesis of results
The results from individual controlled studies, including data from randomized controlled trials and controlled observational studies, can be expressed as odds ratios and displayed in one or more forest plots. Pooled analyses are undertaken using methods similar to those adopted in the meta-analysis of randomized controlled trials. An example is shown in Figure 1.6.3. This shows the odds ratios for each of 12 separate studies, using three different study designs, of the risk of venous thromboembolism with hormone replacement therapy. It has been suggested that Bayesian meta-analyses offer considerable advantages in synthesizing data derived from both randomized controlled trials and observational studies.[23]

### ■ Risk of bias
Interpretation of the results of adverse effects of interventions needs to consider the risk of bias and confounding. Assessing the risks of confounding in observational studies is particularly difficult (see Chapter 1.5) because they may be unpredictable

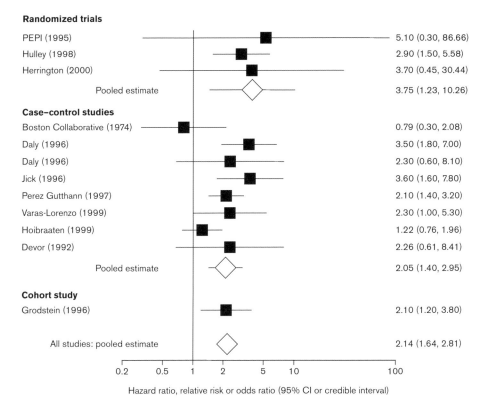

**Figure 1.6.3** Forest plot of the results of 12 studies investigating the risk of venous thromboembolism with hormone replacement therapy.[32]

CI, confidence interval.

and the methods used for their adjustment in the original studies are likely to have been different. Moreover, any residual confounding in individual observational studies is likely to be unknown, and the confidence intervals around point estimates may underestimate the degree of uncertainty. Nevertheless, in a study of the relative risks of harms for the same interventions, comparing data from randomized controlled trials and controlled observational studies yielded a surprising degree of concordance.[24]

■ **Additional studies**

As with systematic reviews of the effectiveness of interventions, those assessing harms may – when there is sufficient information from the individual study reports – include subgroup analyses. When applied appropriately, these can provide important information about the susceptibility factors for particular harms and, as a consequence, be able to propose measures to reduce their frequency. Because of concerns about bias and confounding, *sensitivity analyses* may be undertaken to investigate, for example, whether the results of meta-analyses are overly influenced either by particular studies or by those with apparently weaker design features. If such sensitivity analyses reveal that omitting particular studies results in little change in the pooled estimates, then decision-makers will have greater confidence in the reliability of the findings.

## Conclusions and implications

The results of systematic reviews of harms can lead to important conclusions. First, they may reveal evidence of a significant association between a particular harm and a particular intervention. Whether the association is causal depends on factors that include the extent to which the results could be explained by bias, confounding or chance. The distinctions between association and causation, in the context of both randomized controlled trials and observational studies, are considered extensively in Sections 2 and 3 of this book. Second, the results of a systematic review may provide a more reliable estimate of the incidence of harms than each of the source documents themselves. Finally, subgroup analyses may show whether particular groups of recipients are especially vulnerable, and the extent to which appropriate contraindications in the prescribing literature and in clinical practice should be introduced.

# Systematic reviews based on individual patient data

Conventional systematic reviews and meta-analyses are usually based on analyses on the summary results of studies in the public domain or that are retrieved by the reviewing team. An alternative or additional approach is for the reviewing team to ask each principle investigator of an included report to provide the clinical details of each of the participants on which their study has been based. These 'raw' patient data can then be combined into a single database and subjected to detailed scrutiny and analysis. Individual patient data meta-analyses have been successfully performed with both randomized controlled trials and observational studies.

Analyses based on individual patient data can provide unparalleled opportunities to obtain very precise estimates of the overall effect size and for the effectiveness in subgroups to be explored with consistency. For example, an individual patient meta-analysis of the effectiveness of aspirin in the primary prevention of vascular disease included 95 000 participants who had been previously recruited into six separate randomized controlled trials.[25] Individual patient meta-analyses have been equally informative in the assessment of harms. An individual patient meta-analysis of the risks of breast cancer with hormonal contraceptives,[26] for example, demonstrated the power of this approach. It was based on the results of 43 separate observational studies (six prospective cohort studies and 37 case–control studies) involving a total of 53 297 women with breast cancer and 100 239 controls.

Case study 1.6.1 shows the results of an individual patient meta-analysis of the relationship between upper gastrointestinal haemorrhage and the use of non-steroidal anti-inflammatory drugs.[27] It was based on three previously published case–control studies carried out in Britain, Sweden and Catalonia. The ability of this meta-analysis to distinguish between product and dosage would otherwise have been virtually impossible.

The use of individual patient data in systematic reviews is relatively uncommon; only about two per cent of reviews attempt this.[28] Investigators may be unwilling to relinquish their data, special arrangements are sometimes necessary to maintain patient confidentiality, and merging individual data from disparate sources can be extraordinarily time-consuming. Nevertheless, the approach has considerable power.

# Discussion

In the early years of their evolution, systematic reviews in general and meta-analyses in particular tended to be reviled. One distinguished professor of medicine is alleged to

**Case study 1.6.1** Upper gastrointestinal bleeding with non-steroidal anti-inflammatory drugs: meta-analysis based on individual patient data[27]

| | |
|---|---|
| **Background** | Non-steroidal anti-inflammatory drugs (NSAIDs) are recognized to be causally associated with upper gastrointestinal bleeding. Individual case–control studies have, however, shown considerable heterogeneity, possibly due to differences in the populations studied, patterns of use or methodology. Heterogeneity might also have been due to the differential toxicity of individual NSAIDs, or to the doses used by participants. |
| **Method** | Individual patient data were obtained from the principal investigators of three published case–control studies carried out in Sweden, Catalonia and Britain. Cases were patients admitted to hospital in each place with confirmed upper gastrointestinal bleeding. Catalan controls were selected from acute medical admissions to hospital, Swedish controls were selected from the community, and British controls were selected from both. All controls were matched to cases for age and sex. Individual patient data from each study were entered into a single database. |
| **Results** | The three studies provided information on 2472 cases and 5877 controls. The results indicated marked differences in the risks of upper gastrointestinal bleeding between and within (at different doses) individual NSAIDs. |

| | Odds ratio (95% CI) | | |
|---|---|---|---|
| | **Low dose** | **Medium dose** | **High dose** |
| Paracetamol | 1.2 (1.0, 1.4) | 1.2 (0.8, 1.7) | 1.0 (0.5, 1.9) |
| Ibuprofen | 1.1 (0.6, 2.0) | 1.8 (0.8, 3.7) | 4.6 (0.9, 22.3) |
| Diclofenac | 2.2 (0.8, 5.8) | 3.2 (1.9, 5.5) | 12.2 (5.6, 26.7) |
| Naproxen | 4.8 (1.3, 18.1) | 5.4 (2.9, 9.9) | 15.6 (8.1, 30.2) |
| Indometacin | 3.2 (1.1, 9.5) | 6.8 (3.6, 12.9) | 20.4 (4.2, 99.7) |
| Piroxicam | 9.0 (2.1, 39.2) | 12.0 (6.5, 22.1) | 79.0 (9.9, 631.8) |

| | |
|---|---|
| **Discussion** | The risk of upper gastrointestinal bleeding with NSAIDs was clearly related to both the individual product as well as the dose. Paracetamol, however, was not associated with an increased risk at any dose. The data (not shown here) also indicated that the risk of bleeding is greatest during the first week and declines thereafter, and that the use of more than one NSAID is associated with a super-additive increased risk. |

have stated in the early 1990s that 'Meta-analysis is a bit like combining a case of Chateau Palmer with a thimbleful of vinegar. One is left with a case of vinegar'.[29] It is now widely acknowledged, however, that the approach has much to offer.

The methods that underpin systematic reviews of the *internal validity* of the effectiveness of interventions are well-developed for studies of parallel group randomized controlled trials. They have also proved durable for crossover and cluster randomized controlled trials (see Chapter 3.1). Meta-analyses based on summary statistics are reliable, provided that the original reports include the necessary information and that publication bias can be eliminated.

Conventional systematic reviews of the benefits of interventions, however, have weaknesses. First, only about one-third provide any information on an intervention's harms.[16] This is a serious deficiency because decision-makers need to reach informed conclusions about the balance between an intervention's potential benefits and possible harms. This deficiency lies, in part, in the absence of adequate data on harms in many published reports of randomized controlled trials.[30,31] Even when the information has been recorded and published, it may not be readily retrievable by standard searching of databases. With the increasing adoption of the principles in the CONSORT statement (see Chapter 1.5), this problem will, one hopes, recede. Nevertheless, there appears to be too little appetite among systematic reviewers to couple a full assessment of an intervention's harms alongside an assessment of its benefits. In scrutinizing a systematic review, decision-makers need to consider this omission very carefully.

Second, by avoiding the inclusion of data from observational studies, systematic reviews may deny decision-makers the opportunity to assess the *generalizability* of the findings. Even if observational data are omitted from meta-analyses, they could, where available, provide useful information about the *external validity* of the included randomized controlled trials. Furthermore, observational data are sometimes critical in assessing an intervention's harms.

Third, the problem of using *direct comparisons* – versus indirect and *mixed treatment comparisons* – in the evaluation of competing interventions is now becoming very important. Decision-makers are increasingly being expected to adjudicate between alternative interventions, especially in the use of new (and often very expensive) anticancer agents. Decision-makers should therefore scrutinize carefully the reasons for the inclusion and exclusion of indirect comparators in systematic reviews of competing interventions.

Fourth, too few systematic reviews attempt to incorporate qualitative evidence. There are various ways in which this could be done. The results of qualitative studies could be included in narrative discussion of the quantitative findings; they could help in the interpretation of meta-analyses; or they could be brought formally together in syntheses of qualitative studies in parallel with syntheses of quantitative studies.

The methods that underpin systematic reviews of harms are seriously underdeveloped. Search strategies, the role of the grey literature and the available meta-analytic techniques all require much greater development if the needs of decision-makers are to be properly met. Decision-makers will, rightly, make considerable use of systematic reviews. Nevertheless, systematic reviews vary in quality, and decision-makers have to understand their advantages as well as their limitations. Above all, decision-makers should be aware that the community of systematic reviewers have an overriding fear of bias and a deep suspicion of the exercise of judgement. They are therefore sometimes too critical of studies that fail to meet the high demands they sometimes expect. As Voltaire put it: '*Le mieux est l'ennemi du bien*' ('The best is the enemy of the good').

# References

1. Mulrow CD. The medical review. *Annals of Internal Medicine* 1987;**106**:465–488.
2. Higgins JPT, Green S. *Cochrane Handbook for Systematic Reviews of Interventions*. Chichester: John Wiley & Sons, 2008.
3. Centre for Reviews and Dissemination. *Systematic Reviews: CRD's Guidance for Undertaking Reviews in Health Care*. York: University of York, 2009.
4. Mulrow CD. Systematic reviews: rationale for systematic reviews. *BMJ* 1994;**309**:597–9.

5. Moher D, Liberati A, Tetzlaff J, Altman DG. Preferred reporting items for systematic reviews and meta-analyses: the PRISMA statement. *Journal of Epidemiology* 2009;**62**:1006–12.

6. Liberati A, Altman DG, Tetzlaff J, *et al.* The PRISMA statement for reporting systematic reviews and meta-analyses of studies that evaluate healthcare interventions: explanation and elaboration. *BMJ* 2009;**339**:b2700.

7. Jadad AR, Moore RA, Carroll D, *et al.* Assessing the quality of reports of randomized clinical trials: is blinding necessary? *Controlled Clinical Trials* 1996;**17**:1–12.

8. Jüni P, Wtshi A, Bloch R, Egger M. The hazards of scoring the quality of clinical trials for meta-analysis. *Journal of the American Medical Association* 1999;**282**:1054–60.

9. Hartling L, Ospina M, Liang Y, *et al.* Risk of bias quality assessment of randomised controlled trials: cross sectional study. *BMJ* 2009;**339**:b4012.

10. Aguilar MI, Hart R. Oral anticoagulants for preventing stroke in patients with non-valvular atrial fibrillation and no previous history of stroke or transient ischemic attacks. *Cochrane Database of Systematic Reviews* 2005;**3**:CD001927.

11. Sterne JAC, Egger M, Moher D. Addressing reporting biases. In: Higgins JPT, Green S (eds). *Cochrane Handbook for Systematic Reviews of Interventions*. Chichester: John Wiley & Sons, 2008.

12. Glenny AM, Altman DG, Song F, *et al.* Indirect comparisons of competing effects. *Health Technology Assessment* 2005;**9**:1–134.

13. Bucher HC, Guyatt GH, Griffith LE, Walter SD. The results of direct and indirect treatment comparisons in meta-analyses of randomised controlled trials. *Journal of Clinical Epidemiology* 1997;**50**:683–91.

14. Caldwell DM, Ades AE, Higgins JPT. Simultaneous comparisons of multiple treatments: combining direct and indirect evidence. *BMJ* 2005;**331**:897–900.

15. Schünemann HJ, Oxman AD, Vist GE, *et al.* Interpreting results and drawing conclusions. In: Higgins JPT, Green S (eds). *Cochrane Handbook for Systematic Reviews of Interventions*. Chichester: John Wiley & Sons, 2008.

16. Ernst E, Pittler MH. Assessment of therapeutic safety in systematic reviews: literature review. *BMJ* 2001;**323**:546.

17. McIntosh HM, Woolacott NF, Bagnall A-M. Assessing harmful effects in systematic reviews. *BMC Medical Research Methodology* 2004;**4**:19.

18. Loke YK, Price D, Herxheimer A. Systematic reviews of adverse effects: framework for a structured approach. *BMC Medical Research Methodology* 2007;**7**:32.

19. Golder S, McIntosh HM, Duffy S, Glanville J. Developing efficient search strategies to identify reports of adverse effects in MEDLINE and EMBASE. *Health Information and Libraries Journal* 2006;**23**:3–12.

20. Aronson JK (ed.). *Meyler's Side Effects of Drugs: The International Encyclopaedia of Adverse Reactions and Interactions*, 15th edn. Edinburgh: Elsevier, 2006.

21. Loke YK, Price D, Herxheimer A. Adverse effects. In: Higgins JPT, Green S (eds). *Cochrane Handbook for Systematic Reviews of Interventions*. Chichester: John Wiley & Sons, 2008.

22. Loke YK, Derry S, Aronson JK. A comparison of three different sources of data in assessing the frequencies of adverse drug reactions to amiodarone. *British Journal of Clinical Pharmacology* 2004;**57**:616–21.

23. Speigelhalter DJ, Myles JP, Jones DR, Abrams KR. Bayesian methods in health technology assessments: a review. *Health Technology Assessment* 2000;**4**:1–130.

24. Papanikolaou PN, Christidi GD, Ioannidis JPA. Comparison of evidence of harms of medical interventions in randomized and nonrandomized studies. *Canadian Medical Association Journal* 2006;**174**:635–41.

25. Antithrombotic Trialists Collaboration. Aspirin in the primary and secondary prevention of vascular disease: collaborative meta-analysis of individual participant data from randomised trials. *Lancet* 2009;**373**:1849–60.

26. Collaborative Group on Hormonal Factors in Breast Cancer. Breast cancer and hormonal contraceptives: collaborative reanalysis of individual data on 53 297 women with breast cancer and 100 239 women without breast cancer from 54 epidemiological studies. *Lancet* 1996;**347**:1713–27.

27. Lewis SC, Langman MJS, Laporte J-R, *et al*. Dose-response relationships between individual nonaspirin nonsteroidal anti-inflammatory drugs (NANSAIDs) and serious upper gastrointestinal bleeding: a meta-analysis based on individual patient data. *British Journal of Clinical Pharmacology* 2001;**54**:320–26.

28. Tugwell P, Knottnerus JA. Advantages of individual patient data analysis in systematic reviews. *Journal of Clinical Epidemiology* 2010;**63**:233–4.

29. Ritter JM. Uncertain risks of drug related harms, the precautionary principle and limitations of meta-analysis. *British Journal of Clinical Pharmacology* 2009;**68**:647–50.

30. Loke YK, Derry S. Reporting of adverse drug reactions in randomised controlled trials: a systematic survey. *BMC Clinical Pharmacology* 2001;**1**:3.

31. Ioannidis JP, Lau J. Completeness of safety reporting in randomized trials: an evaluation of 7 medical areas. *Journal of the American Association* 2001;**285**:437–43.

32. Miller J, Chan BKS, Nelson H. *Hormone Replacement Therapy and Risk of Venous Thromboembolism*. Rockville, MD: Agency for Healthcare Research and Quality, 2002.

# SECTION 2
# Randomized controlled trials

# CHAPTER 2.1
## GENERAL PRINCIPLES

The introduction of the randomized controlled trial in the latter half of the twentieth century has unquestionably had a profound impact on medicine and therapeutics. The technique is straightforward in theory but in practice can be extraordinarily complicated – and expensive – to design, undertake and analyze.

At its simplest level a conventional randomized controlled trial involves a comparison of the effects of two or more interventions, allocated randomly to groups of contemporaneously treated patients. After a predetermined interval of time the outcomes of the groups are then compared. The interventions are often pharmaceutical products but may include devices, surgical procedures, psychological treatments or any other therapeutic modality.

## Background

Between 1930 and 1950 there were three major events in the evolution of what we now know as the randomized controlled trial:

- the use of randomization in the allocation of treatments;
- the adoption of 'blinding' in the assessment patient outcomes;
- a formal statistical analysis of the results.

### Randomization

The use of controls in therapeutic research is not (allegedly) new. King Nebuchadnezzar, in 600 BC, compared the effects of vegetarian and royal Babylonian diets over a 10-day period in a group of young men.[1] (Those given the vegetarian diet apparently did better and 'their countenances appeared fairer and fatter in flesh than those which did eat the king's meat'.) James Lind, in the eighteenth century, compared the effects of various treatments (including two oranges and a lemon a day) on the course of scurvy.[2] (After a few days, the sailors treated with citrus fruits were helping to look after the sailors who had been given other, ineffective treatments.)

During the early part of the twentieth century, controls became more common in studies of the *effectiveness* of interventions but were often chosen inappropriately. The famous (or infamous) Lanarkshire milk experiment, for example, was intended to study the benefits of supplementary milk given to school children. Children receiving the additional milk, however, were chosen by head teachers. It subsequently became clear that there had been selection *bias*. Presumably out of kindness, head teachers had selected an excess of malnourished children to receive the supplementary milk.[3]

The concept of randomization in the design of controlled experiments was introduced by Ronald Fisher (1890–1962) in the 1920s in the context of agricultural research. His reasons were largely statistical,[4] because only by randomization would it be possible to guarantee the validity of the statistical test of the significance of the results. During the 1930s and 1940s allocation of treatments in studies of the effects of interventions in humans was primarily based on 'alternation'. In this technique, consecutive patients alternately received the active and control interventions.

Alternation was advocated by Austen Bradford Hill (1897–1991) in a series of articles he wrote for the *Lancet* in the 1930s and in his subsequent book.[5] His intention was 'To ensure that, as far as possible, the control and treated groups are the same in all relevant respects.'

Alternation was used, for example, in trials of serotherapy[6] and sulphonamides[7] for the treatment of pneumonia. It was also the basis on which treatments were allocated in the wartime studies of the effects of sulphonamides by JG Scadding (1907–99) for the treatment of bacterial dysentery.[8]

Allocation of treatments by alternation, if strictly adhered to, would in principle be no different from allocation by randomization. The problem, however, is the potential for selection bias.[9] If the treatment schedules can be identified (and thus ignored or overruled) in advance, there is a serious risk that patient selection will be biased by the preferential allocation of one particular intervention to a particular patient by the investigator (see Chapter 1.5).

During the 1940s allocation of treatments by alternation started, under the influence of Bradford Hill, to become replaced by randomization. Randomization gives better protection against selection bias, provided that the investigator is unaware of which treatment the next patient is to receive. In later life Bradford Hill admitted that he had always been in favour of randomization, even during the 1930s, but was afraid that the notion would 'scare off' the medical profession,[10] and so he settled for alternation as the next best approach.

The first fully randomized trial, published in 1941, appears[11] to have been a study by Joseph Bell (1904–68) designed to examine the effectiveness of immunization against pertussis.[12] Randomization was also used in the Medical Research Council's own trials of pertussis vaccines in the 1940s.[13] The technique, however, became widely accepted around the time of the publication of the Medical Research Council's trial of the use of streptomycin in the treatment of pulmonary tuberculosis.[14]

## Blinding

So-called 'blinding' of trials describes the process whereby either the investigator or the patient is unaware of which treatment has been given until the end of the study. In 'double blind' trials, neither the investigator nor the patient is aware of the particular treatment allocation.

The first double blind clinical trial[3] appears to have been undertaken by Dr Harry Gold (1914–2010) in a study of the effects of antianginal drugs.[15] The technique was successfully adopted by Dr Henry Beecher (1904–76) in studies of the *efficacy* of analgesic agents.[16]

Provided that they are rigorously performed, randomization and blinding largely eliminate selection bias. Blinding of both the investigator and the patient is especially important (see Chapter 1.5) if the benefits are subjective (e.g. in the assessment of hypnotics, analgesics and antidepressants) or if there is a subjective element in the measurement by the investigator of the response (e.g. when using some forms of rating scale).

## Statistical analysis: the frequentist approach

Reports of trials carried out in the 1930s and early 1940s rarely, if ever, included a formal analysis of whether a treatment's apparent effectiveness could have occurred by chance.

For example, the results of the trial of serotherapy in the treatment of pneumonia[6] were described in an entirely descriptive manner, and no attempt at what would now be termed 'hypothesis testing' was made. The mortality rates in patients aged 20–40 years were simply reported as being 14/111 (serotherapy) and 44/194 (controls), but the extent to which the differences might be due to the play of chance were not mentioned. (The *relative risk* (mortality), when calculated, is 0.56 (95% confidence interval (CI) 0.33 to 0.95).)

The Medical Research Council's trial of streptomycin in pulmonary tuberculosis[14] was subjected to more detailed statistical scrutiny. Nevertheless, by modern standards, the description is of charming brevity:

> *Four of the S [i.e. streptomycin] patients (7%) and 14 of the C [i.e. control] patients (27%) died before the end of six months. The difference between the two series is significant; the probability of it occurring by chance is less than one in a hundred.*

The approach used to determine the statistical significance was not stated but was probably a $\chi^2$ test.[17] (Readers may be relieved to know that the relative risk of mortality at 6 months in the streptomycin trial was 0.32 (95% CI 0.11 to 0.86).)

As discussed in Chapter 1.2, the frequentist approach to the statistical analysis of a randomized controlled trial is based on a blend of the ideas of Fisher on the one hand and Jerzy Neyman (1894–1981) and Egon Pearson (1895–1980) on the other. Fisher proposed that the analysis of a study should be based on the 'null hypothesis'. If the probability of obtaining a result is extreme as or more extreme than 1 in 20 (i.e. $P \leq 0.05$), then the null hypothesis could be rejected.

The formulation developed by Neyman and Pearson was based on avoiding two types of error (see Chapter 1.2). A *type I error* (known as $\alpha$) was the chance of incorrectly rejecting the null hypothesis and reaching a false positive conclusion. A *type II error* (known as $\beta$) was the chance of incorrectly accepting the null hypothesis and adopting a false negative conclusion. What also distinguished the approach of Fisher from that of Neyman–Pearson was the latter's suggestion that the rejection of the null hypothesis implied the acceptance of an 'alternative' hypothesis and that the comparator had, indeed, been shown to be better.

A bizarre outcome of what was a bitter dispute between Fisher and Neyman–Pearson is that modern clinical trials – usually designed and analyzed by the frequentist approach – use a combination of the two methods. They are generally designed from a Neyman–Pearson standpoint (with predetermined levels of acceptance of $\alpha$ and $\beta$) but are then analyzed from a Fisherian perspective.

## Statistical analysis: the Bayesian approach

An alternative to the frequentist approach to the design and analysis of randomized controlled trials is one based on Bayes' theorem.[18] In its simplest expression, Bayes' theorem relates the *odds* from what is already known before (*a priori*) a trial to the odds recalculated after the trial (a posteriori). The link between them is the result of the trial itself and is expressed as the *likelihood ratio*. It is expressed thus:

Posterior odds = likelihood ratio × prior odds

### ■ The prior odds

Priors can be derived in several different ways. *Objective priors* may be available from previous studies. In a drug development programme, for example, the results of appropriate phase 1 or 2 studies could provide the prior for a phase 3 trial. Priors can **65** also be derived from historical data or imputed from the effects of an intervention on a *biomarker*. *Subjective priors* are another, more controversial approach. They involve ascertaining the degree of optimism (or pessimism) of relevant experts about the likely effects of a particular intervention. *Default priors*, often described as 'off-the-shelf priors', are probability distributions that conform to one of several potential 'hypotheses'. A 'sceptical prior' will have a mean treatment effect of zero with some spread to indicate the degree of scepticism. An 'optimistic prior' or 'enthusiastic prior' is centred on the alternative hypothesis and with a low chance (say, five per cent) that the true treatment benefit is negative. An 'uninformative prior' has a distribution that gives equal weight to all probability values and therefore provides no preconceived weight to any specific hypothesis. *Robust priors* compare several different priors in a sensitivity analysis.

### ■ Likelihood ratio

The likelihood ratio (also known as the Bayes factor) is the ratio – obtained from the results of a particular study – of the probability of the null hypothesis to the probability of the alternative hypothesis:

$$\text{Likelihood ratio} = \alpha/(1 - \beta)$$

As the likelihood ratio exceeds one, the weight of evidence increasingly favours the null hypothesis. As the likelihood ratio decreases below one, the weight of evidence is increasingly supportive of the alternative hypothesis.

### ■ Posterior odds

The posterior odds, derived using Bayes' theorem, is the product of the prior odds and the likelihood ratio.

An example of the use of a Bayesian approach to the analysis of a clinical trial[19] is shown in Case study 2.1.1.[20] As is common with the reporting of Bayesian analyses, the prior, the likelihood ratio and the posterior are all displayed as probability distributions (see Chapter 1.2). The GREAT (Grampian Region Early Anistreplase Trial) study had suggested that early domiciliary thrombolytic therapy after acute myocardial infarction was accompanied by a substantial further reduction in mortality compared with later hospital treatment.[19] If true, this would have had considerable practical implications for the British National Health Service in arranging for the optimal management of patients with myocardial infarction. The observed 49 per cent reduction in mortality derived from the results of the GREAT trial is the mode of the distribution (Figure b in Case study 2.1.1), and the wide spread of its probability distribution illustrates the inevitable uncertainty, with only a total of 36 deaths. The posterior (Figure c in Case study 2.1.1), however, suggests only modest, if any, advantage.

A Bayesian approach to the design and analysis of randomized control trials has potential advantages. It takes account of previous (prior) information and therefore avoids some of the problems associated with the null hypothesis. It can be used to monitor the progress of a trial without prespecifying strict stopping rules (see Chapter 2.3). Bayesian techniques can also overcome problems relating to power calculations as well as *multiplicity* in the investigation of subgroups (see Chapter 2.4).

Despite these claimed advantages Bayesian approaches have not been used to any great extent in the statistical analysis of randomized controlled trials. This derives, in part, from the distaste of many clinicians for the notion of subjective probability (as discussed in Chapter 1.2). There has also been controversy about the use of subjective priors, although this seems to have lessened with the adoption of objective and default priors.

*Therapeutics, evidence and decision-making*

**Case study 2.1.1** Bayesian reanalysis of the GREAT trial[20]

| | |
|---|---|
| **Background** | The GREAT trial[19] observed a 49 per cent reduction ($P = 0.04$) after acute myocardial infarction when patients were treated with a thrombolytic agent (anistreplase) at home compared with later treatment in hospital. Although early thrombolysis at home might be expected to have some survival advantage, a reduction of almost 50 per cent seemed implausible, given that hospital thrombolytic therapy itself reduces mortality by about 25 per cent. Pocock and Speigelhalter therefore undertook a Bayesian reanalysis of the results. |
| **Methods** | The authors established a prior (Figure a) from previous studies of the effects of this thrombolytic agent. They therefore assumed that a reduction in mortality by 15–20 per cent was highly plausible and that the extremes of no benefit and a 40 per cent reduction were both unlikely. The likelihood (Figure b) was based on the mortality rates in the two groups (23/148 versus 13/163) in the GREAT trial. |
| **Results** | Using Bayes' theorem, the posterior distribution (Figure c) shows that domiciliary therapy is most likely to produce a 24 per cent reduction in mortality, with a 95 per cent credible interval of 0 per cent to 43 per cent. |
| **Conclusion** | The probability derived from a frequentist analysis of the GREAT trial has been 'pulled back' in the light of prior knowledge of the effects of thrombolysis after acute myocardial infarction. The results of the GREAT trial were 'too good to be true'. |

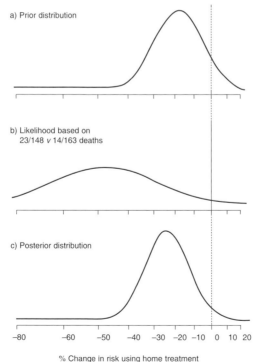

**Figure 2.1.1** Bayesian re-analysis of the GREAT trial showing change (reduction) in mortality from home thrombolytic therapy compared with treatment in hospital.

Bayesian analyses are computationally complex and some statisticians lack familiarity (or confidence) in their use. Some attribute this to statisticians' choice of university.[21] Others, less kindly, believe it to be generational: as one Bayesian has put it: 'Statisticians who were taught to use log books and slide rules can't usually do Bayesian statistics.'[22]

A further important reason why Bayesian approaches are not used widely has been the reluctance of national drug regulatory authorities to concede that they may have advantages. Pharmaceutical companies have, therefore, inevitably been reluctant to submit the results of clinical trials that are based on Bayesian statistics.[22] Nevertheless, manufacturers are increasingly adopting Bayesian approaches in phase 1 and 2 trials and using the results to decide whether to stop the drugs development or to proceed to more expensive phase 3 studies. In the regulation of devices, however, Bayesian approaches have had greater traction with regulators and are now being encouraged.[22]

Although few studies are designed and analysed using Bayesian methods, they have been most frequently used in the supplementary analysis of studies designed from a frequentist standpoint. The reanalysis of the results of the GREAT trial discussed earlier and shown in Case study 2.1.1 is a case in point. Decision-makers should be aware of this legitimate use of Bayesian approaches and should use the results in drawing their conclusions. Scrutinizing the results of a Bayesian analysis, however, needs expert statistical advice.

# Randomization

The critical element of any randomized controlled trial is that patients, at the outset, have an equal chance of receiving each of the interventions. Although other design features, such as blinding of both investigators and patients, are also very important, it is randomization that gives the method its greatest strength. Randomization has several purposes:

- It minimizes selection bias. By ensuring that investigators are unable – either consciously or unconsciously – to allocate treatments based on other factors that might influence the results, randomization provides the best way to make fair comparisons.
- It ensures that patient characteristics that might influence the results, such as age and gender, are likely to be distributed equally among the participants. As already discussed, baseline imbalances may still occur by chance and can be taken into account using techniques such as analysis of covariance (see Chapter 1.4).
- It provides the best opportunity to ensure that unknown patient *confounding* characteristics are distributed evenly between the groups.
- It satisfies statistical theory. In a study with random allocation, the differences between the treatment groups behave like the differences between random samples from a single population. The outcomes in the two (or more) groups can then be compared with what would be expected if the treatments were equally effective (i.e. the null hypothesis).

Randomization in the context of randomized trials has a precise technical meaning.[23] With random allocation each participant has a known probability of receiving each treatment before a treatment is assigned. The actual treatment a participant is given, however, is determined by chance and cannot be predicted in advance.

Randomization is commonly equalized (1:1) so that each participant has an equal chance of receiving each intervention. Unequal randomization, whereby participants have a greater chance of receiving one intervention rather than another, also has a place. Unequal allocation can provide investigators with greater experience of a new treatment with only a modest reduction in power, provided that the inequalities are no more than

2 : 1.[24] It has also been suggested that it might encourage the recruitment of participants as well as reduce the trial costs.[24]

## Techniques of randomization

With *simple randomization* patients are allocated to their treatment groups from a single list in which interventions are arranged in random order. Even if performed rigorously, such randomization can give rise, purely by chance, to significant imbalances. This is most likely with small trials and results in a reduction in the precision of the effect size.

One approach to preventing imbalances is *block randomization*. In this technique treatments are randomized in blocks. If, in a trial comparing two interventions, treatments are randomized in blocks of four, then within each block two patients will receive one intervention and two will receive the other. Block randomization has several advantages. In addition to promoting group balance at the end of the trial, it also ensures periodic balance so that sequential patients are distributed equally between groups. This avoids systematic differences between patients entering at different times during the study. Block randomization is common in multicentre trials where each centre then contributes equal numbers of participants to each of the intervention groups.

Simple and block randomization, however, may still lead to substantial imbalances. One approach to minimizing this is by *stratified randomization*. In this technique separate randomization lists are constructed for each prognostic subgroup. Randomization lists for each prognostic variable, however, need to be within a block design because the resulting allocation would otherwise be no different from that achieved by simple randomization. Stratification can, in theory, be extended to three or more prognostic variables, but the randomization lists then become unmanageable. In practice it is rarely feasible to go beyond stratifying two factors.[25]

An alternative method of achieving comparable treatment groups is by *minimization*. This more complicated approach involves allocating the first patient to one intervention group at random. Subsequent patients are assigned using a randomization that is weighted towards whatever group will minimize any imbalances. After each patient has been entered, the relevant totals for each prognostic factor are updated for the next patient recruited to the study.[26]

## The randomization process

The process by which a random allocation is presented to investigators is important in order to avoid compromising the results of a study. *Unconcealed randomization*, whereby the investigator, the participant or both have prior knowledge about which treatment is to be used, can, as already discussed, lead to conscious or unconscious bias. An investigator may, for example, believe that one form of treatment is particularly suited to a particular patient, or the patient may have some preference for one intervention over another.

*Concealed allocation*, whereby the treatment that a participant will receive is not known in advance, overcomes this limitation. Successful concealed randomization has two components: the generation of an unpredictable allocation sequence, and concealment of the sequence from the investigators who enrol participants. The allocation sequence is usually generated by the use of random numbers (either from published tables or produced electronically). The most common approach to concealment was traditionally the use of sealed envelopes. Investigators were provided with a series of these; after a participant agreed to enter the trial, an envelope was opened and the patient allocated to the revealed treatment.

Concealed allocation of this variety was by no means foolproof. The variety of approaches that individual investigators have used to subvert randomization is extraordinary.[27,28] Investigators have been known to open a series of envelopes until the desired treatment is 'allocated'. Unless the envelopes are opaque, the randomization sequence can be revealed by using a bright light or, easier still, a radiologists 'hot light'. Block randomization itself may enable investigators to predict treatment allocations: towards the end of each block, investigators will be able to guess which treatment the next participant is likely – or even certain – to get.

The preferred approach to randomization is *distance randomization*. This involves an investigator, on recruiting a patient, to contact a central randomization service that notes basic patient details and then issues instructions for treatment. It can be done by telephone, by email or through a dedicated website. Even this technique, though, has been known to be subverted by obtaining the next few allocations all at once.[27]

# Trial configurations

Five types of trial configuration are used in randomized controlled trials:

- parallel group;
- crossover;
- factorial;
- cluster;
- withdrawal.

## Parallel group study

In a parallel group study individuals are randomized to one of two or more interventions. The arms will, at a minimum, include the intervention of interest and either a placebo or an active control. Parallel group studies may also compare two or more doses of a single pharmaceutical product as well as including a placebo. The parallel group study is the one most commonly used in therapeutic research and has wide applicability.

A typical parallel group trial is summarized in Case study 1.4.1 in Chapter 1.4;[29] another, involving the use of streptokinase in the treatment of acute myocardial infarction, is shown in Case study 2.1.2.[30] Although the pooled results of a number of small randomized controlled trials had previously indicated that intravenous streptokinase might reduce early mortality, after acute myocardial infarction, the GISSI (1986) trial was the first definitive study confirming the *effectiveness* of thrombolysis. A criticism of the GISSI study was that the control group did not receive an inert placebo. Nevertheless, distance randomization was adopted for the study; and because it was carried out in a wide range of coronary care units across Italy, the *generalizability* of the trial was strengthened.

## Crossover study

In a crossover study subjects are randomized to a sequence of two (and sometimes more) treatments.[31] Subjects therefore act as their own controls. In a simple $2 \times 2$ crossover study each subject receives each of two treatments in random order. If there are more than two interventions, all subjects may receive each. There are, however, numerous variations, including those where subjects are given a subset of all the possible treatments, and those where subjects receive the same treatment on more than one occasion.

Crossover studies can only be used to study chronic, stable conditions where the intervention is expected to provide symptomatic relief. They have been used, for example,

*Therapeutics, evidence and decision-making*

| **Case study 2.1.2** Intravenous streptokinase in the treatment of acute myocardial infarction[30] |
|---|

| | |
|---|---|
| **Background** | At the time this study was undertaken, there was suggestive evidence that intravenous streptomycin might be effective in reducing the mortality when given 24 hours after the onset of symptoms. This study sought to assess whether intravenous streptokinase was effective and safe under routine conditions. |
| **Methods** | Patients admitted to a coronary care unit within 12 hours of the onset of symptoms with chest pain and electrocardiographic features of acute myocardial infarction were eligible for the study. Patients without contraindications were randomly assigned by a central coordinating centre either to treatment with intravenous streptokinase (1.5 million units infused over one hour) or to a control group (but no placebo). The primary endpoint was in-hospital mortality of the two groups. The causes of death were assessed from the patients' medical records by two cardiologists blind with respect to treatment assignment. Analyses were by intention-to-treat. |
| | Power calculations indicated that to detect a 20 per cent reduction in hospital mortality, with $\alpha = 0.01$ and $1 - \beta = 0.95$, 12 000 patients would need to be recruited. |
| **Results** | A total of 11 806 patients, from 176 Italian coronary care units, were randomized over a 17-month period. The records of 94 randomized patients could not be traced and were therefore omitted from the analysis. The streptokinase and control groups were well-matched with respect to demographic and clinical features. The study results for the all-cause mortality rates are summarized below: |

| | Streptokinase ($n = 5860$) | Control ($n = 5852$) |
|---|---|---|
| In-hospital mortality | 628 (10.7%) | 758 (13.0%) |

| | |
|---|---|
| | Relative risk: 0.81 (95% CI 0.72 to 0.90). |
| | Of the 1386 deaths, 1284 were due to cardiovascular causes. |
| **Conclusion** | The results indicated that intravenous streptokinase given early after the onset of symptoms of acute myocardial infarction, and with no positive contraindications, is associated with a significant reduction in cardiovascular mortality. |

in comparisons of analgesics in chronic pain and of hypnotics in chronic sleep disorders. Crossover studies are used extensively in the pharmaceutical industry to investigate, often in volunteers, the bioequivalence of two formulations of the same medication.

The advantage of the crossover study is that, because participants act as their own controls, the number of subjects needed to investigate a particular hypothesis is therefore much reduced. The resulting reduction of between-patient variation makes it, at least in theory, more efficient. Exquisite care, however, needs to be taken to avoid carry-over effects. This occurs when the residual effects from a previous treatment period influence the apparent response in the next period. As a result there is a danger of bias in the assessment of the treatment comparisons because this carry-over effect cannot be distinguished from the interaction between treatment and period. If a carry-over effect is suspected or demonstrated, one approach is to handle the study as a parallel group design and confine the analysis to the first treatment period. This, of course, immediately reduces the power of the trial.

Carry-over is best avoided by careful preliminary studies showing that the treatment effect is fully developed within the proposed treatment period, and that the washout period between treatments is long enough for the effects of the previous treatment to have been reversed.

The analysis and interpretation of crossover trials can also be complicated by loss of subjects during the trial. There may also be difficulties because of possible carry-over effects in assigning *adverse events* that occur later in the trial to the relevant intervention.

## Factorial study

Factorial designs are used to assess the effects of combinations of treatments given simultaneously. In a $2 \times 2$ factorial design investigating the combination of treatments A and B, subjects are randomly allocated to one of four possible combinations: A alone; B alone: A + B; and neither A nor B.

## Cluster-randomized study

Healthcare interventions are sometimes delivered at organizational or geographical levels rather than to individuals.[32] One example would be health-promotion interventions delivered by schools. In such an instance it would be virtually impossible to randomize individuals to (say) one form of sex education compared with another in the same class. In such circumstances it may be possible to undertake a cluster-randomized trial where, instead of randomizing individual students, it is the participating schools that are randomized and are the unit of analysis.

The number of participants needed in cluster trials is generally much greater than that needed for conventional randomized controlled trials. In a cluster trial, the independent units rather than the participating individuals form the groups. The individuals within the cluster are not independent because they may share common features that influence the outcome. In the case of sex education in classrooms, for example, the school's location may preferentially attract children from a particular socioeconomic group. Estimating the sample size for cluster trials depends on the magnitude of the clustering effect, but this may not be fully apparent until the trial has been completed.

The analysis of the results of a cluster trial may also pose technical difficulties. If the unit of analysis is, for example, the school, then it becomes impossible to adjust for the individual characteristics of the children. A more sophisticated approach is to use a so-called multilevel model that allows for both the characteristics of the children (such as age, gender, religion, socioeconomic status) and relevant features of the school (such as the type and staffing ratio) to be modelled.

There are particular difficulties about the extent to which participants can be blind to their allocation status while, at the same time, be provided with full information about the trial. The extent to which *internal validity* is compromised by this lack of blinding remains uncertain.

## Withdrawal study

In a randomized withdrawal trial patients already receiving an intervention are randomly assigned to continued treatment or to a placebo. The outcome is then reassessed after an appropriate interval of time. Participants may be recruited from an existing cohort of patients who are using the intervention. Alternatively participants may be those who have completed the active arm of a placebo-controlled trial; or, if the trial involves an active comparator, the effects of withdrawal can be studied among participants in both arms.

Randomized withdrawal trials are relatively uncommon. They can provide additional confirmation as to the benefits of an intervention. They have been used in assessing the long-term effectiveness of interventions administered to treat an episode of a potentially recurrent condition (such as depression) and are therefore, in these circumstances, relapse-preventing trials. They have also been used in the assessment of drugs used to suppress symptoms or signs (such as angina pectoris or hypertension) where a protracted placebo-controlled randomized trial would be difficult.

# Trial designs

A variety of designs are used in randomized controlled trials, depending on the objective of the study. They include:

- superiority designs;
- equivalence designs;
- non-inferiority designs;
- futility designs.

## Superiority design

A superiority trial seeks to investigate whether one treatment is more effective than another. The design and analysis is generally based on the null hypothesis; as discussed earlier in this chapter, at the end of the trial the relevant outcomes are compared between the groups. If the probability of observing the observed difference purely by chance is equal to or less than some prespecified value, then the null hypothesis is rejected. If the probability (frequency) that the observed difference in the outcomes is as extreme as or more extreme than the one obtained, then the null hypothesis is rejected. By convention, this specified 'extreme' value is set at less than 1 in 20 (i.e. $P \leq 0.05$). Both the Scandinavian Simvastatin Survival Study[29] (see Case study 1.4.1 in Chapter 1.4) and the GISSI trial[30] (see Case study 2.1.1) are examples of superiority trials.

There are a number of variants of the superiority design that can be used:

- pragmatic trials;
- adaptive design trials;
- preference trials;
- *N*-of-1 trials.

### Pragmatic trials

These are designed to investigate whether a particular intervention is as effective in the circumstances more closely resembling of normal clinical practice.[33] Pragmatic trials are intended to help decision-makers reach conclusions relevant to the 'real world'. They are likely to have greater applicability if they fulfil at least some of the following criteria:[34]

- The participants, communities and practitioners should not be too narrowly selected and should be broadly representative of conventional clinical practice.
- The intervention should be used without special attempts at standardization.
- The comparator group should receive care that is already widely used and known to be effective.

- The outcomes should be those of importance to relevant decision-makers. In particular, it has been suggested that single outcomes may be inadequate to weigh up the benefits, risks and costs that are important to patients and, consequently, that several outcome measures should be incorporated in the design of pragmatic trials.[35]

If multiple scenarios and outcomes are to be analysed in a pragmatic trial, then the statistical power needs to take account of the possibility of false positive and false negative findings. Such trials may therefore have to be of a substantial size. Pragmatic trials can make some contribution to assessing the *generalizability* of the effectiveness of an intervention. Nevertheless, they are usually powered to measure the 'average' effect across the population rather than in specific subgroups.

### ■ Adaptive designs

In these designs the allocation of patients to the interventions in a randomized controlled trial change as the trial proceeds. If, for example, one intervention begins to appear to be superior to another, then the proportion of patients randomized to it is increased as the trial proceeds. Such studies are sometimes described as 'play-the-winner', 'data-dependent' or 'bandit' designs. (The term 'bandit design' is reputed to be analogous to a gambler deciding which arm of a two-armed bandit to pull in order to maximize the expected return.) The alleged advantages of these designs include a reduction in the total number of patients required to be entered into a study, and overcoming the ethical difficulty in continuing to randomize participants to a less effective form of treatment during the course of a study.

Adaptive designs are possible only when the relevant outcomes occur reasonably soon after treatment starts. In a study that is examining mortality over a 5-year period, adaptive designs would obviously be hopeless. In practice adaptive designs have been undertaken only rarely, and their utility is the subject of considerable controversy among statisticians.

### ■ Preference trials

One of the problems with randomized controlled trials is that they only involve patients who agree to be randomized to the study treatments. Omitting patients with a preference for one treatment over another might limit the generalizability of the results. In a study where blinding of participants is virtually impossible (such as a comparison between psychotherapy and drug treatment for depression), those randomized to their less preferred treatment might subvert the protocol by, for example, poor compliance (sometimes called 'resentful demoralization'). On the other hand, those receiving their preferred treatment may comply better than average. In addition, the potentially greater placebo effect among participants randomized to their preferred treatment option may also limit the internal validity of the results. To overcome these potential difficulties, various forms of patient preference trial have been developed.[36] They generally involve comparisons between two active interventions.

The simplest approach is the so-called fully randomized patient preference trial. In this, participants are enrolled in a conventional randomized controlled trial but are asked, after agreeing to take part but before randomization, to indicate their preferred intervention. Irrespective of their preference they continue to be monitored for the duration of the trial. At the end of the study the results are analyzed overall and by preferred treatment.

There are more complicated patient preference designs that allow patients to decide whether their treatment is to be determined by random allocation or whether they are to be allowed to receive their preferred intervention.[36] In these trials, both groups are then followed up in accordance with the trial protocol and the outcomes between the treatments are compared separately in the randomized and preference groups.

*Therapeutics, evidence and decision-making*

Interpreting the results of preference studies is difficult. If the effect sizes between the groups are similar, then patient preference would appear to be unimportant. Such concordance between the groups would also provide some degree of confidence in the generalizability of the results of the overall findings. On the other hand, if the effect size between the groups is greater among participants receiving their preferred treatment compared with those randomized, then there might be several explanations. It could, for example, reflect the influence of known (or unknown) confounders, a subtle placebo effect or something else.

■ *N*-of-1 trials

In a randomized controlled trial, the apparent benefits may vary from patient to patient. This may be due to chance, but it may reflect a true difference between participants in their response. The *N*-of-1 design attempts to obtain a reliable estimate of the effects of an intervention in individual participants. In this approach the interventions – usually a placebo and an active treatment – are assigned in pairs to each participant in random order. The number of pairs varies from two to seven. The number of pairs is often not prespecified, with the participant and investigator stopping when both are convinced that there are important or unimportant differences between the interventions. Ideally the study should be double blind to avoid ascertainment bias, and the outcome(s) should be easily measured.

*N*-of-1 studies are possible only in patients with chronic conditions with stable symptoms, but despite their attractions they are unusual. If they involve a prolonged washout between each treatment, they can be extremely time-consuming for both participant and investigator; and they yield little generalizable information. They have, however, been particularly advocated for the investigation of treatments for very rare diseases.[37]

## Equivalence trials

An equivalence trial is designed to show whether two interventions have similar or equivalent therapeutic effects. It is used, in particular, to assess the efficacy of a new intervention when established alternatives are already available, and when a placebo-controlled trial would deny participants active treatment. If the new intervention is expected to be more effective than an established one, then a superiority trial is the appropriate design. If the new intervention is expected to match existing interventions in terms of efficacy but to have advantages in terms of safety, convenience or cost, then an equivalence trial is likely to be more appropriate.[38]

The design of an equivalence trial is predicated on the fact that absolute equivalence is impossible to demonstrate. Rather, it is possible only to assert that the true difference is likely to be within a range that depends on the size of the trial, the magnitude of the effect and the probability of error. Consequently, in designing an equivalence study, the investigators must decide what degree of 'inequivalence' would be clinically unacceptable – or, put another way, what degree of difference would be clinically unimportant.

An equivalence trial thus reverses the roles of the null and alternative hypotheses. The null hypothesis is that there is a difference of a prespecified, but clinically unimportant, extent; and the relevant alternative hypothesis is that there is no difference between the treatments. Deciding the difference between what is clinically important and unimportant is a matter of judgement but needs to be justified.

Deficiencies in the design and analysis of equivalence studies will tend to undermine any apparent differences in the effect sizes of the two treatments. Unlike superiority trials, where scrupulous attention to detail is often necessary to show a difference between two treatments, sloppy design and analysis of equivalence studies may result in unjustified claims of no difference in effect. Particular attention needs to be given to six factors:[38]

- The reference comparator should be used at a dose and duration that reflects current established clinical practice.
- Both the inclusion criteria and the choice of outcomes should match those used in the original studies of the reference comparator.
- The sample size, which will need to be substantially larger than that required for a superiority trial, needs to be clearly justified.
- Double blinding may be especially difficult if the interventions or treatment regimens are markedly different. This can happen if one treatment is, for example, given orally and the other parenterally. Such difficulties can be overcome by using the 'double dummy' technique, whereby all patients receive both an oral and a parenteral preparation but, depending on their treatment allocation, only one of them is active.
- Analysis of the results using an intention-to-treat approach may be too conservative in equivalence trials. The inclusion of participants who violate the protocol or withdraw from the study will tend to make the results in the two treatment groups appear similar. Consequently, both intention-to-treat and per protocol analyses should be undertaken. If the results are similar in both analyses, equivalence can be inferred with greater confidence.
- The analysis of equivalence trials is generally based on two-sided confidence intervals. Equivalence can be inferred when the entire confidence interval falls within the equivalence margins (see Figure 2.1.2). If the confidence interval covers some points outside the equivalence range, differences of clinical importance remain a real possibility.

There is one additional caveat. If an active comparator trial has been designed and analysed as a superiority study but has shown no statistically significant difference in effect, then it is inappropriate to infer that the result demonstrates equivalence. Such trials often lack the statistical power to rule out important differences.[39]

Case study 2.1.3 describes a well-designed equivalence study comparing the analgesic effects of a corticosteroid (prednisolone) and a non-steroidal anti-inflammatory drug

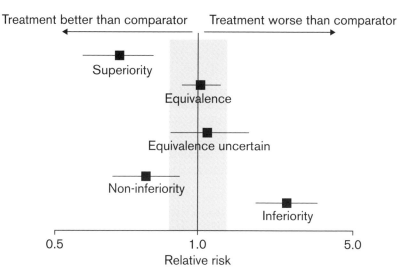

Figure 2.1.2 Some possible treatment scenarios for the results of superiority, equivalence and non-inferiority trials. The error bars are the 95 per cent confidence intervals (95% CI). The shaded area is the zone of equivalence (indifference).

| **Case study 2.1.3** Oral prednisolone versus oral naproxen in the treatment of acute gout: an equivalence trial[40] | |
|---|---|
| **Background** | Acute gouty arthritis has, traditionally, been treated with a non-steroidal anti-inflammatory drug (NSAID). Although effective, NSAIDs carry a range of adverse effects, which restricts their use. There was some evidence that corticosteroids might offer an equivalent degree of pain relief, and this study was designed to examine such a possibility. |
| **Method** | Patients with acute gout, confirmed by the presence of urate crystals in the affected joint, were randomly allocated to treatment with either prednisolone (35 mg once daily) or naproxen (500 mg twice daily). A double dummy design was adopted. Pain in the affected joint was assessed every 12 hours for four days using a 100 mm visual analogue scale, with boundaries of 'absence of pain' and 'the most severe pain ever experienced'. |
| | The trial was designed as an equivalence study. The margin of equivalence was defined as ten per cent and the study was powered to yield $\alpha = 0.05$ and $1 - \beta = 0.8$. Both per protocol and intention-to-treat analyses were undertaken. |
| **Results** | A total of 59 patients were randomized to each treatment group. The mean baseline scores for pain severity were similar in the two groups (61.5 mm and 58.9 mm). The mean difference in pain scores between the groups was 1.3 mm (95% CI –9.8 to +7.1) at 90 hours (the end of the study). |
| **Conclusion** | The similar reduction in pain in the two groups suggests that they can be regarded as of 'equivalent' efficacy. |

(naproxen) in patients with acute gout.[40] It would be reasonable, from the results of this trial, to conclude that the two treatments are similar in their effectiveness.

## Non-inferiority trials

Non-inferiority trials are very similar to equivalence trials but are designed to show that a new therapy is no worse than, rather than equivalent to, a reference therapy. Superiority in a non-inferiority trial is a bonus.

As with equivalence trials the null and alternative hypotheses are reversed, and non-inferiority trials are very similar, in most respects, to equivalence studies. The only major difference is that analysis is based on a one-sided test. Non-inferiority can be inferred if the lower confidence interval lies within the area of indifference (see Figure 2.1.2). The precautions in the design and analysis of non-inferiority trials are similar to those required in equivalence studies.

## Futility trials

Futility trials are, in many respects, variants of equivalence and non-inferiority trials, but with a particular application in drug development. In a futility trial the null hypothesis states that a novel treatment appears to be sufficiently promising to warrant further definitive testing in one or more large phase 3 studies. The alternative hypothesis states that the new treatment lacks the prespecified superiority.[41]

Futility studies have a significant role in drug development where more liberal $P$-values (such as $P < 0.1$) are often adopted. Futility trials have been designed as placebo-controlled trials,[41] but some have used historical controls as comparators.[42] The great advantage of this approach is that it allows some potential new interventions to be discarded at an early stage without incurring the expense of more conventional study designs.[43] When used in this manner as a screening tool, futility trials have merit. They have a reasonable negative predictive value (i.e. a finding of futility) but a weak positive predictive value (i.e. a finding of non-futility).[41] Futility studies are therefore particularly geared to the needs of those who make decisions about whether the development of new products, or indications, should proceed or be abandoned.

# Discussion

The importance of randomized controlled trials in providing decision-makers with reliable evidence on the efficacy of therapeutic interventions is unquestioned. The method has been virtually unchanged – apart from some statistical embellishments – for 50 years. The design follows a linear process and is straightforward. The techniques for frequentist statistical analyses are relatively uncomplicated and are easily performed with modern computers. Drug regulatory authorities worldwide accept the method. There is therefore inertia towards changing the broad approach.

Randomized controlled trials do, however, have practical limitations – stopping rules, subgroup analyses, safety analyses and generalizability – that are discussed extensively in subsequent chapters of this section. There are also additional imperfections:

- the null hypothesis;
- probability;
- cost.

## The null hypothesis

As already described, the design and analysis of the conventional randomized controlled trial is based on the null hypothesis and on the initial assumption that there is no difference between the two or more interventions. Apart from the intellectual difficulty in accepting that 'deductive falsification' (see Chapter 1.1) is a reliable basis for scientific inference, the null hypothesis itself creates several problems.

First, the null hypothesis does not readily lend itself to investigating whether there is no difference, or not much of a difference, between interventions. The equivalence, non-inferiority and futility designs that have already been described require substantial intellectual gymnastics to be made to work. These include reversing the null and alternative hypotheses, the use of one-tailed tests in non-inferiority studies, and the dependency on prior assumptions about the extent to which differences in effect sizes might, or might not, be clinically important in equivalence, non-inferiority and futility studies. Moreover, calling a hypothesis that states there is a difference a 'null hypothesis' is not semantically appealing. It is hardly surprising, therefore, that one systematic review of published equivalence and non-inferiority trials found important deficiencies in their design and analysis.[44]

Second, the null hypothesis may be irrelevant if there have been previous clinical trials showing that a particular treatment has some effect. This is a particularly strange phenomenon in drug development programmes. Phase 2 studies may show that a new product has therapeutic potential but further exploration is necessary in phase 3 studies. Analysing the results of the phase 2 studies based on the null hypothesis has some merit. But analysing the results of the phase 3 studies, and still adopting the null hypothesis, is counterintuitive.

| **Case study 2.1.4** Controlled trial of surgery for temporal lobe epilepsy[50] | |
|---|---|
| **Background** | The value of surgical resection of the non-dominant temporal lobe in the treatment of poorly controlled temporal lobe epilepsy had previously been asserted from the results of case series. This trial was undertaken to assess whether surgery was effective in this indication. |
| **Methods** | Eighty patients with temporal lobe epilepsy agreed to take part in the study. All were at least 16 years of age, and with at least monthly seizures for the past year despite treatment with at least two or more anticonvulsant drugs. They were randomly assigned to either surgical excision of their anterolateral (non-dominant) temporal lobe or continuation of their medical treatment. |
| | The primary outcome was freedom from seizures impairing awareness (i.e. complex partial or generalized seizures) at 1 year. A power calculation indicated that to observe a 34 per cent reduction in the primary outcome, with $\alpha = 0.05$ and $1 - \beta = 0.9$, a total of 40 patients per group would be required. Surgery was performed by one of three experienced neurosurgeons. |
| | Information about the type and frequency of each patient's epileptiform symptoms was assessed every three months after entry into the trial. This was undertaken by two epileptologists (blind to the identity of the patient and the treatment allocation) reviewing the medical records. The analysis was by intention-to-treat. |
| **Results** | Of the 92 patients screened, 86 were eligible. Eighty agreed to participate, and 40 were randomly assigned to each group. There were no imbalances in a variety of demographic and clinical characteristics, apart from a lower quality of life in patients assigned to surgery. |
| | At one year the cumulative proportion of patients free of seizures impairing consciousness was 58 per cent in the surgical group and eight per cent in the medical group (log-rank test $P < 0.001$). The benefit of surgery persisted after adjustment for baseline characteristics, including quality of life ($P < 0.001$). The number needed to treat with surgery to render 1 patient free of seizures impairing awareness was 2 (95% CI 2 to 5). |
| | Four patients in the surgery group suffered adverse effects attributable to the operation (one with a subthalamic infarct, one with a surgical site infection, and two with a significant decline in verbal memory). |
| **Conclusion** | In temporal lobe epilepsy, surgery is superior to prolonged medical therapy. The surgical morbidity was comparable to that observed in previous case series. |

Nevertheless, despite its intellectual and other limitations, it is clear that the null hypothesis will continue to underpin the design and analysis of most randomized clinical trials for the foreseeable future. Greater use of Bayesian statistics in the design and analysis of clinical trials would largely eliminate the 'null hypothesis problem', but the current approaches are unlikely to change very rapidly.

### The P-value

In the frequentist approach to the design and analysis of a randomized controlled trial, the rejection of the null hypothesis – because the outcome between the groups is as extreme as or more extreme than the one observed – leads to acceptance of the alternative hypothesis. That is to say, the results of the study indicate that one treatment is, indeed, more effective than another. The definition of 'extreme' is entirely arbitrary and is often misinterpreted (see Chapter 1.2).

As already discussed, a *P*-value of less than 0.05 does not necessarily mean that one treatment has been 'proven' to be superior to another: the play of chance ('random error') may, for example, be responsible for the findings. Nor if the *P*-value is greater than 0.05 does it necessarily mean that the intervention is ineffective and that the alternative hypothesis should be rejected. The probability of avoiding such a type II error is determined largely by the statistical power of a study, which, in turn, is determined by the size of the difference in outcomes between the two groups, the precision of the estimate of the outcome, and the number of patients studied.

### Cost

The costs of undertaking randomized controlled trials are substantial in money, time and energy and are rising.[22] Trials costing US$50 million are commonplace, and a few cost as much as US$ 500 million. Much of the increase over the past few years has been due to the increasing regulatory burdens imposed on both privately and publicly funded studies.[45] Each measure was introduced with the best of intentions, including a desire to protect patients from unscrupulous investigators and sponsors, to ensure the collection and timely reporting of adverse event data during trials, to audit individual case report forms and thus avoid the consequences of untruthful behaviour by investigators, and so on. As a consequence, even simple studies with products that have been available for many years place a massive bureaucratic challenge to sponsors and investigators alike.

Proposals by an international group of academic clinical investigators indicate that trial costs could be decreased by 40–60 per cent without detriment to their quality.[46,47] Simple measures such as electronic data capture, reduction of the length of case management forms, and modified site management practices would substantially reduce costs.

Randomized controlled trials also impose a substantial carbon footprint. The investigators of the CRASH trial (see Case study 2.2.1 in Chapter 2.2) undertook a carbon audit of their own study.[48,49] During a one-year audit period the total emission of greenhouse gases amounted to 126 tonnes (carbon dioxide equivalents). If the audit year was representative of the six years of the study, then the trial was responsible for about 630 tonnes of carbon dioxide equivalents (corresponding to 525 round-trip flights from London to New York). The authors concluded that a simplified trial design, reduced bureaucracy and greater use of videoconferencing would reap substantial savings.[49] There is a striking concordance between the measures that would reduce the burdens that randomized controlled trials place on healthcare systems and on the planet.

### Judgement

No randomized controlled trial is perfect. All have some deficiency or other, and decision-makers must necessarily exercise judgement in evaluating the implications for routine healthcare. Case study 2.1.4 is an example of one such instance where decision-makers must exercise judgement about the extent to which deficiencies in a randomized controlled trial render it unsuitable for making an informed decision.[50]

This case study summarizes the results of a trial of partial temporal lobotomy in the treatment of patients with temporal lobe epilepsy that was poorly controlled by conventional anticonvulsant agents. Randomized controlled trials in surgery are uncommon but, as this case study indicates, they are not impossible. This particular study was designed as a typical superiority trial with a power that was appropriate to the outcome under investigation. Nevertheless, it has three potential deficiencies.

First, the process of randomization involved the use of sealed, opaque, sequentially numbered envelopes. This method, as discussed earlier, makes it possible for an investigator to decide whether or not to enrol a particular patient before randomization. The evidence suggests, though, that this probably did not occur. The number of patients eligible (total 86) and the number randomized (total 80) indicates that the omission of participants perceived to be unfavourable for randomization was minimal. The reasons for failing to randomizing these six excluded patients are described fully in the original report. Moreover, the baseline characteristics of the two groups are clearly closely matched, except in relation to the quality of life of those randomized to undergo surgical treatment. By any reasonable criteria, although the method of randomization was not ideal, it is unlikely to have biased the results.

The second potential criticism concerns the approach used to assess patients' outcomes in the two groups. In an attempt to minimize ascertainment bias, the patients' progress was assessed by two independent experts from close scrutiny of their medical records. Although they were unaware of the patients' treatment allocations, they necessarily had to rely on the medical records that had been prepared by observers who were not blinded. Participants, too, were not blind to the treatment group to which they had been allocated. Unless the group allocated to continued medical treatment had undergone sham surgery, then it is difficult to imagine any other approach that would have permitted blind ascertainment. Despite this criticism, the magnitude of the reduction in seizures following temporal lobe surgery – with a *number needed to treat* of two – makes it unlikely that ascertainment bias could explain the results.

Third, there must be some doubt about the generalizability of the findings. As with surgical trials in general, the technical skills of the surgeons might not be replicated in wider use. Nevertheless, a reasonable decision-maker might conclude that, in the circumstances of the trial, surgery resulted in substantially better patient outcomes than relying on medical treatment alone and that this form of treatment should be adopted in those centres with appropriate surgical skills.

## Conclusions

Randomized controlled trials can provide decision-makers with many elements of the totality of the evidence required to assess the effectiveness of therapeutic interventions. To regard the technique as the gold standard – as is too often claimed – overemphasizes its place and role.[36,51] The inherent weaknesses include not only those already discussed (the null hypothesis and the dependency on arbitrary *P*-values) but also problems associated with generalizability, stopping rules, and subgroup and safety analyses, which are discussed in subsequent chapters in this section.

# References

1. Daniel 1:11−14. The Bible.
2. Lind J. *A Treatise of the Scurvy*. Edinburgh: Edinburgh University Press, 1953.

3. Rawlins MD. Development of a rational practice of therapeutics. *BMJ* 1989a;**301**:729–733.

4. Armitage P. Fisher, Bradford Hill, and randomization. *International Journal of Epidemiology* 2003;**32**:925–8.

5. Hill AB. *The Principles of Medical Statistics*. London: *Lancet*, 1937.

6. Medical Research Council. The serum treatment of lobar pneumonia. *BMJ* 1934;:**1**:241–6.

7. Evans GM, Gaisford WF. Treatment of pneumonia with 2-(p-amino-benzenesulphonamido)pyridine. *Lancet* 1938;**ii**:14.

8. Scadding JG. Reflections on my studies of the effects of sulphonamides in bacilliary dysentery in Egypt: 1943–1944. *Journal of the Royal Society of Medicine* 2006;**99**:423–6.

9. Chalmers I, Clarke M. J Guy Scadding and the move from alternation to randomization. Oxford, The James Lind Library, 2002. www.jameslindlibrary.org/illustrating/articles/j-guy-scadding-and-the-move-from-alternation-to-randomization.pdf.

10. Hill AB. Memories of the British streptomycin trial in tuberculosis. *Controlled Clinical Trials* 1990;**11**:77–9.

11. Chalmers I. Joseph Asbury Bell and the birth of randomized trials. *Journal of the Royal Society of Medicine* 2007;**100**:287–93.

12. Bell JA. Pertussis prohylaxis with two doses of alum-precipitated vaccine. *Public Health Reports* 1941;**56**:1535–46.

13. Jefferson T. Why the MRC randomized trials of whooping cough (pertussis) vaccines remain important more than half a century after they were done. *Journal of the Royal Society of Medicine* 2007;**100**:343–5.

14. Medical Research Council. Streptomycin treatment of pulmonary tuberculosis. *BMJ* 1948;**2**:769–82.

15. Gold H, Kwit NT, Otto H. The xanthines (theobromine and aminophylline) in the treatment of cardiac pain. *Journal of the American Medical Association* 1937;**108**:2173–9.

16. Denton JE, Beecher HK. New analgesics I: methods in the clinical evaluation of new analgesics. *Journal of the American Medical Association* 1949;**141**:1051–2.

17. Armitage P. A note on the statistical analysis of the 1948 MRC streptomycin trial. Oxford: The James Lind Library, 2009. www.jameslindlibrary.org/illustrating/articles/a-note-on-the-statistical-analysis-of-the-1948-mrc-streptomycin.pdf.

18. Spiegelhalter DJ, Abrams KR, Myles JP. *Bayesian Approaches to Clinical Trials and Health-care Evaluation*. Chichester: John Wiley & Sons, 2003.

19. GREAT group. Feasibility, safety, and efficacy of domiciliary thrombolysis by general practitioners: Grampian region early anistreplase trial 1992;**305**:548–53.

20. Pocock SJ, Spiegelhalter DJ. Grampian region early anastroplase trial. *BMJ* 1992;**305**:1015.

21. Bland JM, Altman DG. Bayesians and frequentists. *BMJ* 1998;**317**:1151.

22. Rawlins MD. *De Testimonium: On the Evidence for Decisions about the Use of Therapeutic Interventions*. London: Royal College of Physicians, 2008.

23. Schulz KF, Altman DG, Moher D. CONSORT 2010 statement: updated guidelines for reporting parallel group randomised trials. *BMJ* 2010;**340**:c332.

24. Matthews JNS. *An Introduction to Randomized Controlled Trials*, 2nd edn. London: Chapman & Hall, 2006.

25. Roberts C, Torgerson D. Randomisation methods in clinical trials. *BMJ* 1998;**317**:1301.

26. Pocock SJ. *Clinical Trials: A Practical Approach*. Chichester: John Wiley & Sons, 1983.

27. Schultz KF. Subverting randomization in controlled trials. *Journal of the American Medical Association* 1995;**274**:1456–8.

28. Kennedy A, Grant A. Subversion of allocation in a randomised controlled trial. *Controlled Clinical Trials* 1997;**18**(Suppl. 3):77–8S.

29. Scandinavian Simvastatin Survival Study Group. Randomized trial of cholesterol lowering in 4444 patients with coronary heart disease: the Scandinavian Simvastatin Survival Study (4S). *Lancet* 1994;**344**:1383–9.

30. Gruppo Italiano per lo Studio della Streptochinasi nell'infarno miocardio (GISSI). The effectiveness of intravenous thrombolytic treatment in acute myocardial infarction. *Lancet* 1986;**i**:397–402.

31. Sibbald B, Roberts C. Understanding controlled trials: crossover trials. *BMJ* 1998;**316**:1719–20.

32. Ukoumunne OC, Gulliford MC, Chinn S, *et al*. Evaluation of health interventions at area and organisation level. *BMJ* 1999;**319**:376–9.

33. Scharz D, Lellouch J. Explanatory and pragmatic attitudes in therapeutic trials. *Journal of Chronic Disease* 1967;**20**:637–48.

34. Zwarenstein M, Treweek S, Gagnier JJ, *et al*. Improving the reporting of pragmatic trials: an extension of the CONSORT statement. *BMJ* 2008;**337**:1223–6.

35. Roland M, Torgerson D. What outcomes should be measured? *BMJ* 1998;**317**:1075.

36. Jadad AR, Enkin MW. *Randomized Controlled Trials*, 2nd edn. London: BMJ Books, 2007.

37. Evans CH, Ildstad ST. *Small Clinical Trials: Issues and Challenges*. Washington, DC: National Academy Press, 2001.

38. Jones B, Jarvis P, Lewis JA, Ebbutt AF. Trials to assess equivalence: the importance of rigorous methods. *BMJ* 1996;**313**:36–9.

39. Piaggio G, Elbourne DR, Altman DG, *et al*. Reporting of noninferiority and equivalence randomized trials. *Journal of the American Medical Association* 2006;**295**:1152–60.

40. Janssens HJEM, Janssen MJ, van Riel PLCM, van Weel C. Use of oral prednisolone for the treatment of gout arthritis: a double-blind, randomised equivalence trial. *Lancet* 2008;**371**:1854–60.

41. Levine B. The utility of futility. *Stroke* 2005;**36**:2331–2.

42. Palech YY, Tilley BC, Sackett DL, *et al*. Applying a phase II futility study design to therapeutic stroke trials. *Stroke* 2005;**36**:2410–14.

43. Schwid SR, Cutter GR. Futility studies: spending a little to save a lot. *Neurology* 2006;**66**:626–7.

44. Le Henanff A, Giraudeau B, Baron G, Ravaud P. Quality of reporting of non-inferiority and equivalence randomized controlled trials. *Journal of the American Medical Association* 2006;**295**:1147–51.

45. Califf RM. Clinical trials bureaucracy: unintended consequences of well-intentioned public policy. *Clinical Trials* 2006;**3**:496–502.

46. Eisenstein EL, Lemons PW, Tardiff BE, *et al*. Reducing the costs of phase III cardiovascular trials. *American Heart Journal* 2005;**149**:482–8.

47. Eisenstein EL, Collins R, Cracknell BS, *et al*. Sensible approaches for reducing clinical trial costs. *Clinical Trials* 2008;**5**:75–84.

48. CRASH Trial Collaborators. Final results of MRC CRASH, a randomised placebo-controlled trial of intravenous corticosteroid in adults with head injury: outcomes at 6 months. *Lancet* 2005;**365**:1957–9.

49. Sustainable Trials Study Group. Towards sustainable clinical trials. *BMJ* 2007;**334**:671–3.

50. Wiebe S, Blume WT, Girvin JP, Eliasziw M. A randomized controlled trial of surgery for temporal lobe epilepsy. *New England Journal of Medicine* 2001;**345**:311–18.

51. Cartwright N. Are RCTs the gold standard? Technical report 01/07. London: London School of Economics and Political Science: Centre for Philosophy of Natural and Social Science, 2007.

# STOPPING RULES

There is a natural desire for investigators to undertake interim analyses during the course of a randomized controlled trial and before the prespecified number of participants have been enrolled:[1]

- The trial may have uncovered serious adverse effects and should therefore be stopped for reasons of unacceptable *safety*.
- The accruing results may suggest that the difference between the intervention and control groups is so unimpressive that the prospect of a positive result is unlikely. The study becomes, in effect, a futility trial (see Chapter 2.1).
- New data may become available from other sources during the course of the trial suggesting that either the intervention is convincingly effective or ineffective or that there are serious safety issues.
- The accruing results may indicate that one intervention is superior to another and that the endpoint(s) for benefit has been reached.

## Ethical issues

If the emerging results of a study indicate unambiguous safety concerns, then there is no ethical dilemma in abandoning it. If interim findings show little or no advantage, then termination may also be appropriate. And if equipoise is lost because of the publication of convincingly positive (or negative) results with the same intervention for the same condition, then abandoning the study may also be fully justifiably.

It has been proposed, however, that there is a basic ethical dilemma in deciding whether to terminate a randomized controlled trial early for benefit.[2] If the emerging results indeed suggest benefit, then the individual ethics of randomizing the next patient may conflict with the collective ethics of making appropriate treatment policies for future patients.

There may, indeed, be substantial disadvantages for future patients in early stopping. First, a statistically significant result might have arisen by chance and would not have been maintained if the trial were to have been continued. In other words, the results could be a false positive finding (or a 'random high', as it is sometimes called). Second, as a result of early termination there is likely to be a wider confidence interval for the observed treatment effect than would have been the case if the trial had been allowed to continue. Premature termination there is therefore likely to result in greater imprecision in the estimate of the effect size. As discussed later, there is empirical evidence to show that for trials stopped early for benefit, this is indeed the case. Third, as a result of early termination, there may be insufficient information to explore the benefits and risks of the intervention in specific subgroups of participants.

It has also been claimed that trials need to be large enough and last long enough to change future medical practice.[2] It has been argued that physicians will be convinced to change their clinical practice only if the results are 'well beyond conventional levels of clinical significance'. This is extremely unconvincing as an ethical basis for continuing trials that might otherwise have met reasonable criteria for stopping early. Obligations to future patients are, indeed, important; but they do not override the rights and interests of current patients.[3] If equipoise has been lost during the course of a trial, it cannot be ethical to continue with a study.

## Statistical issues

### Stopping early for benefit

There are serious statistical difficulties in deciding whether, and when, to terminate a trial early for benefit. With repeated examination of the emerging data, there is an increasing likelihood of rejecting the null hypothesis at a *P*-value of less than 0.05. Indeed, in a very large trial, a *P*-value of less than 0.05 could almost be guaranteed if the data were analysed often enough. This is another example of the problem of *multiplicity* that was outlined in Chapter 1.2.

Various 'stopping rules' have been devised to resolve this particular multiplicity problem. All propose lower, more stringent *P*-values for rejection of the null hypothesis in earlier analyses. Four methods, in particular, have been most widely used and are compared in Table 2.2.1:[4]

■ Pocock's approach adopts a fixed, stringent *P*-value that is the same for the interim and the final analyses.[5] Two particular criticisms have been made of this scheme.[4] First, it may be too easy for a trial to be terminated early using these boundaries. Some argue, with good reason, that a trial should be stopped very early only if there is overwhelming (and unsuspected) evidence of benefit. This would not necessarily be the case with a strict application of Pocock's scheme. Second, the final test of significance, when the trial has been completed, uses a smaller *P*-value (0.0158 in Table 2.2.1) than would have been the case if no interim analyses had been undertaken. A final *P*-value of, say, 0.025, based on the results of the completed trial and assuming the original design proposed a critical *P*-value of 0.05, would no longer be statistically significant. This is seen by some as counterintuitive because if no interim analyses had been undertaken, the result in such an instance would have been regarded as 'statistically significant'.

■ The Haybittle–Peto method uses a constant, but more stringent, *P*-value to determine the stopping boundary during earlier analyses, but a conventional *P*-level of 0.05 for the final one.[6,7] In Table 2.2.1 the *P*-values for each of the interim analyses are all set at less than 0.001 but the final *P*-value remains at less than 0.05. Although this overcomes the difficulties with changing the final *P*-value, which Pocock's scheme advocates, some investigators believe that early termination becomes too difficult with the Haybittle–Peto approach.

■ In contrast to the Haybittle–Peto method, the O'Brien–Fleming scheme changes the stopping rule with each interim analysis (see Table 2.2.1).[8] This approach appeals to some investigators because the very early stopping rules are conservative, with very stringent *P*-values at a time when the results are least stable. This stringency lessens, however, with successive analyses as the results become increasingly reliable. The final *P*-value, under this arrangement, is close to 0.05.

■ The Fleming–Harrington–O'Brien approach (see Table 2.2.1) offers less stringent boundaries for early termination than the O'Brien–Fleming scheme, but with a final *P*-value that is again close to 0.05.[9]

**Table 2.2.1** Comparison of nominal significance levels for interim and final analyses with various stopping rules with $\alpha = 0.05$.[4]

| Analysis | Pocock | Harbottle–Peto | O'Brien–Fleming | Fleming–Harrington–O'Brien |
|---|---|---|---|---|
| Interim 1 | 0.0158 | 0.001 | 0.00005 | 0.0038 |
| Interim 2 | 0.0158 | 0.001 | 0.0013 | 0.0048 |
| Interim 3 | 0.0158 | 0.001 | 0.008 | 0.0053 |
| Interim 4 | 0.0158 | 0.001 | 0.023 | 0.0064 |
| Final | 0.0158 | 0.05 | 0.041 | 0.0432 |

A further approach, the Lan–DeMets method, is more flexible.[10] This approach allows investigators to 'spend' the *type I error* rate (the critical *P*-value) as the trial proceeds; and it permits the number and timing of interim analyses to change during the course of the trial. Because the Lan–DeMets approach tolerates unplanned examinations of the data, direct comparisons with the other methods in Table 2.2.1 are impossible.

The profusion of stopping rules for benefit suggests that none is wholly satisfactory.[4] The methods are probably too formalized to reflect the complexity of the processes involved in deciding whether to terminate a trial – especially a major trial – early. The approaches that accomplish the goals of interim analyses (Harbottle–Peto, O'Brien–Fleming, Fleming–Harrington–O'Brien) without detracting from the overall objectives of the trial are generally to be preferred.[11] Nevertheless, there is no consensus among statisticians about stopping rules, any more than there is about handling multiplicity in general.

## Stopping early for futility

In some studies, interim analyses may indicate that, even at its completion, any benefit from an intervention is unlikely to be demonstrated. Stopping for futility is associated with an abstruse terminology including 'conditional power', 'stochastic curtailment' and 'futility indices'.[2,11]

The CRASH trial (see Case study 2.2.1) is an example of a trial that was abandoned, on the advice of its data monitoring committee, for 'futility'.[12,13] This study was designed to assess the extent to which patients with acute head injuries would benefit from the administration of a corticosteroid in the immediate aftermath of trauma. It showed an excess mortality in patients with acute head injuries treated with intravenous methylprednisolone compared with placebo.[12,13] In this instance, whether the excess deaths were causally associated with corticosteroid treatment or were the 'extreme' play of chance remains controversial. There is no disagreement, however, that treatment with corticosteroids provides no advantage after acute head injuries.

## Stopping early for harms

There is a lack of consensus among statisticians about whether the stopping rules for harms should be the same as those for benefit. In a 'symmetric stopping boundary strategy', the same *P*-values are used in deciding whether a trial should be terminated early for benefit as for harms.

This approach may, however, conflict with the desire to avoid inflicting unnecessary harm on the trial participants. Consequently an 'asymmetric stopping boundary strategy' is sometimes advocated. This involves the use of less stringent *P*-values for decisions about stopping for harms compared with those used in stopping for benefit.

> **Case study 2.2.1** The effectiveness of intravenous methylprednisolone after traumatic head injury (CRASH)[12,13]
>
> **Background** Corticosteroids have been used to treat head injuries for more than 30 years. In 1997, findings of a systematic review suggested that these drugs reduce risk of death by 1–2 per cent. This trial was designed to confirm or refute such an effect.
>
> **Methods** Adults (age 16 years or older) with head injury were screened for inclusion in the study if they were within 8 hour of injury and were noted in hospital to have a Glasgow coma score (GCS) of 14 or less. Eligible patients were randomly allocated to a 48-hour infusion of corticosteroid (methylprednisolone) or placebo.
>
> Power calculations indicated that to detect a two per cent reduction in mortality (for $\alpha = 0.05$ and $1 - \beta = 0.9$), 20 000 participants would be required. The trial protocol specified subgroup analyses for the severity of injury (as assessed from the GCS) and the time after injury that treatment was instituted.
>
> **Results** After 5 years, when 10 008 patients had been recruited, the independent Data Monitoring and Ethics Committee (which had been monitoring the results at yearly intervals) decided to disclose the unmasked findings to the trial steering committee, which decided to terminate the trial. Baseline characteristics indicated that the groups were well-matched.
>
> Mortality at two weeks and six months were:
>
> |  | Corticosteroid ($n = 5007$) | Placebo ($n = 5001$) | Relative risk (95% CI) |
> |---|---|---|---|
> | *Mortality* | | | |
> | 2 weeks | 1052 | 893 | 1.18 (1.09 to 1.27) |
> | 6 months | 1248 | 1075 | 1.15 (1.07 to 1.24) |
>
> There was no evidence that the effect of corticosteroids differed by injury severity or time since injury.
>
> **Conclusions** The results showed unequivocally that the administration of parenteral corticosteroids after head injury has no beneficial effect on mortality. Whether steroids are ineffective or positively harmful has been the subject of some debate.

Thus, in the same trial, the O'Brien–Fleming boundaries might be used in monitoring for benefit, whereas the Peto boundaries might be adopted in monitoring for harms.[11] Although prespecified statistical plans are helpful in deciding whether to stop trials for harms, decisions sometimes have to be based on the unexpected.[2]

# Discussion

It has become increasingly common in randomized controlled trials for an independent data monitoring committee to scrutinize the emerging results.[14] Such committees usually comprise a small number of independent experts with no other involvement in the study, who are supplied with confidential reports of the interim results. This committee then has to advise the trial's steering committee as to whether the trial should continue or whether it should be stopped.[15] Although a data monitoring committee is usually an advisory body, a trial's sponsor would be extremely unwise to overrule its advice. Great responsibility is therefore placed on the members of such committees.

In deciding whether or not a trial should be terminated on grounds of safety, data monitoring committees will base their decisions on judgement and common sense as much as on the results of statistical analyses. The relevance of any adverse safety signals will be balanced against both the emerging evidence of benefit and the nature and frequency of the safety signals themselves. In drawing their conclusions, data monitoring committees also have to balance emerging safety signals with the severity of the condition for which the intervention is targeted. The committee will also wish to take account of the benefits and harms of alternative interventions already in clinical use.

Similar considerations apply in deciding whether to advise that a study should be terminated prematurely for reasons of futility. Case study 2.2.2 provides an example of the complexities surrounding decisions about prematurely terminating trials for lack of benefit.[16] The decision to stop this particular trial had two elements. First, the mortality rate of participants treated with the new modality (neutron therapy) was higher than that in participants treated with conventional therapy (photon therapy). Second, although the treatment difference (*relative risk* 1.52, 95% confidence interval (CI) 0.91 to 2.5) was not statistically significant, the lower 95 per cent confidence interval (0.91) provided no support that neutron therapy represented a viable form of treatment. It had been argued previously that a true mortality reduction of around 30 per cent (relative risk 0.7) was the minimum required to change clinical practice. In this particular instance, it was concluded that a benefit of this magnitude was extremely unlikely, given the interim findings. The investigators considered that to have continued the study in order to gain a better estimate of the treatment difference would have entailed randomizing patients to a treatment (neutron therapy) that was likely to be associated with a worse prognosis.

The greatest challenge for a data monitoring committee is whether, and when, to advise early termination of a randomized controlled trial for benefit. As already discussed, there is a real danger that a random high might lead a committee to recommend the inappropriate early termination of a study. This is not just a theoretical concern. Montori and colleagues surveyed 143 randomized controlled trials published between 1974 and 2004 that had been stopped early for benefit (i.e. 'truncated').[17] The median number of patients on which conclusions were based, at the time of termination, was 66 (interquartile range 23 to 195). The median relative risk (benefit) in these truncated trials was 0.53 (interquartile range 0.28 to 0.66). Montori and colleagues also observed a strong inverse correlation between the number of events and the estimated treatment effects. In other words, among studies terminated prematurely for benefit, those with the lowest relative risks had significantly fewer events on which to base decisions.

A more recent review by Bassler and colleagues compared effect sizes in truncated randomized controlled trials with those of non-truncated randomized controlled trials addressing the same topic.[18] The areas covered included pharmaceutical products intended for the treatment of cardiovascular, neurological and malignant conditions and human immunodeficiency virus (HIV) and acquired immunodeficiency syndrome (AIDS). The pooled ratio of the relative risks in truncated randomized controlled trials versus non-truncated trials was 0.71 (95% confidence interval 0.65 to 0.77). Thus, there was an average 29 per cent greater apparent effect size in truncated compared with non-truncated trials. The effect was independent of the particular statistical stopping rule

| Case study 2.2.2 High-energy neutron treatment for pelvic cancers[16] |
|---|

| Background | In the treatment of locally advanced tumours, high-energy neutron-beam therapy has potential advantages compared with conventional mega-voltage radiotherapy (with photons). There was, however, conflicting evidence of real benefit. |
|---|---|
| Method | Patients with locally advanced pelvic tumours (rectum, cervix, prostate, bladder), but without distant metastases, were randomized to either high-energy neutron-beam therapy or photon-beam therapy. Randomization was initially 3 : 1 (neutron : photon) and unstratified by site. After two years, randomization was changed to 1 : 1 and stratified by tumour site. |
| | The prespecified outcomes included overall survival in relation to the development of metastatic disease and treatment-related morbidity. |
| Results | Four years after the start of the trial, 151 patients had been randomized. The death rates at one year were as follows: |

| | Neutrons ($n = 90$) | Photons ($n = 61$) |
|---|---|---|
| Death rate | 55% | 38% |

| | The relative risk for death after neutron therapy compared with photon therapy was 1.52 (95% CI 0.91 to 2.50). |
|---|---|
| Comment | As a result of these findings, the trial was stopped prematurely. |

that was applied, but it was significantly greater in small trials involving fewer than 500 participants.

Decision-makers should therefore treat the results of randomized trials terminated early for benefit with some scepticism. There will, however, be some occasions when a large treatment effect from an interim analysis indicates that the benefits are substantial and the harms are minimal. To continue the trial would therefore violate the principle of equipoise and deny an effective treatment to many others. Bassler and colleagues have suggested that a threefold approach should be adopted before accepting at face value the findings of substantial benefit in an interim analysis:[1]

- A low *P*-value, such as 0.001, should have been adopted as the threshold for stopping.
- Interim analyses, or at least decisions about early termination, should be avoided until a sufficiently large number of events have accrued.
- Even if an interim analysis fulfils these first two requirements, the trial should continue for at least a further period to ensure that the positive trend is maintained.

The circumstances under which it is appropriate for randomized controlled trials to be terminated prematurely for benefit are still unclear. For the time being, decision-makers would do worse than to adopt the above approach in drawing conclusions about the *effectiveness* of interventions when the relevant trials have been terminated early for benefit.

# References

1. Bassler D, Montori VM, Briel M, *et al.* Early stopping of randomized clinical trials for overt efficacy is problematic. *Journal of Epidemiology* 2008;**61**:241–6.
2. Pocock SJ. When to stop a clinical trial. *BMJ* 1992;**305**:235–40.

3. Beauchamp TL, Childress JF. *Principles of Biomedical Ethics*, 5th edn. Oxford: Oxford University Press, 2001.

4. Matthews JNS. *Introduction to Randomized Controlled Trials.* London: Chapman & Hall, 2006.

5. Pocock SJ. Group sequential methods in the design and analysis of clinical trials. *Biometrika* 1977;**64**:191–9.

6. Harbittle JL. Repeated assessment of results in clinical trials of cancer treatment. *British Journal of Radiology* 1971;**44**:793–7.

7. Peto R, Pike MC, Armitage P, *et al*. Design and analysis of randomized clinical trials requiring prolonged observation of each patient: I. Introduction and design. *British Journal of Cancer* 1976;**34**:585–612.

8. O'Brien PC, Fleming TR. A multiple testing procedure for clinical trials. *Biometrics* 1979;**35**:549–56.

9. Fleming TR, Harrington DP, O'Brien PC. Designs for group sequential tests. *Controlled Clinical Trials* 1984;**5**:348–61.

10. Lan KKG, DeMets DL. Discrete sequential boundaries for clinical trials. *Biometrika* 1983;**70**:659–63.

11. Schultz KF, Grimes DA. Multiplicity in randomised trials II: subgroup and interim analyses. *Lancet* 2005;**365**:1657–61.

12. CRASH trial collaborators. Effect of intravenous corticosteroids on death within 14 days in 10008 adults with clinically significant head injury (MRC CRASH trial): randomised placebo-controlled trial. *Lancet* 2004;**364**:1321–8.

13. CRASH trial collaborators. Final results of MRC CRASH, a randomised placebo-controlled trial of intravenous corticosteroid in adults with head injury: outcomes at 6 months. *Lancet* 2005;**365**:1957–9.

14. Grant AM, Altman DG, Babiker AB, *et al*. Issues in data monitoring and interim analysis of trials. *Health Technology Assessment* 2005;**9**:1–238.

15. DAMOCLES Study Group. A proposed charter for clinical trial monitoring committees: helping them to do their job well. *Lancet* 2005;**365**:711–22.

16. Errington RD, Ashby D, Gore SM, *et al*. High energy neutron treatment for pelvic cancers: study stopped because of increased mortality. *BMJ* 1991;**302**:1045–51.

17. Montori VM, Devereaux PJ, Adhikari NKJ, *et al*. Randomized trials stopped early for benefit: a systematic review. *Journal of the American Medical Association* 2005;**294**:2203–9.

18. Bassler D, Briel M, Montori VM, *et al*. Stopping randomized trials early for benefit and estimation of treatment effects. *Journal of the American Medical Association* 2010;**303**:1180–87.

*Therapeutics, evidence and decision-making*

# CHAPTER 2.3
## ANALYSIS OF SUBGROUPS

The results of a clinical trial will indicate the likely effect of an intervention in the 'average' patient. There will, however, always be some variation – heterogeneity – in the overall response. Exploring this heterogeneity by assessing an intervention's effects in subgroups of patients, such as men and women, or people aged above and below a certain age, can have useful applications:

- Subgroup analyses may be important in answering practical questions. At what stage of the disease is treatment most effective? For how long is thrombolysis effective after a stroke or myocardial infarction? How do the benefits and *harms* relate to common comorbid conditions that may be found in individual patients?
- Heterogeneity may be marked if there are differences in the underlying pathophysiology or biology of the condition. This applies particularly to the influence of gene expression on the effects of some pharmaceutical products and forms the basis of the potential for so-called 'personalized medicine'.[1] The benefits of trastuzumab in breast cancer, for example, are confined to women whose tumours express the human epidermal growth factor 2 (HER2) receptor on the surface of their malignant cells.
- Heterogeneity of *absolute risks* compared with *relative risks* may have important implications in clinical practice. For example, statins reduce the overall risk of major coronary events by 29 per cent. A 45-year-old woman with no risk factors apart from an increased serum cholesterol (> 5.2 mmol/L) has a five per cent chance of a major coronary event over the next decade;[2] statin treatment will reduce this to 3.5 per cent. For a 65-year-male smoker with a family history of heart disease and diabetes, a serum cholesterol of > 6.2 mmol/L and a blood pressure of 160/90 mmHg, the chances of a major coronary event over the next decade are 50 per cent; statin therapy will reduce his risk to 35 per cent. The *absolute risk reductions* – 1.5 per cent for the 45-year-old woman versus 14.6 per cent for the 65-year-old male smoker – are thus strikingly different.[2] Heterogeneity of absolute risks can have an important impact on balancing benefits against harms and on economic evaluation: an intervention that overall is cost-ineffective may be cost-effective in specific subgroups.

Despite these obvious benefits, the extrapolation of the results of clinical trials to particular subgroups is surprisingly unreliable and contentious. Even if the effect sizes of the treatment differences appear to be substantial and potentially important, standard approaches to subgroup analyses are so statistically insensitive that they may be unable to demonstrate them.[3] Conversely, a highly significant effect, using appropriate statistical methods, may still be inadequate for providing good evidence about subgroup-specific treatment preferences.[3]

Some distinguish qualitative from quantitative heterogeneity.[4] *Qualitative heterogeneity* refers to a treatment effect that is directional different in different groups of patients, with benefit for some but harm for others. *Quantitative heterogeneity* refers to situations where an intervention is beneficial or harmful in all subgroups, but the magnitude of the effect differs between them. There is a general (though not universal) agreement that qualitative heterogeneity is very unusual. If it is suspected, then special statistical techniques are needed.[5] Quantitative heterogeneity is the sole focus of discussion in this chapter.

# Handling heterogeneity

Subgroup analyses are bedevilled by the interrelated issues of:

- the failure to undertake the appropriate analysis;
- the lack of statistical power;
- the general problem of handling *multiplicity.*

## Appropriate analytical approaches

In an analysis of subgroups a common (but erroneous) approach is to examine the data separately for each subgroup and draw conclusions based on each of their *P*-values. Case study 2.3.1 provides a famous (and extreme) example of this. This case study describes a *post hoc* reanalysis of the results of a trial that investigated the effects of aspirin on 1-month mortality after an acute myocardial infarction.[6] The reanalysis was done to illustrate the point that such data-mining can give rise to inappropriate (and even ridiculous) conclusions. First, there is no biologically plausible basis for postulating that patients' astrological birth signs would affect their response to aspirin

---

**Case study 2.3.1** Subgroup analysis from a trial of aspirin on the survival at 1 month after acute myocardial infarction[3]

**Background** The Second International Study of Infarct Survival (ISIS-2) trial was a large study examining *inter alia* the effects of aspirin on 1-month survival after acute myocardial infarction.[6] The survival advantage for participants randomized to receive aspirin was striking. Mortality was 804 of 8587 patients allocated to aspirin compared with 1016 of 8600 patients allocated to placebo. The reduction in mortality was 23 per cent ($P < 0.000\,001$).

A *post hoc* subgroup analysis was undertaken to investigate whether the effect of aspirin on the 1-month mortality after acute myocardial infarction was sustained among patients with particular astrological birth signs.

**Method** The 1-month mortality of patients receiving aspirin and placebo with birth signs of either Libra and Gemini was retrieved from the raw data of the ISIS-2 trial.

**Results** The results were as follows:

| Birth sign | Number of deaths (aspirin versus placebo) | *P*-value |
|---|---|---|
| Libra or Gemini | 150 v. 147 | > 0.05 |
| All other birth signs | 654 v. 869 | < 0.000 001 |
| All birth signs | 804 v. 1016 | < 0.000 001 |

**Conclusions** The unwary might conclude that aspirin is ineffective in patients with either Libra or Gemini birth signs, and that patients born under these birth signs should not be given this particular form of treatment.

in this manner. Second, the failure to detect an effect when patients are subdivided in this way is due to the small number of events (deaths at one month) among the Libra and Gemini groups compared with the much larger number of events in those with other birth signs (or, indeed, all birth signs). And third, this approach to subgroup analysis is, anyway, flawed.

The comparisons in Case study 2.3.1 were made between groups but based on analyses carried out separately within each group. This (commonly used) approach is erroneous. The correct method is to compare the differences between the treatments in each group by examining the interactions between subgroups.[7,8] This is undertaken by comparing the mean differences in the effects of treatment in each subgroup.[8,9] ('Interaction' is the term used by statisticians to compare subgroups.)

Flawed conclusions based on inappropriate approaches to subgroup analyses are common. In a review of 50 randomized controlled trials published over a three-month period in the four major weekly international journals, Assmann and colleagues noted that most included subgroup analyses.[10] Less than half of these, however, used statistical tests of interaction; and most relied on P-values for the treatment difference in each separate subgroup. The authors also noted that it was often difficult to distinguish between prespecified and *post hoc* subgroup analyses.

### Power

If trials are powered only to estimate the overall effect of a treatment, most subgroup analyses will, almost by definition, be underpowered. A statistically robust subgroup treatment–effect interaction requires a study to have sufficient power to detect a treatment effect both within and between each subgroup.[11] If a trial has an 80 per cent power to detect the overall effect of treatment, then a reliable estimate of a subgroup interaction with the same effect size might require a fourfold greater sample size.[11,12] To detect interactions that are less than the overall effect size would require even larger trials. The review by Assmann and colleagues of randomized controlled trials with subgroup analyses observed that most trials lacked the power to detect any except very large subgroup effects.[10]

There are many instances where subgroup analyses appear to have claimed to show clinical heterogeneity of treatment effects but where these have subsequently been shown to be erroneous.[12] Such false negative subgroup findings include the apparent ineffectiveness of aspirin in the secondary prevention of stroke in women, and the alleged ineffectiveness of tamoxifen for the treatment of breast cancer in women under 50 years of age.[12]

### Multiplicity

Multiplicity in general is discussed in Chapter 2.2. The multiplicity problem with subgroups is that the greater the number of subgroups that are analysed, the more likely it is that at least one will be statistically significant (P-value < 0.05). This becomes especially egregious if, at the end of a (usually negative) study, investigators pore over the results in an attempt to find a subgroup in which something positive can be found. Such data-dredging has been likened to placing a bet on a horse after watching the race.[4,12]

Approaches that involve adjusting the P-values for multiple testing are available,[13] of which the most well known is the Bonferroni correction. In this, the critical value for statistical significance of the primary outcome (usually $\alpha = 0.05$) is divided by the number of subgroup analyses that are conducted. For example, in a study with ten subgroup analyses, the critical level for acceptance would be 0.05/10 = 0.005. Other approaches have been devised, but they all are widely regarded as conservative and liable to generate false negative conclusions. Indeed, Schultz and Grimes express caution about any adjustments for multiplicity that, they claim, lack substance and often prove unhelpful.[14]

# Discussion

Despite the potential value of subgroup analyses, there is little consensus on the basis by which decision-makers can reach reasonable conclusions.

Some commentators suggest that subgroup analyses should be subject to strict limitations before their uncritical acceptance:

- They should be restricted to a small number of analyses that have been prespecified in the trial protocol.
- The study should have sufficient power to accommodate these prespecified subgroups.
- The final analysis should include a formal interaction test.
- *Post hoc* analyses should be regarded only as exploratory. Further studies should be undertaken to confirm or refute any positive findings.

These guidelines, however, are more honoured in the breach than in the observance. Wang and colleagues examined all 95 randomized controlled trials published in the *New England Journal of Medicine* during a 12-month (2005–06) period.[15] Of the 59 trials that included one or more subgroup analyses, 40 (68 per cent) failed to indicate whether the analyses were prespecified or *post hoc*, and 32 (54 per cent) failed to report whether an interaction test had been undertaken.

The four strict criteria described above are very difficult to achieve. In particular, the cost of undertaking trials with sufficient power to meet all the prespecified subgroups would often be too expensive to contemplate. Nor is the problem of multiplicity resolved by proposing only a 'small number' of prespecified subgroup analyses. The difficulties of interpreting repeated significance tests apply equally to prespecified subgroups and those identified in *post hoc* analyses. In reaching conclusions about the reliability of subgroup analyses, decision-makers should take the following factors into account when drawing conclusions:

- Whether prespecified or *post hoc*, all subgroups should be biologically plausible.
- To have any practical value, subgroups should be able to be identified in future patients before they embark on treatment.
- In the very unusual circumstances where all four of the strict criteria above have been met, decision-makers can reasonably accept their reliability as a basis for drawing conclusions.
- If the subgroups have, indeed, been prespecified and are relatively few in number (less, say, than three or four), reasonable weight can be given to conclusions that may be drawn from them.
- If the results of any *post hoc* subgroup analysis are to be given any credence, decision-makers can reasonably expect to know how many other subgroup analyses were undertaken and how many achieved *P*-values of less than 0.05.
- Where the overall intention-to-treat results suggest benefit, decision-makers should take great care in accepting claims for lack of benefit in some subgroups.
- Where the overall intention-to-treat results suggest either no benefit or even harm, even greater circumspection is required in concluding benefit in any subgroup.

As already noted, even in the absence of significant heterogeneity and with similar relative risk reductions across various strata, absolute risk reductions may be different between subgroups because of underlying differences in absolute risks. This may allow the absolute benefits of a treatment to be better set against the absolute harms and can be invaluable in examining cost-effectiveness in patient subgroups, especially where an intervention is cost-ineffective overall but cost-effective in the relevant patient population.[16]

Decision-makers may derive some comfort from the lack of consensus among statisticians about whether, and when, to accept the results of subgroup analyses. This probably explains the omission of this topic from most books on evidence-based medicine and the perfunctory way in which it is handled in some statistical texts.

# References

1. Collins F. *The Language of Life: DNA and the Revolution in Personalized Medicine*. London: Profile Books, 2010.
2. Sun X, Briel M, Walter S, Guyatt GH. Is a subgroup effect believable? Updating criteria to evaluate the credibility of subgroup analyses. *BMJ* 2010;**340**:850–54.
3. Collins R, Peto R, Gray R, Parish S. Large-scale randomized evidence: trials and overviews. In: Warrell DA, Cox TM, Firth JD, Benz EJ (eds). *Oxford Textbook of Medicine*. Oxford: Oxford University Press, 2010.
4. Yusuf S, Wittes J, Probstfield J, Tyroler HA. Analysis and interpretation of treatment effects in subgroups of patients in randomized controlled trials. *Journal of the American Medical Association* 1991;**266**:93–8.
5. Matthews JNS. *Introduction to Randomized Controlled Trials*. London: Chapman & Hall, 2006.
6. ISIS-2 (Second International Study of Infarction Survival) Collaborative Group. Randomised controlled trial of intravenous streptokinase, oral aspirin, both, or neither among 17,187 cases of suspected acute myocardial infarction: ISIS-2. *Lancet* 1988;**ii**:349–60.
7. Altman DG. *Practical Statistics for Medical Research*. London: Chapman & Hall, 1991.
8. Matthews JNS, Altman DG. Interaction 2: compare effect sizes not *P* values. *BMJ* 1996;**313**:808.
9. Altman DG, Bland JM. Interaction revisited: the difference between means. *BMJ* 2003;**326**:219.
10. Assmann SF, Pocock SJ, Enos LE, Kasten LE. Subgroup analyses and other (mis)uses of baseline data in clinical trials. *Lancet* 2000;**355**:1064–9.
11. Hasford J, Bramlage P, Koch G, *et al.* Inconsistent trial assessments by the National Institute for Health and Clinical Excellence and IQWiG: standards for the performance and interpretation of subgroup analyses are needed. *Journal of Clinical Epidemiology* 2010;**63**:1298–304.
12. Rothwell PM. Subgroup analyses in randomised controlled trials: importance, indications, and interpretation. *Lancet* 2005;**365**:176–86.
13. Lagakos SW. The challenge of subgroup analyses: reporting without distorting. *New England Journal of Medicine* 2006;**354**:1667–9.
14. Schultz KF, Grimes DA. Multiplicity in randomised controlled trials 1: endpoints and treatments. *Lancet* 2005;**365**:1348.
15. Wang R, Lagakos SW, Ware JH, *et al.* Statistics in medicine: reporting of subgroup analyses in clinical trials. *New England Journal of Medicine* 2007;**357**:2189–94.
16. Sculpher M. Briefing paper for methods review workshop on identifying subgroups and exploring heterogeneity. London: National Institute for Health and Clinical Excellence, 2007.

# SAFETY

The statistical theory underpinning the design and analysis of randomized controlled trials is concerned largely with investigating an intervention's benefits rather than its *harms*.[1] Harms are of secondary interest. Indeed, trials are powered to minimize the chances of a false negative conclusion of benefit (*type II error*). Although some potential harms can be anticipated from knowledge of an intervention's mechanism of action, unexpected harms may (and often will) occur. Trials cannot therefore be powered to take account of all possible harms whose frequency, at the design stage, will be unknown. Moreover, unexpected harms may be rare and difficult to detect with confidence. Nevertheless, acquiring information about the *safety* of an intervention is an important objective of any randomized controlled trial.

## Background

The terminology used to describe the harmfulness of interventions is confusing, inconsistent, misleading and sometimes idiosyncratic.[2–4]

Harms are the unwanted, harmful effects of an intervention that are causally related to its use. They broadly fall into two types:[5]

- *Type A* harms are those that can be anticipated from the known biological effects of an intervention. In the case of a pharmaceutical product, this would include excessive bleeding with an anticoagulant, and hypoglycaemia with an antidiabetic agent. The type A harms with pharmaceuticals are generally dose-dependent within the usual therapeutic dose range.
- *Type B* harms are those that are unpredictable from the background knowledge of an intervention's biological effects. Examples include acute anaphylaxis with a penicillin-like antibiotic, and agranulocytosis with a thyrostatic agent. Type B harms with pharmaceuticals are usually dose-independent within the usual range of therapeutic doses.

Type B reactions tend to be less common, but more serious, than type A reactions.[5]

## Harms as primary outcomes

Although the primary outcomes of randomized controlled trials are almost invariably intended to assess the likely benefits of an intervention, the results sometimes indicate not only that an intervention lacks benefit but also that it is positively harmful. The CAST (Cardiac Arrhythmia Suppression Trial) study is an example (see Case study 2.4.1).[6] This trial was designed to assess the benefits of *class 1 antiarrhythmic agents* in patients experiencing ventricular arrhythmias during the weeks and months after acute myocardial infarction. The results showed an excess of deaths and cardiac arrests in patients allocated to the active treatments. A subsequent *meta-analy*sis of 51 randomized controlled trials showed a pooled *odds ratio* of death or cardiac arrest of

1.14 (95% confidence interval (CI) 1.10 to 1.28) for the use of class 1 antiarrhythmic agents following acute myocardial infarction. The Women's Health Initiative Trial of hormone replacement therapy,[7] primarily intended to investigate whether this treatment reduced the *incidence* of coronary heart disease in postmenopausal women (see Case study 2.4.2), is another randomized controlled trial that showed no benefit but, rather, significant harms (including breast cancer).

These case studies demonstrate that randomized controlled trials can, indeed, identify harms. It is important, however, to emphasize two points. First, the original objective of each trial was to assess the benefits of the particular interventions; safety assumed the role of a primary outcome only when the results were analysed. Second, both studies were rightly terminated prematurely – for reasons of safety – on the advice of their data monitoring committees.

## Harms as secondary outcomes

In any large randomized controlled trial, especially those continuing for long periods of time, some participants are likely to experience one or more *adverse events*. There is near

---

**Case study 2.4.1** The CAST trial[6]

| | |
|---|---|
| **Background** | Ventricular arrhythmias are known to be risk factors for cardiac death after myocardial infarction. The CAST trial was designed to test whether suppression of asymptomatic or symptomatic ventricular arrhythmias with class 1 antiarrhythmic agents would reduce the rate of death due to arrhythmia. |
| **Methods** | Patients with a prior history (six days to two years) of myocardial infarction were enrolled if they had an average of six or more ventricular extrasystoles per hour during a minimum of 18 hours continuous electrocardiographic (ECG) monitoring. Eligible patients were randomly assigned to treatment with either encainide, flecainide or placebo. The primary endpoint was death or cardiac arrest due to arrhythmia. |
| **Results** | After the recruitment of 2309 patients, with a mean follow-up of 10 months, the data and safety monitoring board advised that encainide and flecainide should be discontinued in the trial. |

The results were similar for both active treatments and were reported separately and together. Only the overall results of the combined analysis are shown here:

| Relative risk (95% CI) | |
|---|---|
| All deaths and cardiac arrests | 2.38 (1.59 to 3.57) |
| Arrhythmic deaths and cardiac arrests | 2.64 (1.60 to 4.36) |

Kaplan–Meyer survival curves for all-cause deaths and cardiac arrests, and deaths and cardiac arrests due to arrhythmia, showed significant differences compared with placebo (log-rank tests $P = 0.001$ and $P = 0.0004$, respectively).

| | |
|---|---|
| **Conclusions** | The administration of either encainide or flecainide after acute myocardial infarction is associated with an excess of deaths. |

| Case study 2.4.2 Risks and benefits of hormone replacement therapy[7] | |
|---|---|
| **Background** | Observational evidence suggested that hormone replacement therapy reduced the incidence of coronary heart disease. This trial was designed to test this hypothesis and assess the risks of treatment. |
| **Method** | A total of 16608 postmenopausal women aged 50–79 years were randomly assigned to daily treatment with a combination of conjugated equine oestrogen (0.625 mg) plus medroxyprogesterone acetate (2.5 mg) or matching placebo. The primary outcome was non-fatal myocardial infarction or coronary heart disease death. Invasive breast cancer was the primary adverse outcome.

After a mean of 5.2 years follow-up, the data and safety monitoring board advised the stopping of the trial because the test statistic for breast cancer had exceeded the stopping boundary. |
| **Results** | The major clinical outcomes were as follows: |

| | No. of cases | Hazard ratio (95% CI) |
|---|---|---|
| Coronary heart disease | 286 | 1.29 (1.02 to 1.63) |
| Breast cancer | 290 | 1.26 (1.00 to 1.59) |
| Stroke | 212 | 1.41 (1.07 to 1.85) |
| Pulmonary emboli | 101 | 2.13 (1.39 to 3.25) |

| | |
|---|---|
| **Discussion** | Despite a reduced incidence of colorectal cancer and hip fracture (not shown), the overall health risks exceeded the benefits. The results provide no support for the use of hormone replacement therapy in the primary prevention of coronary heart disease. |

universal agreement that this term encompasses any unwanted clinical event that occurs during the course of a study. It may be caused by the intervention, or it may be entirely unrelated to it. Reporting adverse events in randomized controlled trials applies not only to those occurring in participants receiving the intervention under investigation but also those randomized to the comparator (including placebo).

Distinguishing those adverse events that are iatrogenic from those due to intercurrent, unrelated conditions is often difficult. Type A reactions can often be recognized as causally related to the particular intervention. Type B harms with a very obvious temporal relationship (such as acute anaphylaxis occurring a few minutes after the parenteral administration of a drug) can also be recognized as likely to have been caused by the intervention. But, in most instances, the distinction is less clear.

In theory, comparisons of adverse event rates between the two or more groups of participants in a randomized controlled trial should allow a distinction to be made between those that are true harms from those that are unrelated events. The information about adverse events captured during the course of a randomized controlled trial may include:

- newly emergent symptoms (such as nausea or lethargy);
- newly emergent diagnoses (such as thrombocytopenia);
- the results of routine laboratory tests (such as liver function tests);
- the results of special tests (such as electrocardiography);
- withdrawal rates for suspected harms.

*Therapeutics, evidence and decision-making*

## Newly emergent symptoms

Non-specific symptoms of the potential harmful effects of interventions are usually obtained at routine checks that are made during the course of a trial. They can be elicited from participants either using a checklist (or questionnaire) that includes those most likely to be encountered, or from the response to an open-ended question such as 'How have you been since I last saw you?'

Checklists make for consistency and can usefully remind participants of a recent adverse event. They may elicit overreporting, although in a randomized controlled trial this should apply equally to all the interventions (including placebo). Checklists may, however, fail to elicit events that are not listed. The failure of the early randomized controlled trials of angiotensin-converting enzyme inhibitors to recognize the cough that occurs in about 20 per cent of patients receiving this class of drug is an example of this.[8,9] The most reliable approach is to use both a checklist/questionnaire and an open-ended question in the detection of symptoms emerging during the course of a trial. Blinded ascertainment and analysis of such symptomatic adverse events is, of course, very important in ensuring the validity of any findings.

## Newly emergent diagnoses

As well as non-specific symptoms, participants may develop specific conditions during the course of a trial. *Serious adverse events* occurring in association with a new pharmaceutical product are generally scrutinized, to assess likely causality, by a third party (often a member of staff of the company responsible for developing the product) who is unblinded as to treatment allocations. Many in this process use one of several diagnostic algorithms in an attempt to ensure consistency. These algorithms rate the likelihood of the event being causal in a semi-quantitative manner. Although many endorse this approach, decision-makers should be very wary in their interpretation of the results of these attempts at causality assessment: although such tools may identify as harms those diagnoses that are commonly iatrogenic (e.g. anaphylaxis) and those related to a known pharmacological property of the product (e.g. bleeding with an antithrombotic agent),[10] they can be unreliable in determining causality where the event is unexpected.[11]

## Routine laboratory tests

During the development of new pharmaceutical products, routine laboratory tests are undertaken at intervals during the course of the clinical trial programme. These tests typically include urinalysis, full blood count, serum urea and electrolytes, and conventional blood tests of liver function (bilirubin, alkaline phosphatase, transaminases and gamma-glutamyl transpeptidase).

There are several difficulties in interpreting the results of these routine tests. First, all were originally developed as diagnostic tools for individuals with suspected pathology rather than as screening methods for detecting the potential *toxicity* of pharmaceutical products. Their predictive power to detect incipient harms is therefore limited. Second, in multicentre trials, local laboratories may use different analytical techniques and may vary in their normal (or reference) test ranges. This difficulty can be overcome by sending all the samples to a central laboratory, but this incurs a substantially increased cost. Third, examining trends in average values for the various analytes between the groups may conceal large changes in a small number of participants. For this reason, especially in the assessment of liver function tests (which are extremely labile, even within individuals), adverse events are defined as those that are clinically relevant. In the case of liver enzyme tests in particular, it is common to define 'clinically relevant' as those tests that are three times or ten times outside the normal (reference) range.

### Special tests

The preclinical pharmacology or toxicology studies with a pharmaceutical product sometimes indicate that specific harms could be encountered during clinical use. Examples include prolongation of the QT interval (potentially predisposing to torsades de pointes), and evidence of thyroid dysfunction. In these circumstances, special studies may be conducted during a trial to assess the extent to which these may (or may not) become manifest during clinical use. In the examples above, participants would undergo electrocardiographic monitoring or tests of thyroid function at intervals during the course of the study.

### Withdrawal rates

On the completion of a study, rates of withdrawal for suspected adverse effects may also assist in the evaluation of harms.

## Analysis of data about harms

In unusual instances, such as in the CAST study,[6] where the major outcome indicates that an intervention is harmful rather than only ineffective, the analysis is no different from that of primary outcomes in a conventional randomized controlled trial. The interpretation of the results of reports of adverse events, however, poses special difficulties.

As already discussed, randomized controlled trials are powered to detect benefits and not harms. As a consequence, although a trial may be able to identify the more common harms, it may singularly fail to recognize less common harms. As a rule of thumb, the number of participants exposed to an intervention must be three times the reciprocal of the incidence of a particular adverse event to have a 95 per cent chance of seeing it once. In other words, if an adverse event with a particular intervention has an incidence of one per cent, then 300 participants must be studied to have a 95 per cent chance of observing the adverse event once. Even then, this may not be evidence that it is occurring more frequently than in the comparison group unless there are convincing data to show that the expected number (in the comparison group) is close to zero.

With large randomized controlled trials – for example, including 3000 participants – there is a reasonable prospect that harms occurring at a rate of 1 in 100 will be observed. Serious harms occurring at a rate of 1 in 1000 are likely to go unrecognized. The lack of power of most randomized controlled trials to detect less common harms is compounded where these have a long latency. Drug-induced malignancies, for example, may have latencies of many years.[12]

The analysis of randomized controlled trials for harms poses yet another *multiplicity* problem. In large-scale, long-term trials it is almost inevitable that some statistically significant differences in adverse event rates (if the *P*-value is set at < 0.05) between the groups will be observed. The problem is compounded by how adverse events are classified.[13] The medical dictionaries that are routinely used by pharmaceutical manufacturers and drug regulatory authorities have a hierarchical terminology; and at each level there are a number of terms that are used to group reactions. In MedDRA, one of the commonly used dictionaries, there are 26 system organ classes, nearly 1700 high-level terms and over 14 000 preferred terms. This means that if the preferred terms are used, then the potential for multiple significance tests is considerable.[13] On the other hand, if events are classified at a high level, then grouping them may hide a particular problem.

The simplest approach to the assessment of adverse events in the intervention and control groups is by comparison of their proportions, often using a $\chi^2$ test or Fisher's exact test.[13] They can also be expressed as *relative risks*, *odds ratios* and *absolute risk differences* (see Chapter 1.4).

# Discussion

The assessment of harms from the results of randomized controlled trials is fraught with both technical and practical difficulties. The lack of statistical power of such studies to identify less common harms, coupled with the unresolved issues about multiplicity, makes any evaluation as much of an art as a science. The practical problems relate particularly to the inability of most trials to detect less common harms and harms with a long latency.

In large trials, false positive signals may occur. The results of a large long-term placebo-controlled randomized trial of the benefits of pravastatin after acute myocardial infarction illustrate this problem.[14] In this study a greater incidence ($P = 0.002$) of breast cancer was noted in women treated with pravastatin compared with those on placebo. A later systematic review combining the data from seven large randomized controlled trials and nine observational studies failed to show an increased risk of breast cancer after statin use.[15] The original findings can now be reasonably attributed to random error.

How, then, can decision-makers draw conclusions about the safety of an intervention? The following considerations can be helpful in making judgements about the potential or actual harmfulness of interventions:

- Is the suspected harm biologically plausible? Knowledge of the intervention's biological properties can provide some indication of the likelihood that it may be harmful. In the case of pharmaceuticals, the findings from the preclinical pharmacological and toxicological studies, as well as evidence from the results of investigations with similar products, can be helpful. Nevertheless, biological plausibility is relevant only for type A harms and will provide little assistance in confirming or refuting most type B harms.
- Is there a dose–response relationship? A dose–response relationship is a strong signal that an adverse event is caused by an intervention. The absence of a dose–response relationship, however, does not refute a causal association. There may be no, or insufficient, data from the study to infer a relationship with dose; and type B harms, by definition, are not dose-related within the normal therapeutic dose range.
- How large is the effect size? Decision-makers should focus on effect sizes rather than $P$-values. A large effect size (for example, a relative risk in excess of 10) would be a strong signal that an adverse event may be causally related to exposure to an intervention. Nevertheless, a comparatively small effect size may have a significant population impact and should not necessarily be dismissed as unimportant or unconvincing.
- How serious is it? Judgements about the importance or relevance of an adverse event will also be conditioned by its seriousness, especially when balanced against its benefits. Adverse events such as headache or somnolence might be relatively unimportant in

the treatment of malignant disease, but they may be significant for users of, say, non-opiate analgesics or antipruritic agents. The vigour with which adverse events should be pursued for their causality will therefore depend both on the severity of the event and on the proposed indication of the product.

Decision-makers need to accept, however, that their assessment of the safety of (particularly new) interventions will sometimes be flawed. Of the new active substances licensed as medicines in the UK between 1972 and 1994, 22 were withdrawn for safety reasons.[16] The role of judgement in the assessment of harms remains important, but it is also fallible.

# References

1. Senn S. *Statistic Issues in Drug Development*. Chichester: John Wiley & Sons, 1997.
2. Edwards IR, Aronson JK. Adverse drug reactions: definitions, diagnosis and management. *Lancet* 2000;**356**:1255–9.
3. Iannidis JPA, Evans SJW, Gøtzsche PC, *et al*. Better reporting of harms in randomized trials: an extension of the CONSORT statement. *Annals of Internal Medicine* 2004;**141**:781–8.
4. Aronson JK, Ferner RE. Clarification of terminology in drug safety. *Drug Safety* 2005;**28**:851–70.
5. Rawlins MD, Thompson JW. Pathogenesis of adverse drug reactions. In: Davies DM (ed.). *A Textbook of Adverse Drug Reactions*, 2nd edn. Oxford: Oxford University Press, 1981.
6. Echt DS, Liebson PR, Mitchell LB, *et al*. Mortality and morbidity in patients receiving encainide, flecainide or placebo. Cardiac arrhythmia suppression trial. *New England Journal of Medicine* 1991;**324**:781–6.
7. Writing Group for the Women's Health Initiative Trial. Risks and benefits of estrogen and progestin in healthy postmenopausal women. *Journal of the American Medical Association* 2002;**288**:321–33.
8. Coulter DM, Edwards IR. Cough associated with captopril and enalapril. *BMJ* 1987;**294**:1521–3.
9. Fletcher AE, Bulpitt CJ, Hawkins CM, *et al*. Quality of life on antihypertensive therapy: a randomized double-blind controlled trial of captopril and atenolol. 1990;**8**:463–6.
10. Ferner RE, Aronson JK. EIDOS: a mechanistic classification of adverse drug effects. *Drug Safety* 2010;**33**:15–23.
11. Karcg FE, Smith CL, Kerzner B, *et al*. Adverse drug reactions: a matter of opinion. *Clinical Pharmacology and Therapeutics* 1976;**19**:489–92.
12. Hoover R, Fraumani JF. Drug-induced cancer. *Cancer* 1980;**47**:1071–80.
13. Evans SJW. Statistics: analysis and presentation of safety data. In: Talbot J, Waller P (eds). *Stephen's Detection of New Adverse Reactions*, 5th edn. Chichester: John Wiley & Sons, 2004.
14. Sacks FM, Pfeffer MA, Moye LA, *et al*. The effect of pravastatin on coronary events after myocardial infarction in patients with average cholesterol levels. *New England Journal of Medicine* 1996;**335**:1001–9.
15. Bonovas S, Filiousse K, Tsavaris N, Sitaras NM. Use of statins and breast cancer: a meta-analysis of seven randomised clinical trials and nine observational studies. *Journal of Clinical Oncology* 2005;**23**:8606–11.
16. Jefferys DB, Leakey D, Lewis JA, *et al*. New active substances authorised in the UK between 1972 and 1994. *British Journal of Clinical Pharmacology* 1998;**45**:151–6.

# GENERALIZABILITY

*Between measurements based on randomized controlled trials and benefit in the community there is a gulf which has been much under-estimated.*
Archie Cochrane[1]

The methodology underpinning randomized controlled trials is concerned largely with ensuring their *internal validity*. Their design, conduct, analysis and reporting will have been devoted primarily to attempting to make sure the findings of studies are valid for the particular population that has been involved, and with special emphasis on minimizing various *biases* (see Chapter 1.5).

Randomized controlled trials, however, are generally undertaken by experts in a particular disease area, in highly selected populations of participants, and involve a limited number of participants for a finite (often relatively brief) period of time. In clinical practice the intervention will, almost inevitably, be used in a more heterogeneous population of patients, by less expert practitioners, and often for much longer periods of time. The extent to which the findings from randomized controlled trials can be generalized to disparate patient populations – often referred to as *external validity* – has become of increasing concern.[2–4]

## Generalizability for benefit

Three broad influences may limit the *generalizability* of a randomized controlled trial:

- the setting in which the trial has been carried out;
- the patient population enrolled into the study;
- the special characteristics of the intervention.

### *The setting*
#### ■ Country
The country in which the trial is carried out, and that country's own particular arrangements for health and social care, may impede generalizability in other healthcare settings. For example, some trials of the use of cholinesterase inhibitors in patients with Alzheimer's disease appeared to show that their use delayed the need for admission to long-term residential care;[5] another study failed to confirm this.[6] One explanation is that the availability of nursing homes for elderly people and cultural differences in the way families care for their elderly relatives make such transnational comparisons unreliable.

#### ■ Type of care
Randomized controlled trials performed in secondary (hospital) care may have little or no relevance to patients treated in primary (community) settings. Patients with hypertension treated in hospital may be younger and more resistant to conventional antihypertensive therapy than patients managed in primary care;[3] while patients with

depression treated by a psychiatrist in a secondary care setting are likely to have more severe or refractory forms of depression. In both instances, extrapolating the results to the treatment of patients in the community may be unreasonable.

## Patient populations

There are several characteristics about the patient populations enrolled in randomized controlled trials that may prejudice generalizability.

### ■ Age and gender

A number of studies have shown that women and older patients are underrepresented in many trials. These include studies of various cardiovascular interventions[7–9] and treatments for musculoskeletal disorders.[8,10] Despite these discrepancies it is uncertain whether, and when, they are important.

An overview by Bartlett and colleagues suggested that, from the pooled results of the clinical trials of statins, the *effectiveness* in reducing the risk of death and cardiovascular events was similar among women and men.[8] The authors also reported a smaller *relative risk* reduction of cardiovascular outcomes in people aged 70–82 years than that observed in trials of younger people. Nevertheless, the greater *absolute risk* for cardiovascular disease in older people indicates that the benefits of treatment are larger in older people than in younger people.

Evans and Kalra studied the pooled characteristics and outcomes of patients with atrial fibrillation who had been enrolled into three clinical trials of the use of warfarin in preventing stroke; they compared these with three prospective studies among patients receiving routine care in the USA, Canada and the UK (see Case study 2.5.1).[11] Despite the underrepresentation of older people and women (and also people with diabetes and heart failure) compared with people receiving routine care in the randomized controlled trials, the absolute benefits and major bleeding rates were similar in the two populations.

### ■ Ethnicity

There are known to be ethnic differences in the degree of benefit and the risk of harm with some pharmaceutical interventions. The magnitude of the effect of individual antihypertensive agents, for example, differs between black and white Americans.[12] By contrast, the effects of aspirin in preventing recurrent stroke are similar in Europeans and Chinese people.[13–15]

Ethnic differences in response to medicines usually reflect differences in polymorphic pharmacokinetic or pharmacodynamic traits.[16] It is differences in the gene frequencies of these traits themselves, rather than traits unique to a particular ethnic group, that are responsible for these apparent ethnic differences.[16] Ethnicity, to quote Francis Collins, is 'a murky, inaccurate and potentially prejudicial surrogate for the real thing'.[17] Nevertheless, in assessing the generalizability of a randomized controlled trial, it would be reassuring to know that the ethnic profile of the trial population reflected the profile of the target population. The ethnicity of participants appears, however, to be poorly reported in clinical trials.[8]

### ■ Comorbidity

In many clinical trials, especially those undertaken for regulatory purposes, the admission criteria often exclude patients with significant comorbidities. This is designed to allow the assessment of the effectiveness of interventions under 'ideal circumstances'. In practice, however, people often have one or more other conditions (comorbidities). The results of a large US survey showed, for example, that one-third of younger adults

*Therapeutics, evidence and decision-making*

**Case study 2.5.1** Anticoagulation in atrial fibrillation: comparison of the results of randomized controlled trials and routine care[11]

| | |
|---|---|
| **Background** | Randomized trials have shown clear benefits from the use of anticoagulants in patients with atrial fibrillation. Oral anticoagulants, however, are difficult to use because of the possibility of undercoagulation leading to ischaemic stroke and overcoagulation resulting in bleeding. This study compared the effects of warfarin in randomized patient trials with published reports of its effects during routine clinical care. |
| **Methods** | A systematic review of published studies reporting the results of warfarin treatment in patients with atrial fibrillation in actual clinical practice was undertaken. Data from these studies were compared with pooled data from randomized controlled trials. |
| **Results** | Three studies (total 410 patients, 842 patient-years of follow-up) of the effects of warfarin therapy for atrial fibrillation in routine clinical practice were identified. The results of treatment compared with the pooled results of randomized controlled trials were as follows: |

| | Rate (95% CI) per 100 patient-years of anticoagulation | |
|---|---|---|
| | **Controlled trials** | **Routine care** |
| Ischaemic stroke | 1.4 (0.9 to 2.0) | 1.8 (0.9 to 2.7) |
| Intracranial bleed | 0.3 (0.06 to 0.5) | 0.1 (0 to 0.3) |
| Other major bleed | 1.3 (0.8 to 1.8) | 1.1 (0.4 to 1.8) |
| Minor bleed | 7.9 (6.6 to 9.2) | 12.0 (9.7 to 14.3) |

| | |
|---|---|
| | More women were treated in clinical practice than in the trials. Patients undergoing routine care were also significantly older and with more comorbidities. |
| **Conclusion** | Patients who undergo anticoagulation for atrial fibrillation in clinical practice have similar rates of stroke and major bleeding despite different characteristics. The risk of minor bleeding is higher. |

(aged 18–44 years) and two-thirds of middle-aged adults (aged 45–64 years) had one or more chronic conditions; and 88 per cent of those aged over 65 years had at least one chronic comorbid disorder.[18] Comparable results have been observed in similar surveys carried out in European populations. The influence of the presence of such comorbidities on the generalizability of randomized trials will obviously vary with the condition and the intervention. The potential for adverse drug interactions will aggravate these difficulties.

■ **Additional risk factors**

Risk factors that either predispose or adversely affect the response to an intervention are also important considerations in assessing generalizability. For example, clinical trials in asthma commonly exclude patients who are smokers; and yet one study suggests that 30 per cent of an asthmatic population may smoke.[19] Are the results of trials invalid in smokers? Will the benefits be less in smokers compared with non-smokers? If so, by how much?

## The interventions

The nature and use of the interventions, themselves, may limit generalizability.

Randomized controlled trials, even of interventions intended for use over many years, rarely continue for more than two years. Concerns are, therefore, sometimes expressed about whether longer-term benefits can be necessarily assumed. There are three components to this:

- Where an intervention produces relief from the symptoms of a progressive condition – without influencing its long-term course – its benefits are likely to be of limited duration. Examples include the use of non-steroidal anti-inflammatory drugs for the treatment of osteoarthritis of the knees or hips; and the effects of cholinesterase inhibitors for treating Alzheimer's disease. In neither instance do these interventions impede the progression of the underlying disorder.
- There are some interventions that produce a short- to medium-term improvement in the progression of a condition but where the longer-term benefits are elusive. An example are the long-term benefits of the beta-interferons in the prevention of relapses in the relapsing–remitting form of multiple sclerosis. Although the original trials, carried out over a two-year observation period, had shown a reduction in the number of relapses in this form of multiple sclerosis, it was unclear what it would mean over the 10 or more years over which it was likely to be used in the treatment of patients. Would the relapse rate continue to be reduced? Would there be a beneficial effect on the progressive functional impairment?
- There is also the possibility that pharmacological tolerance might occur over the long term. Pharmacological tolerance generally occurs during the first weeks or months of treatment. Examples include the waning effects with time of the effectiveness of opiates and benzodiazepines. Experience shows that tolerance, if it occurs, does so within at most a few weeks.

### ■ Timing

The adherence of patients to a particular intervention may not be as reliable in routine care as it is in a randomized controlled trial. Patients in a trial may feel under a special obligation to take the intervention more reliably than they would in the context of normal practice.

Of particular significance are trials where there is a pre-randomization 'run-in' period to select or exclude participants.[3] In a placebo run-in, all eligible patients are given placebo and those who are poorly compliant are excluded. Although there may be good reasons for doing this, high exclusion rates reduce generalizability. Active run-in treatment periods, in which patients are excluded if they develop suspected adverse reactions or show signs that the treatment is ineffective, will also undermine generalizability.[3]

### ■ Comparators

Many randomized controlled trials use placebo-treated patients as comparators. This is understandable if, often for regulatory reasons, the aim of the trial is to demonstrate *efficacy*. In many instances, however, a decision-maker will seek to know whether the intervention is more or less effective than current practice. In these circumstances, where there is no direct comparator, decision-makers will need to use *indirect comparators* in reaching their conclusions (see Chapter 1.4).

### ■ Skills

The technical skills of those using the intervention in a randomized clinical trial may seriously undermine its generalizability. This particularly applies to surgical and radiological interventionalist techniques. The Asymptomatic Carotid Surgery (ACAS) trial, for example, accepted only surgeons with a good *safety* record and initially rejected 40 per cent of applicants.[20] In such clinical trials, the exclusion of surgeons who are incapable of treating patients safely is clearly reasonable; but selection should not be so exclusive that the results cannot be generalized to routine clinical care.

## Generalizability for *harms*

There are considerable problems in generalizing the results of randomized controlled trials in the assessment of *harms*. They derive from four particular difficulties:

- statistical issues;
- number of participants;
- homogeneity of the participant population;
- limited duration of studies.

### Statistical issues

The statistical problems relating to power and *multiplicity* have already been discussed extensively. In summary, the numbers of participants in randomized controlled trials are generally decided by reference to the magnitude of the benefit that is anticipated or desired. Power calculations that might take account of all possible harms, including those both anticipated and unanticipated, would be virtually impossible to estimate.

### Number of participants

As discussed in Chapter 2.4, the number of participants in any randomized controlled trial is limited by practical issues. Consequently, only harms occurring relatively frequently will be detected.

### Homogeneity of participants

The narrowly drawn inclusion criteria that often define the eligibility for participation in randomized controlled trials are more likely to limit valid extrapolation on harms. This arises because trial populations exclude especially susceptible participants such as very old people, very young people, pregnant women and patients with comorbidities.

### Limited duration

The relatively short duration of many randomized controlled trials, when compared with the likely duration of use in routine clinical practice, will inevitably prejudice any evaluation of long-term harms at the time a new product is placed on the market.

## Discussion

The main difficulty in attempting to assess the generalizability of the results of randomized controlled trials is the lack of empirical research. There have been studies comparing the profiles of patients recruited into trials with those of a target population, but these investigations have rarely explored the extent to which such differences matter.

There are, it is true, some published reports comparing the results from randomized controlled trials with the results obtained during routine care; and the results of one such study, shown in Case study 2.5.1, were considered earlier. There is also some evidence to suggest that the magnitude of the benefits of statins in hypercholesterolaemia, and of angiotensin-converting enzyme inhibitors in hypertension, are similar during routine care as they are in randomized controlled trials.[21,22]

There have, however, been too few such comparisons. It is possible that appropriate case series from which such comparisons could be made already exist in the published literature. Conventional electronic search techniques, however, make these extremely difficult to identify. Probably as a consequence, only passing (if any) reference is made to the assessment of generalizability in standard texts on randomized controlled trials or evidence-based medicine, in the advice from research funding bodies, and in the guidance from regulatory bodies.[3] Nor do the hierarchies of evidence discussed in Chapter 1.1 address the issue in any way. The CONSORT statement, in its advice on the reporting of randomized controlled trials, includes a section of generalizability, comments:

> *External validity is a matter of judgement and depends on the characteristics of the participants included in the trial, the trial setting, the treatment regimens tested, and the outcomes assessed.*[23]

In reaching conclusions about the generalizability of the results of randomized controlled trials, it would be reasonable for decision-makers to base their judgements around four broad themes.

- biological plausibility;
- exclusions and inclusions (patient populations, flowcharts);
- design features (especially multicentre trials and duration);
- effect size and the extent of uncertainty.

## Biological plausibility

There is an assumption that where the biological basis of a condition is similar in different patient populations, comparable effects (other things being equal) can be expected from the use of a particular intervention. There is, unquestionably, some merit to this assertion, but it requires some care in its interpretation. Conditions with the same name can have dissimilar characteristics both between and within populations. We now know that women with breast cancer, for example, may (or may not) have tumour cells expressing oestrogen and human epidermal growth factor 2 (HER2) receptors, and only those that do express these will derive benefit from oestrogen and HER2 antagonists, respectively. Likewise, the successful treatment of malaria will depend on the prevailing patterns of drug resistance in particular geographical regions.

Difficulties often arise when trials have been confined to a single gender, or when the ages of participants exclude elderly or young people. Decision-makers have to make a judgement about whether the results of a trial carried out only in men can reasonably be extrapolated to women with the same condition, or whether the results of trials with an upper age limit of 70 years can be used to presume benefit in older people. Overly rigid decision-makers may prevent some people from accessing effective and cost-effective interventions. Overly liberal decision-makers may place individuals at risk from clinically ineffective, cost-ineffective or potentially harmful interventions.

In general, most interventions are similarly effective in men and women, and benefits are often greater in very elderly people than in younger adults, because their underlying risks (for example, heart disease) are greater. This may, however, be tempered by the increased risk of very elderly people to adverse effects.

Decision-makers have to accept the limits of the available evidence. In the absence of evidence of biological heterogeneity, decision-makers will often have to assume homogeneity but they should recognize that they will sometimes be wrong and that they will, on occasions, draw erroneous conclusions.

*Therapeutics, evidence and decision-making*

## Exclusion and inclusion criteria

Careful examination of the selection criteria imposed by a study's design will provide decision-makers with at least some indication of the extent to which they appear to match the profiles of the likely target population. Common comorbidities likely to occur in subsets of the target population will also require decision-makers to exercise wisdom in deciding the extent to which such individuals are likely to benefit.

Scrutiny of the flow of participants in a randomized controlled trial, from their eligibility to completion and analysis, can often provide some help in assessing generalizability to the target populations. Where there is a significant unexplained discrepancy between the numbers assessed for eligibility and the numbers randomized, generalizability will be less compelling.

Examination of the baseline characteristics of those participants who were enrolled in a trial may also provide useful information.[3] The extent to which there are similarities or dissimilarities with the likely target population will further assist decision-makers in their judgement about generalizability.

## Design features

There are two aspects to the design of a randomized control trial that decision-makers may find particularly helpful. First, the setting in which the trial has taken place will give some indication of the extent to which there is a match with the target population. In trials of antidepressant agents, for example, those conducted exclusively among patients attending hospital may not reflect the likely benefits in patients treated in the community. Second, scrutiny of the eligibility criteria of participants in randomized controlled trials may provide some indication as to whether there are likely to be difficulties achieving similar effect sizes under normal conditions of use.

## Effect size and the extent of uncertainty

It would be reasonable to assume that where effect sizes for benefit are large and with narrow confidence intervals, as estimated from the results of randomized controlled trials, substantial benefits are likely to accrue in normal use. Some care, though, needs to be taken in applying this reasoning: what might seem to be a modest impact of simvastatin on mortality in the secondary prevention of mortality from coronary artery disease (see Case study 1.4.1 in Chapter 1.4) has much greater implications for public health.

Texts on evidence-based medicine or guideline development hardly give generalizability a mention. Although there are elaborate arrangements for post-marketing safety surveillance by regulatory authorities, there is no post-marketing benefit surveillance for benefit. We have made only very modest progress since 1972, when Cochrane penned the quote at the start of this chapter.

## References

1. Cochrane A. *Effectiveness and Efficiency: Random Reflections of Health Services.* London: Nuffield Provincial Hospitals Trust, 1972.
2. Jüni P, Altman DG, Egger M. Assessing the quality of clinical trials. *BMJ* 2001;**323**:42–6.
3. Rothwell PM. External validity of randomised controlled trials: 'to whom do the benefits apply?' *Lancet* 2005;**365**:82–93.
4. Dekkers OM, von Elm E, Algra A, *et al.* How to assess the external validity of therapeutic trials: a conceptual approach. *International Journal of Epidemiology* 2010;**39**:89–94.

5.  Tariot PN, Cummings JL, Katz IR, *et al*. A randomized, double-blind, placebo-controlled study of the efficacy and safety of donepezil in patients with Alzheimer's disease in the nursing home setting. *Journal of the American Geriatric Society* 2001;**49**:1590–99.

6.  AD2000 Collaborative Group. Long-term donepezil treatment in 565 patients with Alzheimer's disease (AD2000): randomised double-blind trial. *Lancet* 2004;**363**:2105–15.

7.  Heiat A, Gross CP, Krumholz HM. Representation of the elderly, women, and minorities in heart failure clinical trials. *Archives of Internal Medicine* 2002;**162**:1682–8.

8.  Bartlett C, Doyal L, Ebrahim S, *et al*. The causes and effects of socio-demographic exclusions from clinical trials. *Health Technology Assessment* 2005;**9**:1–152.

9.  Dhruva SS, Redberg RF. Variations between clinical trial participants and Medicare beneficiaries in evidence used for Medicare national coverage decisions. *Archives of Internal Medicine* 2008;**168**:136–40.

10. Liberopoulos G, Trikalinos NA, Ioannidis JPA. The elderly were under-represented in osteoarthritis trials. *Journal of Clinical Epidemiology* 2009;**62**:1218–23.

11. Evans A, Kalra L. Are the results of randomized controlled trials on anticoagulation in patients with atrial fibrillation generalizable to clinical practice? *Archives of Internal Medicine* 2001;**161**:1443–7.

12. Materson BJ, Reda DJ, Cushman WC, *et al*. Single-drug therapy for hypertension in men: a comparison of six anti-hypertensive agents with placebo. *New England Journal of Medicine* 1993;**328**:914–21.

13. CAST (Chinese Acute Stroke Trial) Collaborative Group. CAST: randomized placebo-controlled trial of early aspirin use in 20,000 patients with acute ischaemic stroke. *Lancet* 1997;**349**:1641–9.

14. International Stroke Trial Collaborative Group. The International Stroke Trial (IST): a randomised trial of aspirin, subcutaneous heparin, both, or neither among 19,435 patients with acute ischaemic stroke. *Lancet* 1997:**349**:1569–81.

15. McDowell SE, Coleman JJ, Ferner RE. Systematic review and meta-analysis of ethnic differences in risks of adverse reactions to drugs used in cardiovascular medicine. *BMJ* 2006;**332**:1177–81.

16. Wood AJJ. Racial differences in the response to drugs: pointers to genetic differences. *New England Journal of Medicine* 2001;**344**:1393–6.

17. Collins F. *The Language of Life: DNA and the Revolution in Personalized Medicine*. London: Profile Books, 2010.

18. Hoffman C, Rice D, Sung H-Y. Persons with chronic conditions: their prevalence and costs. *Journal of the American Medical Association* 1996;**276**:1473–9.

19. Travers J, Marsh S, Williams M, *et al*. External validity of randomised controlled trials in asthma: to whom do the results of the trials apply? *Thorax* 2007;**62**:219–23.

20. Rothwell PM, Guldsrein LB. Carotid endarterectomy for asymptomatic carotid stenosis. *Stroke* 2004;**35**:2425–7.

21. Weiner MG, Xie D, Tannen RL. Replication of the Scandinavian Simvastatin Survival Study using a primary care medical record database prompted exploration of a new method to address unmeasured confounding. *Pharmacoepidemiology and Drug Safety* 2008;**17**:661–70.

22. Tannen RL, Weiner MG, Xie D. Replicated studies of two randomized trials of angiotensin-converting enzyme inhibitors: further empiric validation of the 'prior event ratio' to adjust for unmeasured confounding by indication. *Pharmacoepidemiology and Drug Safety* 2008;**17**:671–85.

23. Altman DG, Schulz KF, Moher D, *et al*. for the CONSORT Group. The revised CONSORT statement for reporting randomized trials: explanation and elaboration. *Annals of Internal Medicine* 2001;**134**:663–94.

# Observational studies

# GENERAL OVERVIEW

The nomenclature describing the range of observational study designs is confused.[1] The defining feature of an observational study is that the allocation of interventions is non-randomized. However, the distinction between those that are sometimes described as 'controlled' and those that are allegedly 'uncontrolled' is unhelpful. Observational studies invariably involve either implicit (informal) or explicit comparisons. Nor are the terms 'cohort studies' or 'quasi-experimental studies' illuminating. The former includes study designs that encompass several distinct entities, while the latter is inadequately and inconsistently defined.

## Observational study designs

There are five distinct varieties of observational study design that can be used to explore an intervention's benefits and *harms*.

- *Historical controlled trials:* these compare the fate of patients treated with a (usually) new intervention; with a group of patients previously receiving standard therapy (which may include 'best supportive care').
- *Concurrent cohort trials:* these compare the fate of patients treated with one intervention with other patients receiving a standard therapy during the same time period but without randomized allocation and (usually) during the course of routine clinical care.
- *Case–control studies:* these compare the use of an intervention in groups with and without a particular condition. The condition is often (though not invariably) a suspected adverse effect.
- *Case series and registries:* these involve the collection and analysis of patient-level data about the consequences of using particular interventions during routine clinical care.
- *Case reports:* these usually describe the harmful effects of interventions in single patients during routine clinical care.

## Observational studies in context

The great advantage of randomized controlled trials in the assessment of the benefits of an intervention is that, when properly designed, conducted and analyzed (see Chapter 2.1), *bias* and *confounding* are minimized. However, randomized controlled trials are limited by their relatively small size, their narrow scope and their *generalizability* (see Chapter 2.1). By contrast, observational studies can encompass a larger number and wider range of patient populations. Moreover, they can provide greater confidence about generalizability. The main limitation of any observational study is the potential for bias and confounding. Randomized controlled trials and observational studies can therefore be regarded as complementary approaches.

A variety of methods have been developed in an attempt to control for known confounding factors.[2,3] These adjust the findings in an attempt to take account of known confounders:

- stratification;
- various forms of regression analysis;
- propensity scoring methods.

*Stratification* involves, for the purpose of the statistical analysis, dividing participants into subgroups with each subgroup having the same or similar baseline characteristics. Stratified analyses thus enable like-for-like comparisons within the subgroups groups. The method is best used when there are only one or two baseline characteristics for which to stratify.[2] *Regression models* estimate how each prognostic factor relates to the outcome (see Chapter 1.4). Linear regression is used for continuous outcomes, logistic regression for binary outcomes, and Cox models if censoring occurs. *Propensity scoring* models how these same covariates relate to treatment allocations rather than, as in regression models, outcomes. The underlying principle is that the propensity score summarizes the manner in which the baseline characteristics are associated with treatment allocations, so that selection bias can be removed when comparisons are made.[2] Further details of these methods can be found in standard statistical texts.

In assessing the results of adjustments based on these techniques it is often helpful to compare the results of the unadjusted and adjusted effect sizes. If they differ markedly, this implies that differences in baseline characteristics have had a substantial effect on the outcome.[3] This should alert decision-makers to the real possibility that other, unknown confounders may still be lurking in the data. If the unadjusted and adjusted effect sizes are reasonably similar, decision-makers can have more confidence in the findings.

## Observational studies: assessing benefits

There is an extensive, and often disputatious, literature on the merits and demerits of randomized and observational studies in exploring the benefits of an intervention.[1] Two problems in particular have bedevilled attempts to systematically review comparisons of these two broad categories of study design.

First, many reviewers have had obvious difficulties in identifying relevant studies. Although most published randomized controlled trials can be found using the full range of electronic databases that are now available, observational studies have been inconsistently tagged. Consequently, there is little reassurance that conventional search strategies can identify them in an unbiased manner. Many reviews of observational studies have consequently relied on personal collections of papers, their own or others' memories, or studies identified in previous systematic reviews. The potential for reviewer bias is therefore considerable.

Second, very few reviews have attempted to distinguish between the varieties of available observational technique. It is by no means self-evident that they are equally reliable or, for that matter, equally unreliable. One review noted, for example, that discrepancies between randomized and observational studies were much less with prospective, as opposed to retrospective, observational designs.[4]

Overall, the available evidence appears to suggest that although the effects of treatments obtained from randomized and observational studies may differ, one method does not give a consistently greater effect than another.[5] Treatment effects measured using each type of study design best approximate when the exclusion criteria are the same, and when confounders are well understood and controlled for in the observational studies. Furthermore, participants excluded from randomized controlled trials tend to have a worse prognosis than those included, which inevitably limits the generalizability of such trials.

Nevertheless, considerable controversy remains. At one extreme there are rugged methodologists who believe that all treatments can be evaluated only by means of one (and preferably more) randomized controlled trial; and at the other extreme there are those who regard anecdotal and clinical experience to be sufficient. Neither of these positions is tenable and decision-makers should take the following issues into account when considering evidence from observational studies:

- The benefits of interventions producing large, dramatic effects can be recognized without the need for a randomized controlled trial.[1,6,7] It is based on the premise that, with very large effects, the influence of bias and confounding can be safely ignored because the effect size would be unlikely to be substantially affected. How large and dramatic such effect sizes need to be is discussed further in Chapter 3.2.
- Randomized controlled trials in patients with very rare diseases may be impractical. It took nine years, for example, to recruit 39 patients into a randomized trial to assess the benefits of itraconazole in preventing serious fungal infections among patients with chronic granulomatous disease.[8] Approaches based on observational methods are needed if people with rare conditions are not to be denied access to safe and effective interventions.[1]
- There are some circumstances when the number of participants needed to be included in a randomized controlled trial make the trial impractical. For example, knowledge of the effects of influenza vaccination in reducing the mortality from epidemic influenza in elderly people has been derived almost entirely from observational studies.[9] To obtain reliable information about vaccine *efficacy* in important subgroups such as elderly people living in the community compared with those resident in nursing homes would be impractical in randomized controlled trials with mortality as the endpoint.
- There are sometimes difficulties in undertaking randomized controlled trials of surgical interventions. Some important randomized surgical trials have, indeed, been carried out and completed successfully. They include trials of coronary artery bypass surgery,[10] carotid endarterectomy,[11] arthroscopy for osteoarthritis of the knee[12] and vertebroplasty for acute osteoporotic vertebral fractures.[13] Nevertheless, randomized controlled trials may not be feasible for ethical reasons or when there are practical difficulties in recruiting patients.[14] In such circumstances observational studies may provide the only practical solution in the assessment of benefit.
- In some instances, particularly in relation to interventional procedures, it may be unnecessary to undertake randomized control trials. Of the 70 interventional procedures evaluated by the UK's National Institute for Health and Clinical Excellence (NICE) between 2002 and 2005, and considered to be sufficiently safe and effective for normal use, 41 (59 per cent) procedures had never been the subject of randomized controlled trials.[15]
- Patients may refuse to take part in randomized controlled trials or, if they do, they may subvert its design. In the 1980s, some patients with human immunodeficiency virus (HIV)/acquired immunodeficiency syndrome (AIDS) who had been enrolled into randomized controlled trials tested their medications to see whether they had been allocated an active intervention or to a placebo. Some of those allocated to placebo were able to obtain the active ingredient from illicit 'buying clubs'.[16]
- Assessing the most effective way to deliver healthcare would be almost impossible by means of randomized controlled trials. There is, for example, a broad consensus, based

on observational evidence, that hospitals treating larger numbers of patients tend to have better outcomes that those treating smaller numbers of patients. Confirming this with a randomized control trial would be ethically dubious and impossible in practice.

- Observational studies are the only way that the results of randomized controlled trials can be shown to be generalizable (see Chapter 2.5).

In addition, the costs of randomized controlled trials (see Chapter 2.1) have become outrageous.[1] Although there are measures that could, and should, be adopted to reduce these costs the demands for randomized controlled trials will always exceed our ability to organize and fund them. We need to prioritize those that will have the maximum impact on healthcare and use observational methods when these are appropriate.

### Observational studies: assessing harms

The use of observational studies in the assessment of harms is much more widely accepted. This, in part, is because in most observational study designs, decisions about treatment allocations are based on patients' expected prognoses and the anticipated beneficial outcomes, rather than the prospect of untoward effects.[17] This reduces (but does not eliminate) the potential for confounding.

The reasons why randomized controlled trials are, as already discussed, relatively weak at identifying and enumerating harms (see Chapter 2.4) can be summarized thus:

- Randomized controlled trials cannot be powered to detect the full extent of an intervention's potential harms. This particularly applies to less frequent harms: the occurrence of Stevens–Johnson syndrome, or toxic epidermal necrolysis, in some patients treated with anticonvulsants is one example.
- Because of their lack of power, randomized controlled trials commonly fail to detect harms that mimic common conditions. The diabetogenic effects of olanzapine during the treatment of psychotic illnesses were undetected during the initial clinical trials.
- Again because of their lack of power, randomized controlled trials are generally poor at identifying particular risk factors among specific subgroups of patients predisposing to particular harms.
- Randomized controlled trials are inevitably limited in their duration: harms with a long latency and that occur only months or even years later will be missed. Examples include the elevated risks of cardiac valvular abnormalities with long-term use of appetite-suppressant drugs, and the increased risk of vaginal clear-cell adenocarcinoma in the daughters of women who had been prescribed diethylstilbestrol during pregnancy.

# Discussion

Many (though not all) methodologists recognize that randomized controlled trials and observational studies are complementary techniques.[18] Both can contribute invaluable evidence about the effects of interventions, but their respective roles will be determined by two factors.

The first will be the extent to which random error, bias and confounding can be adequately addressed. As already discussed, observational studies can often reduce random error by involving very large numbers of individuals and over (in many instances) much longer periods of time – but with a greater potential for bias and confounding.

The second factor, as discussed earlier, relates to the practical difficulties in undertaking some randomized controlled trials. Ethical and logistical problems will often require decision-makers to be pragmatic in deciding whether the results of one or more observational studies provide sufficiently reliable information.

In inferring causal relationships from associations found from observational studies, commentators often refer to the eight factors elaborated in a lecture by Austin Bradford Hill in 1965.[19] They have sometimes been interpreted as 'the criteria' that are required to be met before inferring causality from evidence gained using observational methods. This is incorrect: Bradford Hill clearly indicated that these were factors that should be 'taken into account' when inferring a causal relationship. It is important, however, to appreciate that he was addressing causality in respect of epidemiological studies of the relationship between environmental agents and disease rather than therapeutic interventions. Nevertheless, they are worth rehearsing:

- *The strength of the association:* in modern terminology this would generally be described as the 'effect size'. Bradford Hill emphasized, however, that a cause-and-effect relationship should not be dismissed on the grounds that the effect size appeared to be slight.
- *Consistency:* by this, Bradford Hill meant that causal associations should be replicated in other settings, and with different methodological approaches (such as retrospective versus prospective designs). On the other hand, he argued that failure of replication should not invariably be an argument for rejecting causality.
- *Specificity:* in epidemiology an association between (say) specific groups of workers and particular diseases would be a strong argument in favour of causation but should not be overemphasized.
- *Temporality:* this is concerned with the possibility that exposure to an environmental influence might be as a consequence of a disease rather than its cause. In modern terminology this would be selection bias or confounding by indication.
- *Biological gradient*: in this context Bradford Hill regarded the evidence of a dose–response relationship as strongly suggestive of causation. He suggested that in epidemiological studies, dose–response relationships should invariably be sought, even though it might sometimes be methodologically difficult or impossible to do so.
- *Plausability:* although Bradford Hill regarded biological plausibility as 'helpful' in ascribing causation, he did not consider it essential. As he put it, 'What is biological plausible depends on the knowledge of the day.'
- *Coherence:* Bradford Hill stated that a cause-and-effect interpretation of observational data should not conflict with the generally known facts of the natural history or biology of the disease.
- *Experiment:* occasionally in epidemiology, it is possible to appeal to experimental or semi-experimental evidence.

Bradford Hill also pointed out that no formal tests of significance could answer questions about causality. Although, as he put it, 'they can and should remind us of effects that the play of chance can create', that was as far as he was prepared to go. In subsequent chapters, I provide an indication of the factors that decision-makers should 'take into account' in interpreting the results of observation studies. They do, however, not fully replicate those of Bradford Hill.

Observational studies have an important role in the detection and assessment of both benefits and harms. Although the available techniques require care in their design, conduct, analysis and interpretation, their significance and importance should never be underestimated.

# References

1. Rawlins MD. *De Testimonium: On the Evidence for Decisions about the Use of Therapeutic Interventions*. London: Royal College of Physicians, 2008.
2. Deeks JJ, Dinnes J, D'Amico R, *et al*. Evaluating non-randomised intervention studies. *Health Technology Assessment* 2003;**7**:1–173.
3. Normand S-LT, Sykora K, Li P, *et al*. Readers guide to critical appraisal of cohort studies: 3. Analytical strategies to reduce confounding. *BMJ* 2005;**330**:1021–3.
4. Ioannidis JPA, Haidich A-B, Pappa M, *et al*. Comparison of evidence of treatment effects in randomised and non-randomised studies. *Journal of the American Medical Association* 2001;**286**:821–30.
5. McKee M, Britton A, Black N, *et al*. Interpreting the evidence: choosing between randomised and non-randomised studies. *BMJ* 1999;**319**:312–15.
6. Doll R, Peto R. Randomised controlled trials and retrospective controls. *BMJ* 1980;**280**:44.
7. Glasziou P, Chalmers I, Rawlins M, McCulloch P. When are randomised trials unnecessary? Picking signal from noise. *BMJ* 2007;**334**:349–51.
8. Gallin JI, Alling DW, Malech HL, *et al*. Itraconazole to prevent fungal infections in chronic granulomatous disease. *New England Journal of Medicine* 2003;**348**:2416–22.
9. Jefferson T, Rivettie D, Rivetti A, *et al*. Efficacy and effectiveness of influenza vaccines in elderly people: a systematic review. *Lancet* 2005;**366**:1165–74.
10. Detre KM, Takaro T, Hultgren H, Peduzzi P. Long-term mortality and morbidity results of the Veterans Administration randomized trial of coronary artery bypass surgery. *Circulation* 1985;**72**:V84–9.
11. Mayo Asymptomatic Carotid Endarterectomy Study Group. Results of a randomized controlled trial of carotid endarterectomy for asymptomatic carotid stenosis. *Mayo Clinical Proceedings* 1992;**67**:513–18.
12. Kirkley A, Birmingham TB, Litchfield RB, *et al*. A randomized trial of artroscopic surgery for osteoarthritis of the knee. *New England Journal of Medicine* 2008;**359**:1097–107.
13. Klazen CAH, Lohle PNM, de Vries J, *et al*. Vertebroplasty versus conservative treatment in acute osteoporotic fractures (Vertos II): an open label randomized trial. *Lancet* 2010;**376**:1085–92.
14. McCulloch P, Altman DG, Campbell WB, *et al*. No surgical innovation without evaluation: the IDEAL recommendations. *Lancet* 2009;**374**:1105–12.
15. Campbell WB, Barnes SJ, Kirby RA, *et al*. Association of study type, sample size, and follow-up length with type of recommendation produced by the National Institute for Health and Clinical Excellence Interventional Procedures Programme. *International Journal of Health Technology Assessment* 2007;**23**:101–7.
16. Carpenter D. *Reputation and Power*. Princeton, NJ: Princeton University Press, 2010.
17. Vandenbroucke JP. When are observational studies as credible as randomised trials? *Lancet* 2004;**363**:1728–31.
18. MacMahon S, Collins R. Reliable assessment of the effects of treatment on mortality and major morbidity, II: observational studies. *Lancet* 2001;**357**:455–62.
19. Hill AB. The environment and disease: association or causation? *Proceedings of the Royal Society of Medicine* 1965;**58**:295–300.

*Therapeutics, evidence and decision-making*

# HISTORICAL CONTROLLED TRIALS

In a historical controlled trial the fate of a group of patients treated with a (usually) new intervention is compared with a 'historical' group receiving what was, at the time, the appropriate standard care. The appropriate standard care in this historical group might have been an active treatment or, as is most often the case, so-called 'best supportive care'. Historical controlled trials have been used primarily to assess an intervention's benefits rather than its *harms*. This chapter also includes an account of before-and-after designs because of their close association with historical controlled trials.

The controls in historical controlled trials may be either implicit or explicit.

*Implicit* controls represent established knowledge of the natural history of a particular condition. For example, it had been known for many years that untreated myxoedema led to inexorable death. The introduction of thyroxine (as thyroid extract) almost completely reversed a patient's decline.

*Explicit* controls are specific groups of patients in whom the progress of the condition has previously been observed and documented. In some instances a previous case series may be used as the comparator group. In others, the case records of suitable patients can be retrieved and used specifically for the purpose of constructing the comparator group. The demonstration of the effects of the early antihypertensive agents in preventing renal failure in patients with accelerated (malignant) hypertension relied on explicit controls (see Table 3.2.1).[1] Similarly, the benefits of intravenous *N*-acetylcysteine in the treatment of paracetamol poisoning were shown by a comparison with previous patients attending the Edinburgh Poisons Unit.[2]

**Table 3.2.1** Pharmaceutical interventions with evidence of effectiveness based on historical controlled trials

| Intervention | Year of introduction | Indication |
|---|---|---|
| Thyroxine | 1891 | Myxoedema[10] |
| Insulin | 1922 | Diabetic ketoacidosis[11] |
| Vitamin $B_{12}$ | 1926 | Pernicious anaemia[12] |
| Physostigmine | 1934 | Myasthenia gravis[13] |
| Sulphonamides | 1937 | Puerperal sepsis[14] |
| Penicillin | 1941 | Lobar pneumonia[15] |
| Streptomycin | 1948 | Tuberculous meningitis[16] |
| Ganglion blockers | 1959 | Malignant hypertension[1] |
| Cisplatin + vinblastine + bleomycin | 1977 | Disseminated testicular cancer[17] |
| *N*-Acetylcysteine | 1979 | Paracetamol poisoning[2] |
| Ganciclovir | 1986 | CMV retinitis[18] |
| Imiglucerase | 1990 | Gaucher's disease[19] |
| Imatinib | 2002 | Chronic myeloid leukaemia[20] |
| Imatinib | 2005 | Gastro-intestinal stromal tumours[21] |

# Historical controlled trials: the criticisms

The use of historical controls has sometimes been regarded as a flawed method for establishing the *effectiveness* of an intervention because of the potential for *confounding* and *bias*.[3,4] This view is based on the difficulties in ensuring that the comparisons between the groups are fair. If the groups differ in characteristics, other than the treatment under investigation, they may invalidate any conclusions about an intervention's benefits.

*Confounding by indication*[4] occurs when a treatment is more (or less) frequently provided to individuals who already have features associated with an increased (or decreased) chance of developing the outcome of interest. This may occur if the historical control group has less clearly defined criteria for inclusion; if the treated group is accidentally (or deliberately) drawn from a more restricted patient population; or if the historical control group has been recruited from different sources than the treated group and therefore differs in one or more important respects.

Bias may occur if there are differences in the clinical environment from which the two groups are chosen. The data for the historical group, for example, may have been garnered from patients' routine medical records. These are likely to be inferior to the data collected for the group receiving the new intervention. In addition, the supportive care given to patients receiving the new treatment may be an improvement on the supportive care given to the historical controls. This could contribute in part, or in whole, to any observed improvement. Furthermore, patients on a new intervention may be observed more closely than those comprising the historical group. Added to which, if patients are aware – as they will be – of their participation in a new treatment, this may affect their attitude to their disease and their response to its treatment.

There is no doubt that the inappropriate use of historical controls can have devastating consequences. One of the most controversial uses of the technique was the adoption of high-dose chemotherapy supported by autologous bone marrow transplantation in women with advanced breast cancer.[5] The procedure was introduced during the late 1980s.[6,7] It was based on the premise that high-dose chemotherapy for women with advanced breast cancer carried the prospect of eradicating most, if not all, the patient's malignant cells. Because high-dose chemotherapy would inevitably destroy the patient's bone marrow as well as their malignant cells, fragments of marrow were removed before chemotherapy started and grafted back later.

The clinical evidence to support this practice was based on comparisons with an explicit historical control population of patients with breast cancer, but who were treated only with conventional-dose chemotherapy. The problems with this at the time were obvious.[8] It was very likely that patients fit enough to undergo high-dose chemotherapy followed by autologous bone marrow transplantation were not necessarily comparable with the historical control group. The new procedure was itself associated with a 5–15 per cent early mortality (compared with 1 per cent or less in patients receiving conventional-dose chemotherapy) and only relatively fit patients would be considered for the new treatment. Such patients were therefore likely to have a survival advantage and the comparison was likely to be confounded by indication. So it turned out.[9] The results of a randomized controlled trial published in 2000 showed that high-dose chemotherapy plus autologous bone marrow transplantation had no beneficial effect for women with advanced breast cancer in comparison with conventional-dose chemotherapy.[9] In the meantime, over 40 000 American women had been treated with this new regimen during the 1980s and 1990s, at an estimated cost of US$ 3.4 billion.[5]

# Historical controlled trials: the successes

Despite these criticisms the use of numerous therapeutic interventions of unequivocal effectiveness are based on evidence derived solely from historical controlled trials.

Table 3.2.1 shows examples of pharmacological interventions falling into this category. They include replacement therapies for myxoedema (thyroxine), type 1 diabetes (insulin), Addison's disease (corticosteroids) and congenital growth hormone deifciency (human growth hormone). All are based on clear physiological principles. The table also shows many other examples, including gancyclovir for the treatment of acquired immunodeficiency syndrome (AIDS)-related cytomegalovirus retinitis, enzyme replacement therapy (imiglucerase) for Gaucher's disease, and imatinib for chronic myeloid leukaemia. Table 3.2.2 provides similar examples of a range of interventional procedures whose unquestionable effectiveness has been established from historical controlled trials.

**Table 3.2.2** Some interventional procedures with evidence of effectiveness based on historical controlled trials

| Procedure | Year of introduction | Indication |
|---|---|---|
| Tracheostomy | 1546 | Tracheal obstruction[22] |
| Blood transfusion | 1818 | Haemorrhagic shock[23] |
| Defibrillation | 1948 | Ventricular fibrillation[24] |
| Heimlich manoeuvre | 1975 | Laryngeal obstruction by a foreign body[25] |
| Fundoplication | 1993 | Gastro-oesophageal reflux[26] |
| Parental kiss | 2000 | Nasal obstruction by a foreign body[27] |
| Laser treatment | 2000 | Removal of port-wine stains[28] |

# Before-and-after designs

Before-and-after designs are a special form of historical controlled trial. The technique involves making observations among a group of patients before and after the use of a particular intervention. In this design patients act as their own controls, and any change is attributed to the effect of the intervention.

The design has been used mainly in the assessment of benefit, and the approach forms a part of the evidence base in some historical controlled trials, especially those involving interventional procedures (see Table 3.2.2). As with historical controlled trials more generally, where the natural history of the condition is known and predictable, and where the effect of the intervention is 'dramatic', the technique can be used to provide reliable evidence of effectiveness.

In other circumstances, before-and-after designs are of little value in the assessment of the benefits of an intervention. They have been used to investigate interventions such as the relief of pain in osteoarthritis and rheumatoid arthritis, the reduction in the symptoms of anxiety and depression, and the improvement of the abnormal movements that characterize Parkinson's and Huntington's diseases. However, in each of these circumstances, any improvements may merely reflect the natural course of the condition, the normal day-to-day fluctuations in its symptomatology, regression to the mean, or a manifestation of the Hawthorne effect. All of these influences contribute to the so-called 'placebo effect' of an intervention.[29]

# Discussion

The polarized debate about the role of historical controlled trials in the evaluation of the benefits of interventions is more apparent than real. Most investigators accept that where effects are 'dramatic', historical controlled trials can provide convincing evidence of benefit.[30-32] Even the harshest critics agree that if outcomes are typically poor among untreated patients, and a large proportion derive substantial benefit from a new intervention, then this can constitute reliable evidence of benefit.

The change in attitudes towards historical controlled trials was prompted largely by the emerging human immunodefiency virus (HIV)/AIDS epidemic. In 1992, 22 of some of the world's most respected and experienced clinical investigators accepted that 'some of the traditional approaches to clinical trial design were unnecessarily rigid';[33] they outlined the criteria under which non-randomized trials might provide evidence to support the use of a particular intervention:

- There must be no other treatment appropriate to use as a control.
- There must be sufficient experience to ensure that the patients not receiving treatment will have a uniformly poor prognosis.
- The therapy must not be expected to have substantial *side effects* that would compromise the potential benefit to the patient.
- There must be a justifiable expectation that the potential benefit to the patient will be sufficiently large to make interpretation of the results of a non-randomized trial unambiguous.
- The scientific rationale for the treatment must be sufficiently strong that a positive result would be widely accepted.

When, then, might the effects of an intervention be regarded as 'dramatic'? When might decision-makers reasonably conclude that a historical controlled trial has provided adequate evidence of benefit? I have proposed that historical controlled trials (whether implicit or explicit) should be accepted as reliable evidence for effectiveness provided they meet all of the following conditions:[34]

- *Biologically plausibility*: a biologically plausible basis for the observed benefits would be persuasive evidence, but care should be taken: what constitutes a biologically plausible explanation depends on the state of knowledge at the time. Nevertheless, all the treatments shown in Tables 3.2.1 and 3.2.2 had a plausible basis for their beneficial effects.
- *There should be no appropriate treatment that could be reasonably used as a control*: the term 'appropriate' would exclude, for example, the use of bone marrow transplantation as an alternative to enzyme replacement therapy in the treatment of Gaucher's disease.
- *The condition should have a known and predictable natural history*: for example, advanced breast cancer has a very variable course, and so high-dose chemotherapy with autologous chemotherapy clearly fails this test.
- *The treatment should not be expected to have adverse effects that would compromise its potential benefits*: this is a *sine qua non* and a test that high-dose chemotherapy with autologous bone marrow transplantation, for advanced breast cancer, also fails.
- *There should be a reasonable expectation that the magnitude of the therapeutic effects of treatment will be large enough to make the interpretation of its benefits unambiguous*: a signal-to-noise ratio of ten or more and a *number needed to treat* close to one would appear to be strongly suggestive of a genuine therapeutic effect.

An example of the appropriate use of historical controls is shown in Case study 3.2.1. Imatinib was licensed in the USA and the European Union (EU) for the treatment of chronic myeloid leukaemia (CML) on the basis of its effects on haematological and cytogenetic *biomarkers*. In this instance, the use of historical controlled trials – particularly in assessing the effectiveness of imatinib on survival in the accelerated and blast phases of the disease for the purposes of cost-effectivness analyses – was justified by:

- the plausibility of a beneficial effect of imatinib on the condition (as a result inhibition of BCR-ABL tyrosine kinase);
- the limited effectiveness of alternative treatments (apart from bone marrow transplantation) for patients failing treatment with alfa-interferon;
- the prognosis for the accelerated and blast phases of chronic myeloid leukaemia is uniformly grim;
- the infrequency of adverse effects with imatinib, with less than 5 per cent of patients discontinued from trials for this reason;
- the apparent effect size, which, although not achieving a tenfold signal-to-noise ratio, nevertheless appeared to be very substantial.

---

**Case study 3.2.1** Imatinib in the treatment of chronic myeloid leukaemia[20]

**Background** Imatinib reduces cellular proliferation by inhibiting a specific tyrosine kinase. It was licensed in 2001 for the treatment of the blast, accelerated and chronic phases of chronic myeloid leukaemia (CML) in patients who had failed on treatment with alfa-interferon. Licensing by the European Union (EU) was based on 'exceptional circumstances', and the evidence of efficacy was derived from the results of its effects on haematological and cytogenetic biomarkers. There were no randomized controlled trials and, in the absence of comparators, no evidence of increased survival.

**Method** In order to estimate the effects of imatinib on survival in CML, the fate of patients treated with imatinib was compared with that reported in the placebo arms of randomized controlled trials (RCTs) and case series (i.e. historical controls) of broadly comparable patients treated before imatinib was available.

**Results** Percentage survival at one year in each of the three groups was as follows:

| | | Survival at 1 year (%) | |
|---|---|---|---|
| | RCTs | Case series | Imatinib |
| CML | 96 (range 93–98) | 97.5 (range 87–100) | 97* |
| Accelerated CML | – | 32.5 (range 28–37) | 74 (95% CI 65 to 81) |
| Blast-phase CML | – | 13 (range 6–17) | 30* |

*No range of 95% CI available

**Discussion** Because of the relatively benign course of the chronic phase of CML, no effect on survival with imatinib was discernable. There appeared, however, to be a substantial survival advantage with imatinib in the treatment of the accelerated and blasts phases.

A subsequent randomized controlled trial of imatinib in the chronic phase of CML confirmed its superiority to the combination of cytarabine and alfa-interferon and the durability of the response to therapy.

In the future, there will be circumstances when we should be prepared to accept the evidence of benefit from historical controlled trials. Interventions falling into this category might, for example, include treatments that arrest the premanifest forms of the progressive neurodegeneration seen in Huntington's disease or in the inherited forms of Alzheimer's disease and Creutzfeldt–Jakob disease.[34]

Despite the potential advantages of historical controlled trials there are also circumstances – the corollary to the five conditions necessary for showing effectiveness – when randomized controlled trials remain essential. These comprise the following:

- *Where there is no, or an incomplete, biologically plausible basis underpinning the use of the intervention:* many complementary and alternative medicines fall into this category.
- *Where the condition is self-limiting:* demonstrating effectiveness in conditions where full recovery is likely anyway will make the interpretation of the results of a historical controlled trial almost impossible. Examples include upper respiratory tract infections and soft-tissue injuries.
- *Where the condition has an unpredictable natural history:* examples include relapsing–remitting multiple sclerosis, rheumatoid arthritis, recovery from thrombotic stroke, and death immediately following acute myocardial infarction.
- *Where there are, or are likely to be, pronounced placebo effects:* in these circumstances (such as in the evaluation of treatments for anxiety, depression or pain), the distinction between a placebo effect and a true therapeutic one will be almost impossible to make on the basis of historical controlled trials.
- *Where the magnitude of the benefit (i.e. the effect size) is likely to be modest:* when the effects of an intervention are relatively small, the potential influences of random error, bias and confounding make the interpretation of the results of a historical controlled trial almost impossible to evaluate.

Historical controlled trials have a place in the assessment of the effectiveness of interventions, but they have to be evaluated with appropriate caution.

# References

1. Harington M, Kincaid-Smith P, McMichael J. Results of treatment in malignant hypertension: a seven year experience in 94 cases. *BMJ* 1959;**ii**:969–80.
2. Prescott LF, Illingworth RN, Critchley JAJH, *et al.* Intravenous *N*-acetylcysteine: the treatment of choice for paracetamol poisoning. *BMJ* 1979;**ii**:1097–100.
3. Pocock SJ. *Clinical Trials*. Chichester: John Wiley & Sons, 1983.
4. MacMahon S, Collins R. Reliable assessment of the effects of treatment on mortality and major morbidity, II: observational studies. *Lancet* 2001;**357**:455–62.
5. Mello MM, Brennan TA. The controversy over high-dose chemotherapy with autologous bone marrow transplantation. *Health Affairs* 2001;**20**:101–17.
6. Peters WP, Shpall EJ, Jones RB, *et al.* High-dose combination alkylating agents with bone marrow support as initial treatment for metastatic breast cancer. *Journal of Clinical Oncology* 1988;**6**:1368–76.
7. Williams SF, Mick R, Dresser R, *et al.* High-dose consolidation therapy with autologous stem-cell rescue in stage IV breast cancer. *Journal of Clinical Oncology* 1989;**7**:1824–30.
8. Eddy DM. High-dose chemotherapy with autologous bone marrow transplantation for the treatment of metastatic breast cancer. *Journal of Clinical Oncology* 1992;**10**:657–70.

9. Stadtmauer, EAA, O'Neil A, Goldstein LJ, *et al.* Conventional-dose chemotherapy compared with high-dose chemotherapy plus autologous hematopoietic stem-cell transplantation for metastatic breast cancer. *New England Journal of Medicine* 2000;**342**:1069–76.

10. Murray GM. Note on the treatment of myxoedema by hypodermic injections of an extract of the thyroid gland of a sheep. *BMJ* 1891;**ii**:796–7.

11. Banting FG, Best CH, Collip JB, *et al.* Pancreatic extracts in the treatment of diabetes mellitus. *Canadian Medical Association Journal* 1922;**12**:141–6.

12. Minot GR, Murphy WP. Treatment of pernicious anaemia by a special diet. *Journal of the American Medical Association* 1926;**87**:470–76.

13. Walker MB. Treatment of myasthenia gravis with physostigmine. *Lancet* 1934;**i**:1200–201.

14. Colebrook L, Purdie AW. Treatment of 106 cases of puerperal fever by sulphanilamide. *Lancet* 1937;**ii**:1291–4.

15. Abraham EP, Chain E, Fletcher CM, *et al.* Further observations on penicillin. *Lancet* 1941;**ii**:177–90.

16. Medical Research Council. Streptomycin treatment of tuberculous meningitis. *Lancet* 1948;**i**:582–96.

17. Einhorn LH, Donohue JP. *cis*-Diamminedichlorplatinum, vincristine and bleomycin combination chemotherapy in disseminated testicular cancer. *Annals of Internal Medicine* 1977;**87**:293–8.

18. Collaborative DHPG Study Group. Treatment of serious cytomegalovirus infections with 9-(1,3-dihydroxy-2-propoxymethyl)guanine in patients with AIDS and other immunodeficiencies. *New England Journal of Medicine* 1986;**314**:801–5.

19. Barton NW, Furbish FS, Murray GJ, *et al.* Therapeutic response to intravenous infusions of glucocerebrosidase in a patient with Gaucher disease. *Proceedings of the National Academy of Sciences* 1990;**87**:1913–16.

20. Garside R, Round A, Dalziel K, *et al.* The effectiveness and cost-effectiveness of imatinib in chronic myeloid leukaemia. *Health Technology Assessment* 2002;**6**:1–162.

21. Wilson J, Connock M, Song F, *et al.* Imatinib for the treatment of patients with unresectable and/or metastatic gastrointestinal stromal tumours: systematic review and economic evaluation. *Health Technology Assessment* 2005;**9**:1–142.

22. Lindman JP, Morgan C. Tracheostomy. www.emedicine.com/ent/topic356.htm.

23. Blundell J. The history of blood transfusion medicine. www.bloodbook.com/trans-history.html.

24. Beck CS, Pritchard WH, Feil HS. Ventricular fibrillation of long duration abolished by electric shock. *Journal of the American Medical Association* 1948;**135**:985–6.

25. Heimlich HJ. A life-saving maneuver to prevent food choking. *Journal of the American Medical Association* 1975;**234**:398–401.

26. Cushieri A, Hunter J, Wolfe B, *et al.* Multicentre prospective evaluation of laparoscopic antireflux surgery: preliminary report. *Surgical Endoscopy* 1993;**7**:505–10.

27. Botma M, Bader R, Kubba H. A parent's kiss: evaluating an unusual method for removing nasal foreign bodies in children. *Journal of Laryngology and Otology* 2000;**114**:598–600.

28. Goh CL. Flashlamp-pumped pulse dye laser (585 nm) for the treatment of portwine stains: a study of treatment outcome in 94 Asian patients in Singapore. *Singapore Medical Journal* 2000;**41**:24–8.

29. Finniss DG, Kaptchuk TJ, Miller F, Benedetti F. Biological, clinical and ethical advances of placebo effects. *Lancet* 2010;686–95.

30. Doll R, Peto R. Randomised controlled trials and retrospective controls. *BMJ* 1980;**280**:44.

31. Collins R, Peto R, Gray R, Parish S. Large-scale randomized evidence: trials and overviews. In: Warrell DA, Cox TM, Firth JD, Benz EJ (eds). *Oxford Textbook of Medicine*, 4th edn. Oxford: Oxford University Press, 2003.

32. Glasziou P, Chalmers I, Rawlins M, McCulloch P. When are randomised trials unnecessary? Picking signal from noise. *BMJ* 2007;**334**:349–51.

33. Byar DP, Schoenfeld DA, Green SB, *et al*. Design considerations for AIDS trials. *New England Journal of Medicine* 1990;**323**:1343–8.

34. Rawlins MD. *De Testimonio: On the Evidence for Decisions about the Use of Therapeutic Interventions*. London: Royal College of Physicians, 2008.

# CONCURRENT COHORT STUDIES

In concurrent cohort studies the fate of patients receiving one intervention is compared with that of a group of untreated patients, or a group treated with an alternative intervention, within the same time period. The controls are therefore contemporaneous rather than historical. Concurrent cohort studies may be prospective or retrospective. They are therefore similar in many respects to historical controlled trials. The main difference is that the clinical environment and ancillary treatments of the treated and control populations are more likely to be comparable. In addition, because many of these studies are now often done using routine medical records (including electronic medical records), the clinical observations and the fidelity of record-keeping are also more likely to be comparable. As well as the use of routine medical records for such comparisons, data collected in special registries are sometimes used (see Chapter 3.6). Nevertheless, because the treatments are not allocated randomly, the potential for *bias* and *confounding* remains.

## Assessment of benefit

There have been various comparisons of the results of randomized trials with those obtained from concurrent cohort trials. The conclusions have been varied, in part because of the difficulties in retrieving the relevant literature, as discussed in Chapter 3.1. In addition, as discussed previously, most systematic reviews have combined the findings from studies based on historical controlled and case–control studies with those using concurrent cohort designs. Moreover, many have made comparisons in circumstances where effect sizes have been modest rather than dramatic.

Some reviews have claimed that differences in effects and effect sizes are at worst only minimal.[1,2] Others have concluded that these differences can be as large as, or even larger than, the size of the effects that were to be detected.[3] In a 'review of reviews', this is therefore hardly surprising: 'Results of non-randomized studies sometimes, but not always, differ from results of randomized studies of the same intervention.'[4]

An example of a concurrent cohort study is shown in Case study 3.3.1. Based on the electronic medical records of the UK's General Practice Research Database (see Chapter 3.6), this study sought to determine the extent to which antibiotics reduce the risk of serious complications when given to treat upper respiratory tract infections.[5] Although the results indicated a reduction in rates of pneumonia, otitis media and quinsy in those receiving antibiotics, the benefits were very small, with numbers needed to treat to prevent these serious complications are all in excess of 4000.

In an observational study such as this, with no random allocation of treatments, it is possible that there was some selection bias in the prescribing of antibiotics. In particular, severely affected patients might have been prescribed antibiotics more readily than those less severely affected. Consequently, the results may have underestimated the benefits of antibiotics in these circumstances. Nevertheless, setting these minimal benefits against the likelihood of gastrointestinal and other *harms*, the risk of causing antibiotic

| | | |
|---|---|---|
| **Background** | There is evidence to suggest that the persisting high rates of antibiotic prescribing for upper respiratory tract infections in the community may be due to the perceptions of doctors and patients that this reduces the chances of serious secondary complications. Randomized controlled trials generally have insufficient power to examine the effects of rare outcomes, and the patients included might not reflect those seen in routine practice. | |
| **Method** | Data on antibiotic prescribing for common respiratory tract illnesses were obtained from the electronic records of 162 general practices contributing to the General Practice Research Database. Risk estimates were made of serious complications in patients treated and untreated with antibiotics over the month following an initial diagnosis of upper respiratory tract infection, sore throat or otitis media. | |
| **Results** | The results are based on 1 081 000 episodes of upper respiratory tract infection, 1 065 088 episodes of sore throat, and 459 876 episodes of otitis media. Serious complications were rare and unrelated to age. The adjusted odds ratios with their associated numbers needed to treat for all ages combined were as follows: | |

| | Adjusted odds ratio[*] (95% confidence interval) | Number needed to treat (95% confidence interval) |
|---|---|---|
| Upper respiratory tract infection – pneumonia | 0.68 (0.58 to 0.79) | 4407 (2905 to 9126) |
| Otitis media – mastoiditis | 0.56 (0.37 to 0.86) | 4064 (2393 to 13 456) |
| Sore throat – quinsy | 0.84 (0.73 to 0.97) | 4300 (2522 to 14 586) |
| [*]Adjusted for age, sex and social deprivation. | | |

| | | |
|---|---|---|
| **Conclusion** | The authors concluded that antibiotics are not justified to reduce the risk of serious complications of upper respiratory tract infections, otitis media or sore throat, at any age. | |

sensitivity, and the contributions to antibacterial resistance in the community make routine antibiotic prescribing for such an indication inappropriate.

Case study 3.3.2 is an example of a study requiring a more difficult judgement to be made about the claimed benefits of bilateral versus single lung transplantation in patients with chronic obstructive pulmonary disease.[6] Using data from a registry of lung transplants maintained by the International Society for Heart and Lung Transplants, the authors attempted to compare the survival of patients undergoing each form of transplant surgery.

Overall, the median survival was greater in patients receiving bilateral versus single transplants, and the adjusted *hazard ratios* were similar irrespective of the statistical techniques that were used. Moreover, the results of the unadjusted and adjusted hazard ratios were not widely divergent. The conclusion, however, of a true difference in the consequences of the two procedures is less clear. The hazard ratios themselves are not large, and they translate at five years into a 4.0–6.3 per cent better chance of survival for bilateral versus single lung transplant.[6] Consequently, despite the reassuring results of the statistical adjustments, residual confounding might still explain the findings.

**Case study 3.3.2** Survival after bilateral versus single lung transplantation for patients with chronic obstructive pulmonary disease[6]

| | |
|---|---|
| **Background** | Patients with severe chronic obstructive pulmonary disease may be offered lung transplantation. Single lung transplantation is technically easier and allows for economy of organs, since the lungs from one donor can be transplanted into two patients. Both single and bilateral transplantation yield similar benefits in terms of exercise capacity, but there are reports that bilateral transplantation is associated with better survival. |
| **Methods** | The survival of 3525 patients with severe chronic obstructive pulmonary disease and undergoing bilateral lung transplantation was compared with that of 6358 patients undergoing single lung transplantation between 1987 and 2006. Attempts to account for selection bias were made by a variety of adjustments (analysis of covariance, propensity-score risk adjustment and propensity-based matching). |
| **Results** | The median survival times after bilateral and single lung transplants were 6.4 years (95% CI 6.02 to 6.88) and 4.6 years (95% CI 4.41 to 4.76). The effects on estimates of the hazard ratio after the use of various techniques to allow for selection bias are shown below: |

| | Hazard ratio (95% CI) |
|---|---|
| Unadjusted | 0.76 (0.70 to 0.83) |
| Analysis of covariance | 0.83 (0.78 to 0.92) |
| Propensity decile | 0.84 (0.79 to 0.90) |
| Propensity decile + covariates | 0.86 (0.81 to 0.93) |
| Propensity-based matching | 0.89 (0.80 to 0.97) |

| | |
|---|---|
| | Further analyses suggested that the benefit of bilateral versus single lung transplantation was inapparent in people aged over 60 years (hazard ratio 0.95, 95% CI 0.81 to 1.13) and that the benefit appeared to be restricted to people aged under 60 years. |
| **Conclusions** | The authors concluded that bilateral transplantation leads to longer survival than single lung transplantation, especially in people aged under 60 years. |

The apparent effect of age could be due to decreased statistical power as a result of the subgroup analyses.

Confronted with such evidence, a decision-maker might also consider an additional aspect. The availability of lungs suitable for transplantation is very limited. Although bilateral transplantation may offer an advantage to a single individual, single lung transplants would benefit two patients. Put another way, depending on the prognosis of non-transplanted patients, one patient receiving a bilateral lung transplant (with an average survival of 6.4 years) will deprive two patients of single lung transplants (average survival of 4.6 years each, giving a combined total of 9.2 years).

## Assessment of harm

The role of concurrent cohort studies in the assessment of an intervention's harms is a less contentious use of the technique. Nevertheless, care needs to be taken to avoid misinterpretation as a result of selection bias and confounding.

The problems are shown in Case study 3.3.3. This study was instigated, in part, because of the possibility that the use of omeprazole might be associated with increased rates of upper gastrointestinal malignancies.[7] It was postulated that omeprazole might mask early symptoms; that it might influence the frequency of oesophageal adenocarcinoma occurring in association with Barrett's ulcer; or that the raised plasma gastrin levels in response to reduced acid production might act as a growth promoter and increase the *incidence* of gastric neoplasms.

As can be seen in this case study, from a superficial examination, the initial results appeared alarming. The ratios of observed to expected deaths from oesophageal and gastric neoplasms were 6.9 and 6.1, respectively, indicating an excess of upper

---

**Case study 3.3.3** Omeprazole and upper gastrointestinal tract malignancies[7]

| | |
|---|---|
| **Background** | There had been suspicions, based largely on theoretical considerations, that long-term treatment with protein pump inhibitors such as omeprazole might increase the frequency of upper gastrointestinal malignancies. |
| **Methods** | A cohort of 17 936 patients resident in one of six UK conurbations and prescribed omeprazole by their family doctor were registered between 1993 and 1995. Causes of death over the following four years were obtained from the family doctors' records and from the patients' death certificates. Observed death rates were compared with expected population rates matched for gender and age. |
| **Results** | The numbers of deaths from oesophageal and gastric malignant diseases that were not present at the time of registration, as well as the ratio of observed to expected deaths over the four years following registration, are shown below: |

|  | Study year Conclusions | | | |
|---|---|---|---|---|
|  | **1** | **2** | **3** | **4** |
| *Oesophageal neoplasms* | | | | |
| Number of deaths | 36 | 17 | 8 | 15 |
| Ratio observed/expected | 6.9* | 3.3* | 1.6 | 2.9* |
| *Gastric neoplasms* | | | | |
| Number of deaths | 25 | 15 | 7 | 4 |
| Ratio observed/expected | 6.1* | 2.5* | 1.2 | 0.9 |
| *P<0.02. | | | | |

There was no evidence that patients with more severe oesophageal symptoms or Barrett's ulcer had higher rates of upper gastrointestinal malignancies than those with less severe oesophageal disease. There was no evidence of a dose–response relationship (as determined from the number of prescriptions issued).

| | |
|---|---|
| **Conclusions** | The excess of oesophageal neoplasms in the first two years is very likely to have been due to confounding by indication. The findings indicate that the nature of the underlying oesophageal disease is the major, and probably the sole, cause of the increased risk of oesophageal cancer deaths in people taking omeprazole. Similar conclusions apply to the apparent early increased risk of gastric cancer. |

*Therapeutics, evidence and decision-making*

gastrointestinal malignancies among patients taking omeprazole. The fact that the observed-to-expected mortality rates for malignancies at both sites reduced substantially over the four-year period of observation strongly suggests that the original findings were due to confounding by indication and that patients with early symptoms of either oesophageal or gastric cancer were prescribed omeprazole. This case study emphasizes the potential difficulties that may be encountered in the interpretation of the results of concurrent cohort studies. Careful examination of the data is invariably necessary to avoid, as in this instance, the influence of confounding by indication.

A more recent concurrent cohort study, based on information from linked computerized data, is summarized in Case study 3.3.4. This study was undertaken in the light of intense controversy about the relative cardiovascular toxicities of pioglitazone and rosiglitazone

---

**Case study 3.3.4** Adverse cardiovascular events during treatment with rosiglitazone and pioglitazone[8]

**Background** The glitazones are established as effective treatments for the control of type 2 diabetes. They have, however, been associated with increased risks of fluid retention and heart failure in both randomized controlled trials and observational studies. Rosiglitazone in particular has also been associated with an increased risk of acute myocardial infarction. This study was designed to assess whether the two drugs have differential cardiovascular risks.

**Methods** The study population was based on Ontario residents aged 66 years or older who started treatment with either rosiglitazone or pioglitazone between 1 April 2002 and 31 March 2008. Prescription data and clinical outcomes were obtained using linked computerized databases. The primary (composite) outcome was death or hospital admission for either acute myocardial infarction or heart failure. A secondary analysis for each outcome separately was also undertaken.

During the study period 39 736 patients were started on treatment with a glitazone. The median period of follow-up was similar for the two groups (294 days pioglitazone, 292 days rosiglitazone). During the six-year study period the results of the primary and secondary analyses were as follows:

| | Pioglitazone (*n* = 16 951) | Rosigliatzone (*n* = 22 785) | Hazard ratio (unadjusted) | Hazard ratio (adjusted*) |
|---|---|---|---|---|
| Primary outcome | 895 (5.3%) | 1563 (6.9%) | 0.81 (0.74 to 0.87) | 0.83 (0.76 to 0.90) |
| *Secondary outcomes* | | | | |
| Death | 377 | 645 | 0.82 (0.73 to 0.94) | 0.86 (0.75 to 0.98) |
| Heart failure | 461 | 869 | 0.75 (0.67 to 0.84) | 0.77 (0.69 to 0.87) |
| Myocardial infarction | 273 | 425 | 0.91 (0.78 to 1.06) | 0.95 (0.81 to 1.11) |

*Adjusted for demographic factors, clinical factors and drug dose with Cox proportional hazards regression.

**Conclusions** Among older patients with diabetes, pioglitazone is associated with a significantly lower risk of heart failure and death compared with rosiglitazone.

in the treatment of type 2 diabetes.[8] It was designed primarily to assess the relative frequency of a composite endpoint (see Chapter 1.4) comprising death, heart failure and myocardial infarction with each of these two products. The study population was large, the statistical analyses were exhaustive, and the adjustments for confounding were extensive. The complete absence of *P*-values in the published report is admirable!

In assessing the results of a study such as this, however, decision-makers must nevertheless exercise considerable judgement. As the authors of the report admit, there is a possibility of confounding by indication and that those patients prescribed pioglitazone rather than rosiglitazone had a greater risk of cardiovascular complications. The comparability at baseline of the two groups provides some reassurance, as do the similarities between unadjusted and adjusted hazard ratios.

# Discussion

The role of concurrent cohort studies in the assessment of benefit has been controversial, but too much has probably been made of their disadvantages. Selection bias and confounding can obviously undermine the conclusions from such studies, but decision-makers should avoid rejecting this study design out of hand. By contrast, concurrent cohort studies have an established place in the identification of harms.

When should decision-makers be prepared to accept the results of concurrent cohort studies as reliable forms of evidence? Taking the following factors into account provides some help:

■ *Biological plausibility:* a biologically plausible basis for the observed benefits of harms would be persuasive, but care should be taken. What constitutes a biologically plausible explanation is, itself, a judgement. For example, the authors of Case study 3.3.4 claimed a biologically plausible explanation for the differential harmfulness of rosiglitazone and pioglitazone based on their relative potencies.[8]
■ *Selection bias and confounding:* as has been discussed extensively, the potential for selection bias and confounding to distort the results of concurrent cohort studies is substantially greater than for randomized controlled trials. Selection bias is less likely in studies of harms than of benefits. Decision-makers will have greater confidence in the results of concurrent cohort studies if appropriate adjustments have been carried out, and where the unadjusted and adjusted outcomes are not too dissimilar.
■ *Dose–response relationship:* the demonstrations of a dose–response relationship can provide a strong indication of a causal relationship between exposure to the intervention and a particular outcome. Many studies, however, will be insufficiently powered to enable dose–response relationships to be established, and type B harms (see Chapter 3.1) are, anyway, independent of dose.
■ *Effect size:* as discussed in Chapter 3.1, in interpreting the results of historical controlled trials it is assumed that the influences of bias and confounding will be dwarfed by a large effect size.
■ *Replication:* confidence in the results of a concurrent cohort study will be increased if similar results have been observed in other studies, and especially in those using different methodological approaches.

In their evaluation of the results of a concurrent cohort study, decision-makers should avoid taking a too formulaic approach. These factors are ones that decision-makers should take account of when reaching conclusions rather than rigid criteria to which strict adherence must be applied.

*Therapeutics, evidence and decision-making*

# References

1. Concato J, Shah N, Horwitz RI. Randomized, controlled trials, observational studies and the hierarchy of research designs. *New England Journal of Medicine* 2000;**342**:1887–92.
2. Benson K, Hartz AJ. A comparison of observational studies and randomized controlled trials. *New England Journal of Medicine* 2000;**342**:1878–86.
3. Kunz R, Oxman AD. The unpredictability paradox: review of empirical comparisons of randomised and non-randomised clinical trials. *BMJ* 1998;**317**:1185–90.
4. Deeks JJ, Dinnes J, D'Amico R, *et al*. Evaluating non-randomised intervention studies. *Health Technology Assessment* 2003;**7**:1–173.
5. Petersen I, Johnson AM, Islam A, *et al*. Protective effect of antibiotics against serious complications of common respiratory tract infections: retrospective cohort study within the UK General Practice Research Database. *BMJ* 2007;**335**:982–7.
6. Thabut G, Christie JD, Ravaud, P, *et al*. Survival after bilateral versus single lung transplantation for patients with chronic obstructive pulmonary disease: a retrospective analysis of registry data. *Lancet* 2008;**371**:744–51.
7. Bateman DN, Colin-Jones D, Hartz S, *et al*. Mortality study of 18,000 patients treated with omeprazole. *Gut* 2003;**52**:942–6.
8. Juurlink DN, Gomes T, Lipscombe LL, *et al*. Adverse cardiovascular events during treatment with pioglitazone and rosiglitazone: population based cohort study. *BMJ* 2009;**339**:b2942.

# CHAPTER 3.4

## CASE–CONTROL DESIGNS

Case–control studies are the reverse of other methods for examining the effects of interventions. In other designs, the effects of an intervention are compared between groups of patients. In a case–control study the comparison is the exposure status to the intervention interest in groups with and without specific conditions or outcomes.

## Background

At its most simple, a case–control study involves identifying a group of individuals with a specific condition – the cases – and comparing their exposure to a particular intervention with that of a group – the controls – without the same condition. The controls should represent the population at risk of the condition and, if they did have it, they would have become cases. As discussed later, the choice of controls can be critical for the reliable conduct of a case–control study.

If no attempt has been made to match the cases with the controls (an 'unmatched' study), the results of a case–control study can be represented as a straightforward $2 \times 2$ contingency table (see Table 3.4.1).

**Table 3.4.1** $2 \times 2$ table for an unmatched case–control study

| Exposure status | Cases (with condition) | Controls (without condition) |
|---|---|---|
| Exposed group | a | b |
| Non-exposed group | c | d |

The *odds ratio* for exposure (see Chapter 1.4) can then be calculated thus:

$$\text{Odds ratio} = \frac{(a/c)}{(b/d)} = ad/cd$$

and is usually reported with its 95 per cent confidence intervals (CIs). Adjustments for *confounding* can be undertaken using logistic regression or Mantel–Haenszel methods, which weight the confounders.

Very commonly, however, each case is matched with one or more controls chosen to reflect one or more confounding factors. It would, for example, be inappropriate for controls to be drawn from a general population to study whether oral contraceptive use is associated with the development of venous thromboembolism. Such a case–control study would, as a minimum, need to match cases of thromboembolism with controls of the same age and gender. In a matched case–control study the analysis has to take matching into account using Mantel–Haenszel methods or conditional logistic regression analysis (a variant of logistic regression that compares cases with controls in a matched set). Overmatching, on the other hand, will reduce statistical efficiency and can introduce *bias*.

When exposure among cases of interest is rare, the odds ratio and the *relative risk* are approximate (see Chapter 1.4). Where exposure is common, the precise interpretation of the odds ratio estimated in a case–control study depends on the sampling scheme used

to select the controls.[1]

# Case–control studies of benefit

The utility of case–control studies for benefit, like other observational designs, can be compromised by selection bias and confounding. Case study 1.5.2 in Chapter 1.5 provides an example. Enthusiasm for, and the widespread use of, hormone replacement therapy during the 1990s was based on the results of case–control studies comparing the frequency of cardiovascular events in long-term users with non-users. As shown in this case study, a *meta-analysis* suggested that hormone replacement therapy reduced coronary heart disease by 44 per cent (95% CI 39 per cent to 50 per cent). It subsequently became clear from the results of large, well-conducted randomized controlled trials that such treatment has no beneficial effects in the prevention of coronary heart disease.[2] The discrepancies between the results of the case–control studies and the randomized controlled trials of the perceived benefits of hormone replacement therapy were very largely due to the influence of *confounding* by indication.[3] Subsequent analyses showed that if the case–control studies had taken account of the influence of age, socioeconomic status, smoking habits and duration of use, most of the alleged advantages would have disappeared.[3] Some women, however, paid a high price for the inappropriate use of long-term hormone replacement therapy because of the *harms* (venous thromboembolism and breast cancer) to which they were exposed.[4]

The failure of case–control studies to provide reliable information about the benefits of hormone replacement therapy contrasts with the success of the technique in other circumstances. During the 1960s and 1970s, emerging evidence from case–control studies suggested that maternal vitamin deficiency – specifically, folate deficiency – was associated with the development of neural tube defects in the offspring.[4] A concurrent controlled trial indicated that vitamin supplementation that included folic acid at around the time of conception to women who had previously given birth to one or more infants with a neural tube defect was associated with a substantial reduction in the *incidence* of these congenital abnormalities. A small randomized study showed a non-significant benefit in preventing neural tube defects. The results of a large multicentre randomized control trial carried out under the auspices of the Medical Research Council and published in 1991 confirmed that periconception folate supplementation reduced the incidence of neural tubes in at-risk mothers to an extent similar to that seen in observational studies.[5]

There are also other circumstances where case–control studies have provided significant indications of the benefits of interventions. A case–control study confirmed by randomized controlled trials first noted the effects of aspirin in the prevention of acute myocardial infarction.[6] The relationship between sleeping posture and sudden infant death syndrome was also established by case–control studies;[7] the widespread implementation of this finding has prevented numerous deaths in infancy.

Case–control studies published in the late 1980s and early 1990s suggested that the regular use of aspirin and other non-steroidal anti-inflammatory drugs reduced the risk of colorectal cancer.[8] These observations spawned a number of randomized controlled trials and concurrent controlled studies focusing on this protective effect of aspirin. The analysis and interpretation of these studies have been complicated by their clinical and methodological heterogeneity; in the definitions of regular use, dose and duration of use; and by the assumption that the prevention of colorectal polyps was a valid surrogate for the prevention of colorectal cancer. Overall, however, there is a consensus that aspirin reduces the incidence of colorectal polyps and colorectal cancer, especially if used for more than ten years.[9]

Case–control studies can, indeed, provide evidence to support the use of therapeutic interventions, although considerable care needs to be taken to avoid drawing false positive conclusions.

## Case–control studies of harms

In contrast to some of the difficulties encountered in assessing benefits, case–control studies have been invaluable in the identification of harms. Case study 3.4.1 provides an example.[10] This study was designed to investigate the gastrointestinal *toxicity* of non-steroidal anti-inflammatory drugs. Although it was known that the therapeutic class generally was associated with an increased risk of bleeding from peptic ulceration, there was little evidence as to whether there were differential risks between products or between dosages. The results of the study indicated substantial differences in the risk of bleeding from peptic ulcer between various members of the class and between doses. It also confirmed that paracetamol (which is not a non-steroidal anti-inflammatory drug) was not associated with gastrointestinal toxicity. The fact that such wide-ranging conclusions could be drawn from such a study demonstrates the power of the technique.

In addition (not shown in Case study 3.4.1), this investigation demonstrated that the risk of bleeding peptic ulceration was associated with the duration of use. The *odds ratio* for patients who had been using non-aspirin non-steroidal drugs for three months or longer (4.8, 95% CI 3.8 to 6.0) was half that for patients starting within the previous month (9.6, 95% CI 5.5 to 16.8) of the time of admission. In other words, patients are more likely to develop bleeding peptic ulceration shortly after starting treatment. This is an example of 'healthy survivor bias' and can occur if no account is taken of the duration for which treatments, given for long periods of time, may have been used. A similar phenomenon has been observed with the risk of venous thromboembolism with oral contraceptives: thromboembolic disease is more likely to occur shortly after embarking on therapy than after longer-term use.

Table 3.4.2 shows some examples of other case–control studies that have identified harms with pharmaceutical products. At the time these harms were recognized in case–control studies, none had been identified from randomized controlled trials. The associations between hormone replacement therapy and both venous thrombosis and breast cancer were later confirmed by large randomized controlled trials.

Case study 3.4.2, however, provides a warning. It summarizes one of three similar studies[23–25] published in the same edition of the *Lancet* in 1974. Each of these studies described an association between long-term use of reserpine (and other Rauwolfia derivatives) and the development of breast cancer. Investigators in the USA had discovered the association serendipitously a year earlier;[24] because of its implications they (commendably) contacted centres in the UK and Finland to see whether their findings could be replicated. All three of these original studies demonstrated an association with breast cancer, with a relative risk ranging from two to four. Over the next six years, however, a further nine case–control and concurrent controlled studies failed to confirm the findings. It is now widely accepted that the initial claims of causal association were erroneous.

The most likely explanation appears to have been in the choice of controls. In two of the original studies,[24,25] controls but not cases were excluded if they had any form of cardiovascular disease. Repeating these studies in another setting showed that excluding controls with cardiovascular disease gave rise to an odds ratio of 2.5 (95% CI 0.9 to 7.3), but including controls with cardiovascular disease reduced the odds ratio to 1.1 (95% CI 0.5 to 3.3).[26] It was postulated that a false association may have been produced by so-called 'exclusion bias'.[26] Irrespective of the explanation, decision-makers need to be aware that even the most distinguished epidemiologists (the senior author of the UK study was the late, very great Sir Richard Doll) can fall into error.

Case–control studies have also provided reassurance that putative adverse effects 'signalled' in case reports (either in the literature or to national drug regulatory

| **Case study 3.4.1** Bleeding peptic ulceration associated with non-steroidal anti-inflammatory drug therapy[10] |
|---|

| | |
|---|---|
| **Background** | Upper gastrointestinal haemorrhage from a bleeding peptic ulcer is a common cause of admission to hospital. A significant proportion of patients will be undergoing treatment with a non-steroidal anti-inflammatory drug (NSAID). This study was designed to assess the contribution of individual NSAIDs for the risk of bleeding peptic ulceration. |
| **Methods** | The study was designed as a prospective case–control investigation. Information about the previous use of NSAIDs was sought from 1144 patients aged 60 years or older admitted to hospitals in five large UK cities with bleeding peptic ulceration, and compared with prior use among 1126 and 989 matched community controls. |
| **Results** | The hospital and community controls were similar and therefore were combined in the analyses of the results. The odds ratios for use of aspirin, non-aspirin NSAIDs and paracetamol were as follows: |

| Drug | Unmatched odds ratio (95% CI) | Matched odds ratio* (95% CI) |
|---|---|---|
| Aspirin | 2.9 (2.4 to 3.5) | 3.1 (2.0 to 4.8) |
| Non-aspirin NSAIDs | 3.8 (3.1 to 4.5) | 3.5 (2.4 to 5.3) |
| Paracetamol | 1.1 (0.8 to 1.3) | 1.1 (0.7 to 1.7) |

Matched odds ratios for some common non-aspirin NSAIDs were as follows:

| Drug | Matched odds ratio* (95% CI) |
|---|---|
| Ibuprofen | 2.0 (1.4 to 2.8) |
| Diclofenac | 4.2 (2.6 to 6.8) |
| Naproxen | 9.1 (5.5 to 15.0) |
| Indometacin | 11.3 (6.3 to 20.2) |
| Piroxicam | 13.7 (7.1 to 26.3) |

Matched odds ratios by dose (using British National Formulary definitions) were as follows:

| | Matched odds ratio* (95% CI) |
|---|---|
| Low | 2.5 (1.7 to 3.8) |
| Medium | 4.5 (3.3 to 6.0) |
| High | 8.6 (5.8 to 12.6) |

*Adjusted (logistic regression analysis) for alcohol use, smoking, previous peptic ulcer disease and dyspepsia.

| | |
|---|---|
| **Conclusions** | There is a clear association between exposure to NSAIDs and admission to hospital with bleeding peptic ulceration, with evidence of heterogeneity between individual NSAIDs and between dose. |

**Table 3.4.2** Some harms confirmed by case–control studies[4]

| Intervention | Year of publication | Harm |
|---|---|---|
| Oral contraceptive agents | 1967 | Venous thromboembolism[11] |
| Diethylstilboestrol during pregnancy | 1972 | Genital tract carcinoma in female offspring[12] |
| Aspirin in children | 1985 | Reye's syndrome[13] |
| L-Tryptophan | 1990 | Eosinophilia-myalgia syndrome[14] |
| Non-steroidal anti-inflammatory drugs | 1994 | Bleeding peptic ulceration[15] |
| Hormone replacement therapy | 1996 | Venous thromboembolism[16,17] |
| Hormone replacement therapy | 1997 | Breast cancer[18] |
| Selective serotonin reuptake inhibitors | 1999 | Upper gastrointestinal bleeding[19] |
| Anticonvulsants | 1999 | Stevens–Johnson syndrome[20] (toxic epidermal necrolysis) |
| Olanzapine | 2002 | Diabetes[21] |
| Fluoroquinolones | 2002 | Achilles tendon disorders[22] |

---

**Case study 3.4.2** Association between the use of Rauwolfia derivatives and breast cancer[23]

**Background** This study was undertaken because the authors were aware of an unpublished report describing an association between the use of reserpine and the development of breast cancer.

**Methods** Patients with breast cancer, and control patients with other neoplasms, first referred to hospitals in the Bristol area and registered in 1971 and 1972 formed the two study populations. Three controls were matched for age and year of registration. Where there were more than three matching patients, three were selected at random. For each patient, information on all drug therapy at the time of initial presentation was obtained by examination of the patients' hospital and general practitioner medical records.

**Results** Adequate drug-therapy data were obtained for 708 patients with breast cancer and 1430 controls. An association between breast cancer and the use of Rauwolfia derivatives was found, with a relative risk of 2.0 (95% CI 1.2 to 3.4). No association was observed between breast cancer and the use of any other antihypertensive agent, or the use of other products known to enhance the release of prolactin.

**Conclusions** The study showed a significant positive association between prior Rauwolfia derivative use and breast cancer. Although biased identification or selection of cases and controls might explain these findings, these factors did not appear to account for the association.

---

authorities) do not have (or are extremely unlikely to have) a iatrogenic basis. Examples include suspected associations between bisphosphonates and the development of atrial fibrillation,[27] and the use of sympathomimetic bronchodilators with excess asthma deaths.[28]

# Discussion

There is no doubt that case–control methods have contributed greatly to epidemiology generally, and in particular to studies of the effects of therapeutic interventions.

Their place in providing evidence of the benefits of an intervention is mixed. There are instances where the method has singularly failed (such as in the alleged benefits of hormone replacement therapy on coronary heart disease). Equally, there are examples of where the approach has correctly predicted benefits (such as the effects of folate in the prevention of neural tube defects).

In the assessment of harms, case–control designs have been extraordinarily helpful in eliciting and elucidating the harmfulness of interventions. This is, in part, because the potential for confounding by indication is reduced. Yet, as discussed, they are also capable of generating false positive results.

The factors decision-makers should take account of in concluding causal relations from the results of case–control studies include the following:

- *Biological plausibility:* as discussed in Chapter 3.2, biological plausibility is neither necessary nor sufficient. It does, however, help.
- *Effect size:* the greater the magnitude of the effect, the more likely it is that an association – either for benefit or for harm – is causal.
- *Minimization of bias and confounding:* appropriate measures in the design and analysis of the study should have been taken to reduce the influence of bias and confounding. Large differences between the unadjusted and adjusted odds ratios may indicate residual confounding (see Chapter 3.1).
- *Dose–response relationship:* as discussed in Chapter 3.1, a dose–response relationship strongly assists in the interpretation of causality (see Case study 3.4.1).
- *Reproducibility:* reproducibility of the findings in other settings, and with different methodologies, can increase confidence in claims of causality.

None of these factors individually has an overriding influence, but the effect size is probably the most important. In assessing the results of a historical controlled trial, it was suggested (in Chapter 3.2) that the signal-to-noise ratio should be ten or more. By analogy, in the evaluation of a case–control study for benefit, odds ratios of around ten or more should be regarded as very encouraging. Lower odds ratios should not, however, necessarily be dismissed as showing a causal relationship of benefit.

In the evaluation of harms, much lower odds ratios can provide confidence in the results. There have been suggestions that odds ratios of more than three in case–control studies are required to provide good evidence for the harmfulness of interventions, but there is little empirical evidence to support this assertion.

Decision-makers need to exercise judgement on the totality of the evidence from one or more case–controlled studies in concluding whether benefits or harms are associated with an intervention are causal. Strict, arbitrary rules about odds ratios should play little part in this.

## References

1. Rodrigues L, Kirkwood BR. Case–control designs in the study of common diseases: updates on the demise of the rare disease assumption and the choice of sampling scheme for controls. *International Journal of Epidemiology* 1990;**19**:205–13.

2. Beral V, Banks E, Reeves G. Evidence from randomised trials on the long-term effects of hormone replacement therapy. *Lancet* 2002;**360**:942–4.

3. Petitti DB, Freedman DA. How far can epidemiologists get with statistical adjustment. *American Journal of Epidemiology* 2005;**162**:415–18.

4. Rawlins MD. *De Testimonio: On the Evidence for Decisions about the Use of Therapeutic Interventions*. London: Royal College of Physicians, 2008.

5. MRC Vitamin Study Research Group. Prevention of neural tube defects: results of the Medical Research Council Vitamin Study Group. *Lancet* 1991;**338**:131–6.

6. Boston Collaborative Drug Surveillance Group. Regular aspirin intake and acute myocardial infarction. *BMJ* 1874;**i**:440–43.

7. Gilbert R, Salanti G, Harden M, See S. Infant sleeping position and sudden infant death syndrome: systematic review of observational studies and historical review of recommendations from 1940 to 2002. *International Journal of Epidemiology* 2005;**34**:874–87.

8. Sturmer T, Glynn RJ, Lee I-M, *et al*. Aspirin use and colorectal cancer: post-trial follow-up data from the Physicians Health Study. *Annals of Internal Medicine* 1998;**128**:713–20.

9. Dubé C, Rostom A, Lewin G, *et al*. The use of aspirin for primary prevention of colorectal cancer: a systematic review prepared for the US Preventative Services Task Force. *Annals of Internal Medicine* 2007;**146**:365–75.

10. Langman MJS, Weil J, Wainwright P, *et al*. Risks of bleeding peptic ulcer associated with individual non-steroidal anti-inflammatory drugs. *Lancet* 1994;**343**:1075–8.

11. Medical Research Council. Risk of thromboembolic disease in women taking oral contraceptives. *BMJ* 1967;**ii**:355–9.

12. Herbst AL, Kurman RJ, Scully RE, Poskanzer DC. Clear-cell adenocarcinoma of the genital tract in young females. *New England Journal of Medicine* 1972;**287**:878–81.

13. Hurwitz ES, Barrett MJ, Bregman D, *et al*. Public Health Service study on Reye's syndrome and medications: report of the pilot phase. *New England Journal of Medicine* 1985;**313**:849–57.

14. Eidson M, Philen RM, Sewell CM, *et al*. L-Tryptophan and eosinophilia-myalgia. *Lancet* 1990;**335**;645–8.

15. Langman MJ, Weil J, Wainwright P, *et al*. Risk of bleeding peptic ulcer associated with individual non-steroidal anti-inflammatory drugs. *Lancet* 1994;**343**:1075–8.

16. Daly E, Vessey MP, Hawkins MM, *et al*. Risk of thromboembolism in users of hormone replacement therapy. *Lancet* 1996;**348**:977–80.

17. Jick H, Derby LE, Myers MW, *et al*. Risk of hospital admission for idiopathic venous thrombosis among users of postmenopausal oestrogens. *Lancet* 1996;**348**:981–3.

18. Collaborative Group on Hormonal Factors in Breast Cancer. Breast cancer and hormone replacement therapy: collaborative reanalysis of data from 51 epidemiological studies of 52 705 women with breast cancer and 108 411 women without breast cancer. *Lancet* 1997;**350**:1047–59.

19. De Abajo FJ, Rodríguez FAG, Montero D. Association between selective serotonin reuptake inhibitors and upper gastrointestinal bleeding: population based case control study. *BMJ* 1999;**319**:1106–9.

20. Razny B, Correia O, Kelly JP, *et al*. Risk of Stevens–Johnson syndrome and toxic epidermal necrolysis during first weeks of antiepileptic therapy: a case–control study. *Lancet* 1999;**353**:2190.

21. Koro CE, Fedder DO, L'Italien GJ, *et al*. Assessment of independent effect of olanzapine and risperidone on risk of diabetes among patients with schizophrenia: population based nested case–control study. *BMJ* 2002;**325**:243–7.

22. Van der Linden PD, Sturkenboom MCJM, Herings RMC, *et al*. Fluoroquinolones and risk of Achilles tendon disorders: case–control study. *BMJ* 2002;**324**:1306–7.

23. Armstrong B, Stevens N, Doll R. Retrospective study of the association between use of rauwolfia derivatives and breast cancer in English women. *Lancet* 1974;**ii**:672–7.

24. Boston Collaborative Surveillance Programme. Reserpine and breast cancer. *Lancet* 1974;**ii**:669–71.

25. Heinonen OP, Shapiro S, Tuominem L, Turunen MI. Reserpine use in relation to breast cancer. *Lancet* 1974;**ii**:675–7.

26. Horwitz RI, Feinstein AR. Exclusion bias and the false relationship of reserpine and breast cancer. *Archives of Internal Medicine* 1985;**145**:1873–5.

27. Sørensen HT, Christensen S, Mehnert F, *et al*. Use of bisphosphonates among women and risk of atrial fibrillation and flutter: population based case–control study. *BMJ* 2008;**336**:813–16.

28. Anderson HR, Ayres JG, Sturdy PM, *et al*. Bronchodilator treatment and deaths from asthma: case–control study. *BMJ* 2005;**330**:117–24.

# CHAPTER 3.5

# DATABASES

Databases are becoming powerful tools for research. The information they provide has underpinned some of the case studies in the preceding chapters of this section. However, to be useful in studying the effects of interventions, databases must necessarily include, as a minimum, patient-level data about the use of one or more particular intervention(s) and the subsequent outcome(s).

## Background

The terminology used to describe the variety of databases available for evaluative research is confused and inconsistent. Here I distinguish 'case series' from 'case registries'. *Case series* comprise data collected as part of the routine provision and administration of normal healthcare. *Case registries* are disease-specific or intervention-specific databases of patient information collected and maintained specifically for research. Most databases are now stored and maintained in electronic format. Case series tend to have less information than registries, but they provide greater coverage than most clinical registries.[1] Case registries often contain more detailed information about their participants but tend to be smaller and with a more restricted coverage. Consequently, although case series may have wider *generalizability*, the information they provide can pose difficulties in controlling for *bias* and confounding.

### Case series

Case series may be assembled from single datasets. The UK's General Practice Research Database, for example, comprises healthcare information at an individual level from the records of patients' general practitioners.[2] It contains the primary care records of over eight million people and has proved to be a valuable resource for evaluating care.

Particularly in North America, administrative databases from multiple sources have been linked to create research databases of considerable power. The sources of data may include electronic health records, billing claims and dispensing records from pharmacies and a complete dataset can be assembled for evaluating the effects of interventions in very large populations. The data used for the comparison of the cardiovascular *toxicity* of pioglitazone and rosiglitazone (see Case study 3.3.4 in Chapter 3.3), for example, were assembled by linking the electronic prescription records of the Ontario Public Drug Benefit Plan, the National Ambulatory Care Reporting System, the Canadian Institute for Health's Information Discharge Abstract Database (to provide information about hospital admissions), the Ontario Diabetes Database, and the Ontario's Registered Persons Database (for basic demographic data, including the date of death).[3] From this database, the details of 39 736 patients starting treatment with pioglitazone or rosiglitazone were retrieved.

The Medicines Monitoring Unit (MEMO) in Tayside, Scotland has established a database linking all prescriptions dispensed in the community; hospital discharge data; and the NHS Information Services database in Edinburgh. This was used to investigate the gastrointestinal and renal toxicities of 131 410 patients prescribed non-selective non-steroidal anti-inflammatory drugs between 1989 and 1996.[4]

Despite the potential power of such databases to provide information about benefits and *harms* (including rare adverse outcomes), they can have limitations:[5]

- Although information on drug use avoids the problem of poor patient recall, the validity of the data may be compromised by misclassification of exposures and outcomes. Nor will the data capture patients' use of over-the-counter medicines. These deficiencies can lead to bias.
- Unless the clinical data are based on patients' electronic medical records, there may be a lack of relevant clinical information. Comorbidities, for example, may not be documented accurately.
- Such databases may provide a limited ability to control for confounding.

## Case registries

Case registries are systems comprising patient-level data specifically created for one or more purposes. They may seek to describe the natural history of a disease or condition; they may have been established to determine the clinical or cost-effectiveness of healthcare products or services; they may be designed to monitor and measure *safety* and harm; or they may attempt to measure the quality of care. Government agencies, specialist medical societies and the sponsors of manufactured interventions (such as pharmaceutical companies) may be responsible for their finance and management. The essential requirements for the development and maintenance of registries have been described in some depth.[6]

A survey of UK registries noted that they exist in almost all areas of healthcare, but with a special emphasis on cancer and surgery.[7] Most of these UK registries have the potential to provide data for the evaluation of interventions, but they vary considerably in the quality of their content. Nevertheless, in general, appropriately designed and maintained registries have the potential to provide richer information about patients than can be provided by routine sources.

The registry maintained by the International Society for Heart and Lung Transplantation, for example, was used to provide data for Case study 3.3.2 in Chapter 3.3.[8] This database collects 240 variables related to the characteristics of individual patients at the time of transplantation. Moreover, this case study was based on analysis of 9883 patients undergoing single or bilateral lung transplantation. Despite their deliberately narrow focus, and often smaller size, registries may be better able to provide data that will allow better control of *confounding* and bias.

# Uses of databases

In evaluating the effects of interventions, case series and case registries have three potential applications. They can provide further information about the generalizability of the results of formal studies; they may provide additional data about an intervention's benefits; and they can be tools for the further evaluation of an intervention's harms.

## Generalizability

As discussed extensively in Section 2, and specifically in Chapter 2.2, one of the most significant limitations of randomized controlled trials is their uncertain generalizability. To what extent are their results likely to be replicated during routine clinical practice?

In theory, case series and case registries could help to answer this question. Case study 2.5.1 in Chapter 2.5 is an example: Merging the findings of several case series allowed comparisons to be made of the rates of ischaemic stroke in patients with atrial fibrillation and treated with anticoagulants in routine clinical practice, with stroke rates reported in randomized controlled trials.[9] Similarly, registries of patients undergoing thrombolytic therapy for acute stroke have been useful in demonstrating the generalizability of the positive results of randomized controlled trials in this indication. In the UK, despite an uneven provision of services, the outcomes and complication rates (particularly of intracerebral haemorrhage) were similar to those reported in clinical trials.[10]

## Benefits

Databases have been used in some instances to assess the long-term benefits of an intervention.

Fabry's disease is a rare progressive multisystem disorder caused by a deficiency of the lysosomal enzyme $\alpha$-galactosidase. Renal failure, cardiomyopathy and cerebrovascular disease are the main causes of death. The benefits of enzyme replacement therapy were established from small-scale randomized controlled trials of relatively short duration. The Fabry's Outcome Survey, a database of patients receiving replacement treatment with agalsidase alfa, was used to assess the benefits of treatment over a period of five years.[11] Prolonged treatment resulted in a sustained reduction of left ventricular mass, a reduction in the rate of the decline of renal function, significant pain relief, and an increased quality of life.[11] Although the numbers involved were modest (total 181 patients), the results indicate that the long-term benefits of agalsidase alfa are probably substantial.

Another example of the use of a registry is the Swiss HIV Cohort Study.[12] The individual patient-level data in this registry were used to impute the long-term benefits of highly active antiretroviral therapy (HAART) in the treatment of people with human immunodeficiency virus (HIV) infection. The HAART regimen combines at least three different antiviral agents. Its presumed *efficacy* in randomized controlled trials was based largely on its effects on surrogate outcomes (CD4 count and viral load).

In order to study the *effectiveness* of HAART, data from the registry were used to estimate the regimen's effectiveness compared with no treatment or treatment with a two-drug regimen.[12] The analyses were based on observations of 3437 patients for a median follow-up time of 54 months. After adjusting for a variety of confounding factors, the results (progression to acquired immunodeficiency syndrome (AIDS) or death) provided estimates of the *hazard ratios* for HAART versus no treatment of 0.14 (95% confidence interval (CI) 0.07 to 0.29) and for HAART versus two-drug treatment of 0.49 (95% CI 0.31 to 0.79). It is inconceivable in a condition such as this that such information could ever have been obtained from a randomized controlled trial.

## Harms

Databases have proved to be most valuable in identifying and enumerating the harms associated with a variety of interventions.

Paul Dieppe and colleagues were able to use MEMO's linked database to investigate the risks of acute renal failure in patients receiving non-steroidal anti-inflammatory drugs.[13] Acute renal failure had not been observed in any of the randomized trials for use in osteoarthritis, and yet the *incidence* observed in the data provided by MEMO was 2.2

*Therapeutics, evidence and decision-making*

per patient-years during routine clinical use. The disparity between the results of the randomized controlled trials and the observations from routine clinical care are almost certainly due to the underrepresentation of elderly people in the controlled trials:[14] below the age of 60 years no increase was observed during routine care; but in people aged 60–69 years the *relative risk* of acute renal failure was 2.31 (95% CI 1.68 to 3.18), in people aged 70–79 years it was 4.70 (95% CI 3.49 to 6.33), and in people aged 80 years or over it was 8.79 (95% CI 6.55 to 11.8).

Condition-specific registries can also make important contributions to patient safety. The UK Epilepsy and Pregnancy Register, for example, has collected data since 1996 about pregnant women with epilepsy – whether or not they were taking antiepileptic drugs – and who are referred before the outcome of their pregnancy was known.[15] These two features avoid selective reporting of pregnancies with bad outcomes (a form of ascertainment bias). The results show, for example, differences in major malformation rates (per pregnancy) between both drugs and dosages. Table 3.5.1 shows the major malformation rates for three of the most commonly used antiepileptic agents.

**Table 3.5.1** Overall major malformation rates from the UK Epilepsy and Pregnancy Register

| Antiepileptic drug | Major malformation rate (95% confidence interval) | | |
|---|---|---|---|
| | Low dose | Medium dose | High dose |
| Carbamazepine | 1.7 (0.8 to 3.6) | 2.6 (1.4 to 4.7) | 3.3 (1.1 to 9.2) |
| Valproate | 4.1 (2.3 to 7.3) | 6.1 (3.7 to 9.8) | 9.1 (5.8 to 14.1) |
| Lamotrigine | 1.3 (0.4 to 4.7) | 1.9 (0.8 to 4.8) | 5.4 (3.3 to 8.7) |

After Morrow J, Russell A, Guthrie E, *et al*. Malformation risks of antiepileptic drugs in pregnancy: a prospective study from the UK Epilepsy and Pregnancy Register. *Journal of Neurology, Neurosurgery and Psychiatry* 2006;**77**:193–8.[15]

Data from this registry have been used in the development of national guidelines on the management of epilepsy during pregnancy, and to inform potential parents of the extent of the risks of major congenital malformations in mothers taking antiepileptic agents.[16] The registry has also been important in identifying pharmaceutical products whose risk to the fetus appears to be minimal.

Databases may also provide reassurance about the potential harmful effects of an intervention. A study based on another well-validated British general practice database, The Health Impact Network database (THIN), compared the outcomes after more than eight years in 129 288 patients receiving statins compared with 600 241 matched controls.[17] After adjusting for potential confounders no effect was observed for a wide range of outcomes (including a variety of cancers), apart from vascular endpoints. For these endpoints, the hazard ratios were comparable to those observed in large randomized controlled trials. This study not only provides reassurance about the overall safety of this widely prescribed product but also confirms the generalizability of the original estimates of the effectiveness of statins.

## Discussion

Databases are becoming an increasingly powerful tool for assessing the benefits and particularly the harms of therapeutic interventions. As with other observational techniques, however, they suffer from potential bias and confounding, particularly in the assessment of benefit. Decision-makers should therefore view the results of studies based on databases with caution. Nevertheless, as already shown, they can provide confidence in the long-term benefits of interventions for which there is evidence only of short-term benefits in randomized controlled trials. They have also proved to be powerful for the identification and enumeration of harms.

As electronic databases become more widespread in routine healthcare, it is likely that their uses for research will expand too. There is an urgent need for the development of registries to demonstrate the generalizability of the results of randomized controlled trials and in the evaluation of new interventional procedures.[18]

In drawing conclusions based on evidence derived from databases, decision-makers need to take two factors into account. First, they should reassure themselves that the database itself is fit for purpose. Because of the importance of the minutiae of its construction, this is not easily accomplished. Decision-makers can, however, be more confident if a particular database has been shown previously to be reliable in other studies. Second, decision-makers need to assess the potential for bias and confounding. This includes the characteristics of the population studied and whether the findings and conclusions are generalizable. Furthermore, in order to avoid survival bias (see Chapter 3.4), the outcomes should relate to events from the time of an intervention's first use in the particular patient cohort.

# References

1. Raftery J, Roderick P, Stevens A. Potential uses of routine databases in health technology assessment. *Health Technology Assessment* 2005;**9**:1–92.
2. Walley T, Mantgani A. The UK General Practice Research Database. *Lancet* 1997;**350**:1097–9.
3. Juurlink DN, Gomes T, Lipscombe LL, *et al*. Adverse cardiovascular events during treatment with pioglitazone and rosiglitazone: population based cohort study. *BMJ* 2009;**339**:b2942.
4. Dieppe P, Bartlett C, Davey P, *et al*. Balancing benefits and harms: the example of non-steroidal anti-inflammatory agents. *BMJ* 2004;**329**:31–4.
5. Schneeweiss S, Avorn J. A review of uses of health care utilization databases for epidemiological research on therapeutics. *Journal of Clinical Epidemiology* 2005;**58**:323–37.
6. Gliklich RE, Dreyer NA (eds). *Registries for Evaluating Patient Outcomes*. Rockville, MD: Agency for Healthcare Research and Quality, 2007.
7. Black N, Barker M, Payne M. Cross sectional survey of multicentre clinical databases in the United Kingdom. *BMJ* 2004;**328**:1478–83.
8. Thabut G, Christie JD, Ravaud P, *et al*. Survival after bilateral versus single lung transplantation for patients with chronic obstructive pulmonary disease: a retrospective analysis of registry data. *Lancet* 2008;**371**:744–51.
9. Evans A, Kalra L. Are the results of randomized controlled trials on anticoagulation in patients with atrial fibrillation generalizable to clinical practice? *Archives of Internal Medicine* 2001;**161**:1443–7.
10. Lees KR, Ford GA, Muir KW, *et al*. Thrombolytic therapy for acute stroke in the United Kingdom: experience from the safe implementation of thrombolysis in stroke (SITS) register. *Quarterly Journal of Medicine* 2008;**101**:863–9.
11. Mehta A, Beck M, Elliot P, *et al*. Enzyme replacement therapy with agalsidase alfa in patients with Fabry's disease: an analysis of registry data. *Lancet* 2009;**374**:1986–96.
12. Sterne JAC, Hernàn MA, Ledergerber B, *et al*. Long-term effectiveness of potent antiviral therapy in preventing AIDS and death: a prospective cohort study. *Lancet* 2005;**366**:378–84.

13. Dieppe P, Bartlett C, Davey P, *et al.* Balancing benefit and harms: the example of non-steroidal anti-inflammatory drugs. *BMJ* 2004;**329**:31–4.

14. Bartlett C, Doyal L, Ebrahim S, *et al.* The causes and effects of socio-demographic exclusions from clinical trials. Health Technology Assessment 2005;**9**:1–152.

15. Morrow J, Russell A, Guthrie E, *et al.* Malformation risks of antiepileptic drugs in pregnancy: a prospective study from the UK Epilepsy and Pregnancy Register. *Journal of Neurology, Neurosurgery and Psychiatry* 2006;**77**:193–8.

16. Aylward RLM. Epilepsy: a review of reports, guidelines, recommendations and models for the provision of care for patients with epilepsy. *Clinical Medicine* 2008;**8**:433–8.

17. Smeeth L, Doyle I, Hall AJ, *et al.* Effect of statins on a wide range of health outcomes: a cohort study validated by comparison with randomized trials. *British Journal of Clinical Pharmacology* 2008;**67**:99–109.

18. Lyratzopoulos G, Patrick H, Campbell B. Registers needed for new interventional products. *Lancet* 2008;**371**:1734–6.

# CHAPTER 3.6
## CASE REPORTS

There is a long tradition of the publication by physicians of case reports describing the effects of interventions in either an individual patient or as a small case series. It has been claimed, however, that new ideas from such reports are rarely sustained by further research, that they often contain misleading elements, and that by emphasizing the bizarre they do 'more harm than good'.[1]

To dismiss case reports in this manner misses the point. The first indications of the teratogenicity of thalidomide came in a letter to the *Lancet*,[2] and the first report of the oculomucocutaneous syndrome with practolol, the first licensed selective beta-adrenoceptor antagonist, was published in the *British Medical Journal*.[3] Vandenbroucke has defended case reports on the grounds that they have permitted the discovery of unexpected beneficial and adverse effects of interventions and played a role in the discovery of new diseases and a better understanding of disease mechanisms.[4]

What role, then, can case reports play in contributing to the evidence base of modern therapeutics in the discovery of benefits or in the detection of *harms*?

## Case reports: the detection of benefits

Single case reports on their own have a very limited place in identifying the benefits of an intervention. It is true that, very occasionally, a particular intervention produces a spectacular benefit in circumstances where there appears to be no other explanation. The response of the first patient with myxoedema to be given thyroid extract[5] might fall into this category; but most decision-makers would expect to see at least a case series to ensure that this initial success was not due to a mistaken diagnosis or some other factor.

The 'parental kiss' (sometimes described as the 'mother's kiss') is another example of an anecdote that might have given rise to claims of unequivocal benefit from a single case report: in a child with a nostril blocked by a foreign object, occluding the unblocked nostril while the parent blows into the child's mouth can relieve the obstruction.[6] The results of a small case series describing similar benefits in 15 of 19 children with nasal obstruction due to a foreign body give much stronger support to the benefits of the manoeuvre than a single case report.[7]

Episodes such as these, though, are very rare. Nevertheless, there are occasions where individual case reports or small case series have prompted formal investigations that have subsequently demonstrated novel benefits for an intervention. Examples include the disease-modifying effects of rituximab in a single patient with rheumatoid arthritis, and of penile erections in volunteers given sildenafil. The appropriate response to anecdotes about the benefits of an intervention is to undertake a formal study.

## Case reports: the detection of harms

There is a distinction to be made between case reports published in medical journals and those solicited by and reported to national drug regulatory authorities.

## Published case reports

As has been pointed out, published case reports for detecting harms have an established place. Case reports of reactions that mimic rare, naturally occurring conditions, instances where adverse effects appear on rechallenge, and instances for which the evidence of causality is unequivocal by other means (see Case study 3.6.1[8]) can provide evidence that such harms may be causally related with a particular product.

Many journals still publish case reports of suspected *adverse drug reactions*, although their value has been questioned. Geoffrey Venning showed that of 52 reports of adverse drug reactions published in four major journals during 1963, 35 had been validated 18 years later.[9] A more recent review was less optimistic.[10] Of the 63 reports of suspected adverse drug reactions published in five of the journals that accept such publications (including the *BMJ* and the *Lancet*), only seven had been evaluated further; of these seven, only four had been shown unequivocally to be adverse effects of the particular products.

Irrespective of the merits of published single case reports to the clinical community, their value to decision-makers is slender. Such reports cannot distinguish readily

| **Case study 3.6.1** Extensive cutaneous *Mycobacterium abscessus* infection[8] | |
|---|---|
| **Background** | A 48-year-old woman with insulin-dependent diabetes presented with multiple injection-site lesions. She had been dependent on insulin for 27 years and had evidence of microvascular disease (early diabetic nephropathy, sensory peripheral neuropathy and grade 1 retinopathy). Her management included injections of neutral insulin and isophane insulin but her diabetic control was poor. |
| **Examination** | She was afebrile but had multiple erythematous, non-tender plaques on the anterior aspects of her thighs corresponding to the sites of injection of isophane insulin. Her anterior abdominal wall injection sites were unremarkable. |
| **Investigations** | Biopsy of a lesion was culture-negative for common pathogens but positive for *Mycobacterium abscessus*, which was confirmed by phenotypic and genotypic testing. Microbiological testing of her injection devices revealed the presence of *M. abscessus* in the barrel of her isophane injection pen but in no other injection devices. *M. abscessus* isolates from her lesions and her insulin pen were indistinguishable by genetic analyses. |
| **Treatment** | She was treated initially with amikacin, cefoxitin and clarithromycin for two weeks. She then underwent nine months treatment with clarithromycin alone. All her lesions resolved. She discarded her insulin and insulin delivery devices and replaced them with fresh insulin and new injection pens. No new lesions appeared during three years' follow-up. |
| **Discussion** | *M. abscessus* infections are usually sporadic and linked to environmental sources, including medical equipment. Treatment is difficult because of multidrug resistance, but response to long-term clarithromycin is generally seen. |
| | There can be virtually no doubt that this patient's infection at the injection sites of isophane insulin was due to *M. abscessus*-contamination of her insulin pen. |

between those that are 'clinical curiosities' from those that portend greater problems during wider use. In addition, once a journal has published one case report of a putative adverse reaction, it is very unlikely to publish any more unless as part of a large case series. As a result decision-makers are unable to make any assessment of the frequency of the reaction. Moreover, journals will publish single case reports of an adverse reaction only when there is a very high likelihood of a causal relationship. Yet, because of the difficulties of diagnosis, especially for *adverse events* mimicking common conditions, suspected adverse reactions are unlikely to be accepted for publication by journals even though they will be of interest to decision-makers.

## National reporting schemes

The limitations of published case reports led national drug regulatory authorities to establish in the 1950s and 1960s national schemes for the reporting of adverse drug reactions. Such schemes ask doctors and, depending on the scheme, other health professionals such as nurses and pharmacists to report any suspected adverse reactions that they encounter in their patients with marketed products. Some reporting schemes also accept reports from patients. In addition, pharmaceutical manufacturers in most countries have a legal obligation to report any suspected adverse reactions to their products of which they have been made aware.

Such reporting schemes have two purposes. First, they alert drug regulatory authorities to possible adverse reactions that have not, hitherto, been described. They thus provide signals that may require further evaluation to assess whether there is a causal relationship. Second, reports can sometimes provide regulatory authorities with some intimation of the scale of the problem, in relation to the frequency and the severity of the particular reaction. There are numerous examples of the discovery of previously unsuspected adverse reactions that have first been detected by spontaneous reports to national regulatory authorities.[11–13]

In some instances spontaneous reports have been hypothesis-generating and have subsequently been confirmed by formal studies. For example, a series of reports to regulatory authorities of cough associated with angiotensin-converting enzyme inhibitors[14] was later confirmed by the results of randomized controlled trials that specifically asked patients about this symptom.

Spontaneous reports of suspected adverse reactions to pharmaceutical products have simultaneously been both hypothesis-generating and hypothesis-confirming. Examples include the recognition of a causal relationship between the occurrence of acute dystonia in patients embarking on treatment with the antiemetic metoclopramide,[15] and recognition of acute angio-oedema early in the course of treatment with angiotensin-converting enzyme inhibitors.[16] Indeed, between 1990 and 2003, 18 pharmaceutical products were withdrawn from the US market as a result of reports to the US Food and Drug Administration (FDA); Table 3.6.1 shows some examples.[17]

Spontaneous reporting schemes have limitations, however. Reporting by health professionals and patients is voluntary. Consequently, whether reports are made at all is partly dependent on the reporters' energy and enthusiasm and their ability to make a distinction, in individual patients, between an adverse drug reaction and some intercurrent unrelated event. Agencies have tried to overcome this problem by asking health professionals to report suspected reactions. However, this level of distinction requires a degree of judgement that varies between individual healthcare professionals.

*Therapeutics, evidence and decision-making*

**Table 3.6.1** Some pharmaceutical products removed from the US market for safety reasons with evidence from spontaneous reports[17]

| Year | Product | Indication | Reason |
|------|---------|------------|--------|
| 2001 | Rapacuronium | Hypercholesterolaemia | Bronchospasm |
| 2001 | Cerivastatin | Anaesthesia | Rhabdomyolysis |
| 2000 | Alosetron | Irritable bowel syndrome | Ischaemic colitis |
| 2000 | Cisapride | Heartburn | Arrhythmias |
| 2000 | Troglitazone | Diabetes mellitus | Hepatotoxicity |
| 1999 | Grepafloxacin | Antibiotic | Arrhythmias |
| 1999 | Astemazole | Antihistamine | Arrhythmias |
| 1998 | Bromfenac | Non-steroidal anti-inflammatory | Hepatotoxicity |
| 1998 | Mibefradil | Antihypertensive | Cardiac events |
| 1997 | Terfenadine | Antihistamine | Arrhythmias |

Spontaneous reporting schemes are also susceptible to reporting *bias*, especially when there has been media (professional or lay) interest in a particular *safety* issue. In these circumstances reports of specific adverse reactions can increase substantially. It has been alleged that only 10 per cent of suspected adverse reactions are reported through national spontaneous reporting schemes, but there is little empirical evidence to support this claim.

For these reasons, regulatory authorities have had difficulties, at least in the past, in deciding whether a group of reports of a particular reaction reflect a signal that might be assumed to be causally related or whether it is a reflection of 'background noise'. The approach for many years was to express the numbers of adverse events in relation to the prescription volume of the product.[18] Apart from the biases associated with the number of reports (the numerator), prescription volumes are extremely poor proxies for the numbers of users of a product. This is especially the case if the product has been available for many years or if it can be purchased as an over-the-counter medicine. The difficulty in distinguishing between first and repeat prescriptions of the product overestimates the numbers of users. In the face of widespread over-the-counter use, prescription data alone will underestimate numbers of users.

## Signal detection techniques

Substantial advances have been made over the past few years in overcoming some of the difficulties of identifying signals of adverse reactions from background noise in assessing spontaneous reports. Various approaches are used, but most involve assessing whether there are disproportionate numbers of reports of particular suspected reactions to a specific product compared with those in the totality of the database. This involves comparing the ratio of numbers of reports of a particular reaction to the total reports of all other reactions to a specific product, with the ratio of the total number of reports of the same particular reaction to the total number of reports to all other products in the spontaneous reporting database.

### ■ Proportional reporting ratios

The most widely used approach is to calculate the proportional reporting ratio.[19] The principle can be displayed in a typical $2 \times 2$ contingency table (see Table 3.6.2).

**Table 3.6.2** Spontaneous reports classified by reaction and drug

| | Particular reaction | All other reported reactions | Total |
|---|---|---|---|
| Product of interest | $a$ | $b$ | $a + b$ |
| All other drugs | $c$ | $d$ | $c + d$ |
| Total | | | $(a + c)/(b + d)$ |

The proportional reporting ratio is calculated as follows:

$$\text{Proportional reporting ratio} = \frac{[a/(a + b)]}{[c/(c + d)]}$$

A closely related measure is the reporting *odds ratio* (see Chapter 1.4):

$$\text{Reporting odds ratio} = \frac{(a/c)}{(b/d)} = ad/bc$$

It is possible to estimate the 95 per cent confidence intervals for the proportional reporting ratio and the reporting odds ratio. The proportional reporting ratio and the reporting odds ratio will approximate when $b$ and $d$ are both much larger than $a$ and $c$, as is usually the case. A $\chi^2$ statistic can also be calculated for the proportional reporting ratio.

Various approaches have been used to determine whether a proportional reporting ratio (or reporting odds ratio) for a particular reaction is a signal requiring further investigation.[20] Many adopt as a threshold a proportional reporting ratio of greater than two together with a $\chi^2$ value of greater than four and a minimum of three reports of the same reaction to the specific product.[19] Some use the lower limit of the 95 per cent confidence interval of the proportional reporting ratio as the basic signal.

Apart from technical issues,[19] the interpretation of a proportional reporting ratio (or the reporting odds ratio) signal depends on the circumstances. The nature and severity of the reaction, and the product's indications, will indicate whether there is merit in further investigation. Using proportional reporting ratios in a study of 15 marketed drugs, Evans and colleagues established that 70 per cent of spontaneous reports were known adverse reactions, 13 per cent were likely to be a complication of the underlying disease, and 17 per cent represented signals requiring further evaluation.[19]

### ■ Bayesian approaches

The so-called 'disproportionality approach' on which proportional reporting ratios are based is capable of being analysed using Bayesian techniques. The World Health Organization (WHO) Bayesian Confidence Neural Network,[21] based on the natural logarithm of the proportional reporting ratio, gives similar results to those provided by the proportional reporting ratio and the reporting odds ratio when the number of reports is greater than three. The method used by the US FDA, the so-called 'empirical Bayesian gamma method', is also Bayesian in approach.[22] This estimates the geometric mean of the proportional reporting and, as with the WHO method, uses the lower 95 per cent confidence limit as the boundary for signal detection. It is probably more reliable than the frequentist estimates of the proportional reporting ratio when the numbers of reports are few (below three). With larger numbers of reports the two approaches lead to similar conclusions.

### ■ Self-controlled case series method

This is a retrospective cohort method applied to a defined observation period.[23] It is conditional on the number of events experienced by each individual over the observed time period. It has proved to be especially useful in studying the potential adverse effects of vaccines.[24]

## Discussion

As discussed earlier, a single case report claiming novel benefit almost never provides decision-makers with sufficient evidence to inform the wider use of an intervention. Published single case reports about the adverse effects of an intervention also have significant limitations and are unable to provide any estimate of *incidence*. Although any indication that a treatment might have a harmful effect should not be ignored, a balance has to be struck between responding to each report of a potential adverse effect and trying to eliminate uncertainty before acting. Isolated case reports of harms in the medical literature should not normally cause decision-makers undue concern. If they are worried, then the appropriate course of action is to check the report against one or more of the databases held by national drug regulatory authorities.

National spontaneous reporting schemes are an important resource and many can be accessed through the Internet. The staff of national drug regulatory agencies regularly interrogate their own databases, and some agencies have automated methods. These national schemes can also provide some reassurance about the safety of marketed products. Although the absence of reports of a particular reaction to a specific product does not necessarily imply the lack of a causal relationship, such data can in some circumstances give decision-makers information that can contribute to their conclusions.

The main limitation with these schemes is the requirement for health professionals to report their clinical experiences. For this reason the US FDA is exploring the use of existing databases including electronic medical records and medical claims databases as a potential replacement for reliance on reporting by healthcare professionals. Coupled with an automated estimate of one of the versions of disproportionate ratio methods, this could allow an automated approach to the detection, confirmation or refutation of adverse reactions to new pharmaceutical products.[25]

## References

1. Hoffman JR. Rethinking case reports. *Western Journal of Medicine* 1999;**170**:253–4.
2. McBride WG. Thalidomide and congenital abnormalities. *Lancet* 1961;**ii**:1358.
3. Wright P. Untoward effects associated with practolol administration: oculomucocutaneous syndrome. *BMJ* 1975;**i**:595–8.
4. Vandenbroucke JP. In defense of case reports and case series. *Annals of Internal Medicine* 2001;**134**:330–34.
5. Murray GM. Note on the treatment of myxoedema by hypodermic injections of the thyroid gland of a sheep. *BMJ* 1891;**ii**:796–7.
6. Glasziou P, Chalmers I, Rawlins M, McCulloch P. When are randomised trials unnecessary? Picking signal from noise. *BMJ* 2007;**334**:349–51.
7. Botma M, Bader R, Kubba H. A parent's kiss: evaluating an unusual method for removing nasal foreign bodies in children. *Journal of Laryngology and Otology* 2000;**114**:598–600.
8. Bates TR, Keenher T, O'Reilly LC, *et al.* Extensive cutaneous *Mycobacterium abscessus* infection due to contaminated insulin delivery system. *Quarterly Journal of Medicine* 2009;**102**:881–4.

9. Venning GR. Validation of anecdotal reports of suspected adverse drug reaction: the problem of false alarms. *BMJ* 1982;**284**:249–52.
10. Loke YK, Price D, Derry S, Aronson JK. Case reports of suspected adverse drug reactions: systematic literature follow-up. *BMJ* 2006;**332**:335–9.
11. Rawlins MD. Spontaneous reporting of adverse drug reactions. I: uses. *British Journal of Clinical Pharmacology* 1988;**26**:8–13.
12. Rawlins MD. Pharmacovigilance: paradise lost, regained or postponed? *Journal of the Royal College of Physicians* 1995;**29**:41–9.
13. Davies S, King B, Raine JM. Spontaneous reporting: UK. In: Mann RD, Andrews EB (eds). *Pharmacovigilance*, 2nd edn. Chichester: John Wiley & Sons, 2007.
14. Coulter DM, Edwards IR. Cough associated with captopril and enalapril. *BMJ* 1987;**294**:1521–3.
15. Bateman DN, Rawlins MD, Simpson JM. Extrapyramidal reactions with metoclopramide. *BMJ* 1985;**291**:930–32.
16. Wood SM, Mann RD, Rawlins MD. Angio-oedema and urticaria associated with angiotensin converting enzyme inhibitors. *BMJ* 1987;**294**:91–2.
17. Wysowski DK, Swartz L. Adverse drug event surveillance and drug withdrawals in the US, 1969–2002. *Archives of Internal Medicine* 2005;**165**:1363–72.
18. Rawlins MD. Spontaneous reporting of adverse drug reactions. I: the data. *British Journal of Clinical Pharmacology* 1988;**26**:1–7.
19. Evans SJW, Waller PC, Davis S. Use of proportional reporting ratios (PPRs) for signal generation from spontaneous adverse drug reaction reports. *Pharmacoepidemiology and Drug Safety* 2001;**10**:483–6.
20. Deshpande G, Gogolak V, Smith SW. Data mining in drug safety: review of published threshold criteria for defining signals of disproportionate reporting. *Pharmaceutical Medicine* 2010;**24**:37–43.
21. Bate A, Lundqvist M, Edwards IR, *et al.* A Bayesian neural network method for adverse reaction signal generation. *European Journal of Clinical Pharmacology* 1998;**54**:315–21.
22. DuMouchel W. Bayesian data mining in large frequency tables, with an application to the FDA spontaneous reporting system. *American Statistician* 1999;**53**:177–90.
23. Whitaker HJ, Farrington CP, Spiessens B, Musonda P. Tutorial in biostatistics: the self-controlled case series method. *Statistics in Medicine* 2006;**25**:1768–97.
24. Farrington CP, Nash J, Miller E. Case series analysis of adverse reactions to vaccines. *American Journal of Epidemiology* 1996;**143**:1165.
25. Platt R, Wislo M, Chan A, *et al.* The new sentinel network: improving the evidence for medical product safety. *New England Journal of Medicine* 2009;**361**:645–7.

# SECTION 4
# Qualitative research

## APPROACHES AND METHODS

The traditional approach to assessing the *effectiveness* of interventions has relied largely on research designs that express the results in a quantitative manner. Indeed, the preceding chapters have been devoted almost exclusively to such methods. There are, however, some research questions that are unsuitable for this approach and that require the use of qualitative techniques if useful answers are to be obtained. This type of research is concerned with the subjective world and offers insights into social, emotional and experiential phenomena.[1] It aims to draw out understandings and perceptions, to explore social contexts and cultural values, and to understand the linkages between processes and outcomes. Qualitative research has been used widely in anthropology and sociology, and the methods used in its medical applications are derived largely from studies in these disciplines. Qualitative research is essentially inductive. It is not concerned with testing hypotheses but, rather, with gathering data and then formulating general premises that explain them.

## Methods

In qualitative research, data are obtained using a variety of techniques.[2] In some studies several methods are used simultaneously to check on the validity of the findings (a technique known as 'triangulation'). The methods used include:[1,2]

- interviews (individuals or groups);
- field observation (direct or indirect);
- document analysis.

The term 'action research' is also used in the qualitative literature.[3] This is a style of research rather than a specific method and involves working with, and for, people rather than undertaking research on them. The distinction between 'researcher' and 'researched' that is found in other forms of investigation may thus be less apparent in action research. Citizens' juries and the Citizens' Council of the UK's National Institute of Health and Clinical Excellence (NICE), described below, are examples of action research.

### Interviews

Much qualitative research is based on interviews.[4] The *one-to-one interview* is probably the most widely used qualitative research method in medical research. Structured interviews, in which interviewers ask closed questions in a standard manner, are used in surveys and the responses are generally analysed quantitatively. In qualitative research interviews are either semi-structured or depth interviews.

Semi-structured interviews are conducted using a loose framework of open questions that define, at least initially, the area to be explored. As the interview progresses, however, the interviewer (or interviewee) will diverge from the original outline questions in order to explore particular ideas or issues in greater detail. Depth interviews are less structured and cover only one or two issues, but interviewers need to exercise considerable skill if they are to ensure that interviewees talk fully and freely.

Both semi-structured and depth interviews are interactive. They must be responsive to the language of the interviewees, and they need to be conducted with a flexible agenda. Interviewers therefore need to be very skilful if they are to get below the surface of the topic that is under discussion and if they are to uncover ideas that were unanticipated at the time the investigation was started.

*Group interviews* are in some ways similar to one-to-one interviews, with a facilitator who invites the participants to consider a particular topic. Group interviews can be useful with members of ethnic minorities for whom one-to-one interviews can be unfamiliar experiences.[4] In a *focus group*, the facilitator tries to encourage participants to explore and clarify their views about a particular issue over a period of usually not more than half a day. The range and number of members in a focus group will depend on the nature of the topic and the resources available but is usually between six and 12. Group work can help investigators use the various forms of communication that people adopt in day-to-day interactions, including jokes, anecdotes, teasing and arguing. These forms of communication are useful because people's knowledge and attitudes are rarely encapsulated by reasoned responses to direct questions.[5] Focus groups are particularly suited to the study of how knowledge and ideas develop within a given cultural context,[5] and they encourage participants to deliberate about particular issues. The data from focus groups can also inform the nature and wording of questions used in subsequent opinion polls, thus bridging the gap between qualitative and quantitative research methods.

An extended form of the focus group methodology is the *citizens' jury*. These comprise 10–20 members of the general public selected, in so far as is possible, at random. They meet for 2–4 days to consider a particular question (sometimes, as in a criminal trial, called a 'charge') posed by the organization commissioning the study. As in a criminal trial, members of the citizens' jury hear evidence from appropriate witnesses and deliberate among themselves before reaching their 'verdict'. A facilitator tries to ensure that the deliberative process runs smoothly, that members retain their focus, and that the views of less assertive members are heard. The approach has been used to study healthcare policy in the UK.[6,7] A variant of the citizens' jury is used by NICE in eliciting the social value judgements that inform the prioritization decisions the institute is required to make.[8,9] Both citizens' juries and the NICE Citizens Council are forms of action research.

Consensus methods are further extensions of the role of groups in qualitative research. They are concerned primarily with deriving quantitative estimates through qualitative approaches.[10] Consensus methods are of special value when there is conflicting scientific evidence. They aim to determine the extent to which experts or lay people can agree about a given issue. Their advantage, compared with conventional open committee meetings, is that they avoid domination by one individual or groups of individuals. The three common methods are:[10]

- the Delphic process (which takes its name from the Delphic Oracle's skills of interpretation and foresight);
- the nominal group technique (also known as the expert panel);
- the consensus development conference.

Details of these approaches are beyond the scope of this book but can be found elsewhere.[10,11]

## Field observation

The purpose of field observation is to observe and record social phenomena directly and prospectively in their natural settings.[12] There are two basic approaches:[1] direct observation by investigators and indirect observation by audiotape or videotape recording. Observational techniques are also categorized according to the role of the investigator.[1] In non-participant observation the researcher stays relatively uninvolved in the social interactions that are observed and attempts to be a 'fly on the wall'. In participant observation the researcher is part of the social setting.

In both participant and non-participant field observation, controlling for the effects of the investigator is almost impossible. The presence of a researcher or even audiotape/videotape equipment may influence participants' behaviour. Interactions between investigators and those they study are, paradoxically, regarded as both a useful source of data and a potential source of *bias*.[1] The use of more than one observational technique is sometimes used to enhance the validity of any findings.

## Document analysis

Documents, including charts, journals, correspondence, and studies of information patterns on the Internet[13] can provide qualitative data.[1,2] These have been especially useful in policy, historical and organizational studies of healthcare but have been little used to investigate the influences and effects of interventions.

# Validity, reliability and generalizability

Various strategies are used in qualitative research to limit bias and enhance reliability.[14,15]

## Triangulation

Triangulation compares the results from two or more different methods (such as interviews and observation) or from two or more different sources (such as interviews with members of different interest groups). This approach to validity seeks patterns of convergence to develop or corroborate an overall interpretation of the findings.

This, however, is a controversial test of validity.[15] It assumes that weaknesses in one method will be compensated by strengths in another, and that it will be possible to adjudicate between different accounts. Triangulation is therefore perhaps better seen as a way to ensure comprehensiveness than as a test of validity.

## The sample

The sample should be relevant to the particular problem. Qualitative research is often concerned with specific groups of people with certain characteristics, or who live in circumstances relevant to the social phenomena under study. Informants should therefore be those who are able to explore a particular aspect of behaviour or attitude that is relevant to the research. There may be circumstances when a random sample of a population is needed to enhance the reliability of a study. This can be achieved with methods similar to those used in randomized controlled trials.

## Respondent validation

Investigators sometimes report their findings to participants to ensure that they represent a reasonable account of their experience. Alternatively, researchers may use interviews or focus group meetings with participants so that their reactions to the evolving analysis become part of the emerging research data. Some investigators believe this to be the strongest check on the validity and credibility of a qualitative research project.[15] Nevertheless, the account of one participant may differ from that of another because of their different roles in the research. Respondent validation is therefore seen by others as part of the process of error reduction, which also generates further data.

A related issue is concerned with how investigators examine and explain 'negative' or 'deviant' cases. This especially applies to participants whose responses contradict investigators' emerging explanatory hypotheses. Reports should include a fair account of these instances and attempt to provide an explanation.

### Methods of data collection and analysis

In many forms of qualitative research the raw data are collected in a relatively unstructured manner.[14] The reliability of any findings is therefore dependent on the maintenance of meticulous records of interviews and observations and documentation of the process of analysis. If the data are in the form of tape recordings or transcripts, the reliability of the analysis can be enhanced by an independent assessment and then the extent of agreement compared with the investigator.

### Reflexivity

Reflexivity is the term used by qualitative researchers to describe the extent to which the potential prejudices and biases of the investigator(s) may have influenced the design, conduct and analysis of the study. Personal and intellectual biases need to be stated at the outset in order to enhance the credibility of the findings.[15] The possible influences of personal characteristics such as age, gender and socioeconomic status need to be discussed, as do the relationships between the investigator and the participants.

## Discussion

To many clinical scientists qualitative research is unscientific and anecdotal.[16] Yet the beliefs, attitudes and preferences of both patients and practitioners are (or should be) important to decision-makers. It is only by understanding these aspects of the application of quantitative evidence, and about its use in routine clinical practice, that decision-makers can draw conclusions for both individuals and populations. Recognizing the limits of quantitative research, such as randomized controlled trials and studies with observational designs, does not imply rejection of these investigative techniques. Rather, it emphasizes the fact that different questions require different research methods. In evaluating a qualitative study, reference to a checklist such as that shown in Table 4.1.1 will provide some help.

Qualitative research can provide answers to a variety of questions that are relevant to decision-makers. They include the following:

■ Why do patients agree, or decline, to take part in randomized controlled trials?
■ Why do patients default on life-saving treatments in the full knowledge of the consequences?
■ In the face of resource constraints, what social values does society place on the differing priorities that are available for the prevention and treatment of disease?

These questions are of no lesser important to decision-makers than the effective size or adverse reaction profile of a new intervention.

**Table 4.1.1** Checklist for evaluating the report of a qualitative research study[15]

| Item | Question |
|------|----------|
| Worth or relevance | Was the research worth doing? |
| | Has it contributed usefully to knowledge? |
| Clarity | Was the research question clear? |
| | Did the investigator(s) acknowledge their preconceptions? |
| Design | Would a different study design have been more appropriate? |
| Context | Was the context or setting adequately described? |
| | Could the reader relate the findings to other settings? |
| Sampling | Did the sample include the full range of possible cases? |
| | Were efforts made to obtain data from participants who might have provided contradictory findings? |
| Data collection and analysis | Were data collected and analysed systematically? |
| | Was an 'audit trail' provided so that someone else could repeat each stage? |
| | How well did the analysis incorporate all the observations? |
| | Did the investigator(s) search for contradictory cases? |
| Reflexivity | Did the investigator(s) explicitly assess the likely impact of the methods used on the data obtained? |
| | Were the data provided in the report sufficient for the reader to assess whether the analytical criteria had been met? |

# References

1. Giacomini MK, Cook DJ. Users' guide to the medical literature: XXIII. Qualitative research in health care A: are the results of the study valid? *Journal of the American Medical Association* 2000;**284**:357–62.
2. Britten N, Jones R, Murphy E, Stacy R. Qualitative research methods in general practice and primary care. *Family Practice* 1995;**12**:104–14.
3. Meyer J. Using qualitative methods in health related action research. *BMJ* 2000;**320**:178–81.
4. Britten N. Qualitative research: qualitative interviews in medical research. *BMJ* 1995;**311**:251–3.
5. Kitzinger J. Qualitative research: introducing focus groups. *BMJ* 1995;**311**:299–304.
6. Lenaghan J, New B, Mitchell E. Setting priorities: is there a role for citizens' juries? *BMJ* 1996;**312**:1591–5.
7. McIver S. *Independent Evaluation of Citizen's Juries in Health Authority Settings: Excecutive Summary*. London: Kings Fund, 1998.
8. Rawlins M. Background to NICE's Citizens Council. In: Littlejohns P, Rawlins M (eds). *Patients, the Public and Priorities in Healthcare*. Oxford: Radcliffe Publishing, 2009.
9. Rawlins MD, Culyer AJ. National Institute for Clinical Excellence and its value judgements. *BMJ* 2004;**329**:224–7.
10. Jones J, Hunter D. Qualitative research: consensus methods for medical and health services research. *BMJ* 1995;**311**:376–83.
11. Stocking B, Jennet B, Spiby J. *The History and Impact of Consensus Development Conferences in the UK*. London: King's Fund, 1991.
12. Mays N, Pope C. Qualitative research: observational methods in health care settings. *BMJ* 1995;**311**:182–5.
13. Eysenbach G, Till JE. Ethical issues in qualitative research on internet communities. *BMJ* 2001;**323**:1103–5.

14. Mays N, Pope C. Qualitative research: rigour and qualitative research. *BMJ* 1995;**311**:109–13.
15. Mays N, Pope C. Assessing quality in qualitative research. *BMJ* 2000;**320**:50–52.
16. Green J, Britten N. Qualitative research and evidence based medicine. *BMJ* 1998;**316**:1230–32.

# CHAPTER 4.2

## USES IN THE EVALUATION OF THERAPEUTIC INTERVENTIONS

The impact of research studies using qualitative techniques has been broadly threefold: such studies have provided important insights into improving the design and conduct of quantitative research studies; have been used to investigate the *generalizability* of conventional clinical trials in ways that would have not been accomplished using quantitative methods; and have been invaluable in eliciting the priorities and social values of the public so as to inform decision-makers about the use of alternative or competing interventions in the face of resource constraints.

## Design and conduct of quantitative studies

There are a number of ways in which qualitative research has been used to inform and enrich quantitative research.

### Enrolment

A number of studies have explored the reasons why participants have, or have not, agreed to take part in randomized controlled trials.[1–4]

Some studies have used the information obtained from these investigations to enhance recruitment rates. A qualitative component to enhance recruitment was included in the ProtecT trial protocol.[5] This is a randomized controlled trial, scheduled to last 10–15 years, of either surgery, radiotherapy or active monitoring ('watchful waiting') in men aged 50–69 years with localized prostate cancer.[5] The qualitative component was included in the original protocol to assess the processes by which participants were offered the opportunity of taking part in the study.[6] Using a combination of audiotaped recordings of recruitment appointments and in-depth interviews with patients, the qualitative findings showed that recruiters had difficulty in discussing equipoise and in presenting the three treatments equally.[6] Recruiters were also unknowingly using terminology that was misinterpreted by participants. The findings led to a change in the presentation and content of the information given to potential participants. As a consequence participation rates increased from 30–40 per cent during the first seven months of the study to 70 per cent a year later.

Some studies have sought the views of individuals who might, at some future date, be asked to take part in a specific study. In the late 1990s, for example, there was uncertainty about the relative benefits and risks of thrombolytic therapy in the early treatment of thrombotic stroke. Although further trials were warranted, there were concerns that patients with acute stroke might be unwilling to be recruited. In order to explore the likely responses of future stroke patients if asked to participate in a randomized controlled trial, discussions were held with older people to identify the relevant issues.[7] Two formal focus group meetings then followed. After considering the evidence, and a revision of the patient information and consent procedures, most participants (89 per cent) agreed that they would be prepared to enrol in a randomized trial.

Apart from their value in assisting recruitment to specific studies, qualitative investigations have also exposed some general issues relating to the willingness (or otherwise) of people to take part in trials. The reason why people are prepared to take part in clinical research is only partly altruistic. Although a willingness to help others and a desire to contribute towards furthering medical knowledge are important, such reasons are not the only motivators. Participants also appear to take account of the personal benefits to themselves. The advantages of more frequent clinic visits and closer expert monitoring appeared to be important motivators. The terms 'weak altruism'[8] and 'conditional altruism'[4] have been used to describe this tendency to agree to take part in clinical research provided it also offers perceived personal benefits.

The language used to explain research studies can be challenging to potential participants. The most difficult concepts for patients to comprehend appear to be those of 'clinical equipoise', 'randomization' and 'clinical trial'. A qualitative study among some of the participants in a randomized trial comparing transurethral resection of the prostate, laser therapy and conservative treatment for the treatment of benign prostatic hypertrophy (the CLasP study) demonstrates this well.[9] Some potential participants could not understand why it was necessary to undertake 'a trial' that included transurethral prostatectomy. 'It's longstanding, isn't it?' In relation to randomization, one participant said, 'Well, it was a bit confusing. If it was an operation, or if it could have been cured by medication, they would have decided there and then'. A third participant expressed disappointment at the randomization process itself: 'When she first explained it, she said "you'll be given an envelope and take your pick", apparently, and that never happened ... the treatment they more or less picked out for me'.

Accounts of treatment allocations in randomized controlled trials can cause confusion among potential participants. In the CLasP study,[9] some participants believed that 'random' implied treatment allocations were without purpose or control. Moreover, at least some participants regarded a 'trial' as something being tried and tested. In the context of the 'longstanding' use of transurethral prostatectomy for the treatment of benign prostatic hypertrophy, it appeared strange for this procedure to be included in a trial. Confusion is more likely to arise from participants' attempts to make sense of their own experience of taking part in a clinical trial rather than the apparently contradictory accounts provided by investigators. Nevertheless, it emphasizes the importance of the manner in which both written and verbal information is provided to potential participants.

## Outcomes

Qualitative studies can offer insights into what outcomes are important to participants in a clinical trial. Indeed, the development of reliable instruments that capture the potential symptomatic benefits of therapeutic interventions should begin with qualitative research into what outcomes are most significant to patients.

The *effectiveness* of interventions for the treatment of rheumatoid arthritis, for example, has traditionally been assessed using clinical measures of disease activity. They include tender and swollen joint counts, raised blood levels of inflammatory markers, the development of erosions on plain radiographs, and a health status questionnaire.[10] Case study 4.2.1 provides an example of qualitative research designed to capture benefits not identified using the conventional methods for assessing outcomes in rheumatology trials. The findings of this study – that patients' outcomes were far broader than those assessed using the conventional clinical tools – have subsequently been confirmed and amplified.[11,12]

**Case study 4.2.1** Perceptions of treatment with anti-tumour necrosis factor therapy for rheumatoid arthritis: a qualitative study[10]

| | |
|---|---|
| **Background** | Rheumatologists caring for patients with rheumatoid arthritis noted that the response to anti-tumour necrosis factor (TNF) therapy not only included improvements in conventional measures of disease activity; the patients also often felt well in themselves, often for the first time in many years. This study was designed *inter alia* to understand the patients' experience of this new form of treatment, and their impressions of its benefits or otherwise. |
| **Methods** | The authors conducted two focus groups involving patients ($n = 17$) with rheumatoid arthritis who had been treated with either infliximab or etanercept. The topic guide used for these focus groups covered, (among others), the following themes:<br><br>■ their expectations of treatment;<br>■ their experience of treatment;<br>■ their concerns about taking a new drug.<br><br>The authors also discussed the patients' feelings about the inclusion of their data in a national registry and whether the costs of the drugs – £9295 + VAT per year – represented good value for money. For reasons of space, these themes have been excluded from this case report.) |
| **Results** | The responses of patients for these three themes were broadly as follows:<br><br>■ *Expectations of treatment*: most had high expectations of anti-TNF therapy from what they had read or been told.<br>■ *Experience of treatment*: most patients were extremely positive:<br><br>*Patient N:* 'I just couldn't believe it.'<br>*Patient O:* 'Now I can go sometimes four or five hours shopping like everyone else.'<br>*Patient E:* 'It's marvellous ... My life is 99 per cent better.'<br>*Patient K:* 'It's like being a normal person.'<br>*Patient N:* 'It's just lovely to be able to get out of bed quicker and not have the anxiety of not getting to the loo in time.'<br><br>■ *Concerns about a new drug*: there was little concern about the lack of clinical experience, although one participant stated: 'I was really scared at the beginning. I didn't know what to expect, with it being a new drug ... I was scared but quite excited.' |
| **Discussion** | The findings of this qualitative study provided a fuller picture of the benefits of anti-TNF therapy. The benefits particularly appreciated by patients were the improvements to the quality of their lives and their independence in undertaking every day tasks, and the knock-on psychological effects. The patients were also more dynamic socially and they could perform tasks that previously were beyond them. |

## Analysis

It is possible to undertake a synthesis of qualitative and quantitative evidence using Bayesian approaches (see Chapter 2.1). A study designed to investigate the factors influencing the uptake of childhood immunization in developed countries,[13] for example, combined the evidence from 11 qualitative and 32 quantitative studies. The analysis (a Bayesian *meta-analysis*) involved deriving prior probabilities from the results of the qualitative studies and using the findings from the quantitative studies to estimate the posterior probabilities.

## Generalizability

Qualitative studies have been particularly useful in assessing why patients under the circumstances of routine clinical care fail so frequently to use interventions as prescribed or recommended. Two examples will suffice to explain the importance of qualitative research in identifying the issues that contribute to such non-adherence.

Chronic hepatitis C virus infection occurs mainly, in developed countries, in people who inject drugs. Its treatment involves a prolonged (6–12 months) course of antiviral therapy comprising a combination of parenteral interferon and oral ribavirin. The treatment has varying effectiveness (50–80 per cent) and is associated with a range of unpleasant adverse effects. Of those who enter treatment regimens, many fail to complete the full course. A systematic review of qualitative studies examining the experience of intravenous drug users undergoing hepatitis C treatment revealed three interplaying themes.[14] First, participants not only saw themselves stigmatized by their healthcare systems but also 'felt stigma' and believed themselves to 'deserve' to be cast as deviant. Second, participants experienced so-called 'biographical adaptation' – perhaps better expressed as 'psychological adaptation' – to their hepatitis C infection. In this context, participants saw their hepatitis as oscillating between a socially accommodated risk and a spoiled identity. Third, studies described an overwhelmingly poor experience of both diagnosis and treatment from their healthcare system. Even a casual reading of this systematic review suggests that the effective treatment of hepatitis C infection among injecting drug users requires substantial efforts to be made to restore dignity and self-worth and to ensure a sympathetic and non-condemnatory environment.

Tuberculosis is a major contributor to the global burden of disease (two million deaths per annum) especially in low- and middle-income countries. Treatment involves 6–8 months of directly observed antitubercular therapy, but up to half of all patients fail to complete their course. A systematic review of qualitative research designed to explore the factors contributing to medication adherence (non-adherence) showed that structural, patient and healthcare factors had impacts on treatment-taking behaviour.[15] Patient adherence was influenced by interactions between these three factors.

## Healthcare priorities

All healthcare systems are constrained in the range and scope of the services they can provide by the availability resources. In setting healthcare priorities, both scientific and social judgements have to be made.[16]

Scientific value judgements are concerned with interpreting the significance and reliability of the available scientific and clinical data.[17] Although such evidence (rather than prejudice and intuition) is crucial to decision-making, it is never enough: experts have to make judgements about issues such as the validity of a particular surrogate endpoint as an indicator of therapeutic benefit, and whether the results of a randomized controlled trial can be generalized to routine clinical care.

*Therapeutics, evidence and decision-making*

Social value judgements relate to society rather than to basic or clinical science.[16] They take account of the ethical principles, preferences, culture and aspirations that should underpin the nature and extent of the services provided by healthcare systems.[17] They include matters such as whether resources should be deployed in a way that gives special priority to children and young people, and whether a healthcare system should be prepared to pay a premium price for drugs to treat very rare diseases.

Ascertaining the public's preferences in setting healthcare priorities requires a qualitative approach. Quantitative techniques such as opinion polls and surveys can, when undertaken competently, elicit the public's immediate preferences on particular issues. Responses, however, may be coloured by inaccurate media activity, and there is no opportunity for considered thought or deliberation. Responses, moreover, are exquisitely sensitive to the precise manner in which the question has been phrased or framed.

A better understanding of the public's preferences can be elicited from focus groups. These provide insights into why members of the public feel as they do. Focus groups used in this way are an extended form of polling, and the time available (usually no more than 2–4 hours) does not allow much opportunity for debate, discussion or deliberation.

A more promising approach has been the use of citizens' juries (see Chapter 4.1). These have been widely used to obtain the views of informed members of the public on a wide range of policy issues in the USA, Germany and Britain.[18] Coote and Lenaghan showed that UK citizens can engage and deliberate on difficult matters relating to healthcare, and that they can reach well-argued and, in some cases, novel conclusions.[19]

The UK's National Institute for Health and Clinical Excellence (NICE) has adapted the citizens' jury methodology to provide a forum – the Citizens Council – where the social value judgements that should underpin the setting of healthcare priorities can be discussed and debated. As with citizens' juries, members of the Citizens Council are asked a specific question. They have the opportunity to listen to and cross-examine experts, and they discuss and deliberate over 2–3 days before reaching their conclusions and formulating their advice. The NICE Citizens Council, however, has a larger number of participants; to achieve continuity, members serve for three years, with one-third retiring annually.[20] The topics considered by the NICE Citizens Council are shown in Table 4.2.1.[21] The Citizens Council's reports (available from the NICE website) have formed the basis of a guideline on social value judgements, to which NICE advisory bodies are expected to conform.[22]

## Discussion

Despite earnest efforts, qualitative research has yet to make its fullest contribution to the evaluation, assessment and appraisal of the benefits and *harms* of therapeutic interventions. Both the *British Medical Journal*[23] and the *Journal of the American Medical Association*[24] have, to their credit, attempted to introduce the methodology and significance of qualitative research to their readers; and the Cochrane Collaboration[25] and the NHS Centre for Reviews and Dissemination[26] have provided advice on incorporating evidence from qualitative studies into systematic reviews. Yet no hierarchy of evidence includes qualitative findings apart from, at the lowest level, so-called 'expert opinion'.

**Table 4.2.1** Topics considered by the National Institute for Health and Clinical Excellence (NICE) Citizens Council

| Year of publication | Topic |
|---|---|
| 2003 | Clinical need |
| 2004 | Age |
| 2004 | Confidential enquiries |
| 2005 | Ultra-orphan drugs |
| 2005 | Mandatory public health measures |
| 2006 | Rule of rescue |
| 2006 | Health inequalities |
| 2007 | Only in research |
| 2007 | Patient safety |
| 2008 | Quality-adjusted life-years (QALYs) and the severity of illness |
| 2008 | Departing from the threshold |
| 2009 | Smoking and harm reduction |
| 2009 | The nature of innovation |
| 2010 | Incentives |

The resistance to incorporating qualitative evidence in the evaluation of therapeutic interventions is multifaceted. It is an approach that is almost entirely inductive; its methodology is embedded in the social sciences; it is regarded, pejoratively, as providing only anecdotal evidence; and its findings cannot be reduced to quantitative expressions. Yet, as already discussed, it can have considerable value when used alongside quantitative research studies, and it has a distinctive role to play in answering questions beyond the scope of conventional quantitative research techniques.

Qualitative research methods have a particular role in the evaluation of 'complex' interventions.[27] *Complex interventions* are interventions that include several components; examples include cognitive–behavioural therapy for depression, and health promotion methods to reduce alcohol consumption and support dietary change. Complex interventions are, inherently, subject to more variation than are pharmaceutical products. In a trial of cognitive–behavioural therapy, for example, the outcomes might vary with the personality and style of the therapist, the content of the behavioural therapy, the setting in which therapy is conducted, and the background of the patient. Many of the components of the intervention can be defined at the outset, using focus groups, surveys or case studies,[27] so that the main study addresses all the significant issues. Qualitative studies of the processes in each of the study arms of the main trial can help show the validity of the findings.[27]

It is therefore disappointing that in a systematic review of the use of qualitative studies alongside randomized controlled trials is still relatively uncommon in the evaluation of complex interventions.[28] Most of the qualitative studies were carried out before or during the trials, and few were used to explain the results. Many of the qualitative studies also had major methodological shortcomings.

Where available, decision-makers should take the findings from qualitative research seriously as part of their scrutiny and appraisal of the totality of the evidence. Clearly, such studies should be both relevant and robust; but, provided decision-makers can put aside any remaining prejudices they might hold about induction, and data for which no summary statistics can be provided, qualitative research can provide them with invaluable information.

*Therapeutics, evidence and decision-making*

# References

1. Ashcroft RE, Chadwick DW, Clark SRL, *et al.* Implications of socio-cultural context for the ethics of clinical trials. *Health Technology Assessment* 1997;**1**:1–165.
2. De Sallis I, Tomlin Z, Toerin M, Donovan J. Qualitative research to improve RCT recruitment: issues arising in establishing research collaborations. *Contemporary Clinical Trials* 2008;**29**:663–70.
3. Shah JY, Phadtare A, Rajgor D, *et al.* What leads Indians to participate in clinical trials? A meta-analysis of qualitative studies. *PLoS ONE* 2010;**5**:e10730.
4. McCann SK, Campbell MK, Entwistle V. Reasons for participating in randomized controlled trials: conditional altruism and considerations for self. *Trials* 2010;**11**:31–41.
5. National Institute for Health Research Health Technology Assessment Programme. The ProtecT trial: evaluating the effectiveness of treatments for clinically localised prostate cancer. www.hta.ac.uk/project/1230.asp.
6. Donovan J, Mills N, Smith M, *et al.* Improving the design and conduct of randomized controlled trials by embedding them in qualitative research: ProtecT (prostate testing for cancer and treatment) study. *BMJ* 2002;**325**:766–9.
7. Koops L, Lindley RI. Thrombolysis for acute ischaemic stroke: consumer involvement in the design of new randomised controlled trial. *BMJ* 2002;**325**:415–19.
8. Edwards S, Braunholtz D. Can unequal be more fair? A response to Andrew Avins. *Journal of Medical Ethics* 2000;**26**:179–82.
9. Donovan JL, Peters TJ, Neal DE, *et al.* A randomized trial comparing transurethral resection of the prostate, laser therapy and conservative treatment in men with symptomatic benign prostatic enlargement: the CLasP study. *Journal of Urology* 2000;**164**:65–70.
10. Marshall NJ, Wilson G, Lapworth K, Kay LJ. Patients' perceptions of treatment with anti-THF therapy for rheumatoid arthritis. *Rheumatology* 2004;**43**:1034–8.
11. Edwards J. An exploration of patients' experiences of anti-TNF therapy. *Musculoskeletal Care* 2004;**2**:40–50.
12. Sanderson T, Morris M, Calnan M, *et al.* What pharmacological outcomes are important to people with rheumatoid arthritis? Creating the basis of a patient core set. *Arthritis Care Research* 2010;**62**:640–46.
13. Roberts KA, Dixon-Woods M, Abrams KR, Jones DR. Factors affecting the uptake of childhood immunization: a Bayesian synthesis of qualitative and quantitative evidence. *Lancet* 2002;**360**:1596–9.
14. Treloar C, Rhodes T. The lived experience of hepatitis C and its treatment among injecting drug users: qualitative synthesis. *Qualitative Health Research* 2009;**19**:1321–34.
15. Munro SA, Lewin SA, Smith HJ, *et al.* Patient adherence to tuberculosis treatment: a systematic review of qualitative research. *PLoS Medicine* 2007;**4**:e238.
16. Rawlins MD, Culyer AJ. National Institute for Health and Clinical Excellence and its value judgements. *BMJ* 2004;**329**:224–6.
17. Rawlins MD. Pharmacopolitics and deliberative democracy. *Clinical Medicine* 2005;**5**:471–5.
18. Chambers R. *Involving Patients and the Public*. Abingdon: Radcliffe Press, 2000.
19. Coote A, Lenaghan J. *Citizens Juries: Theory into Practice*. London: Institute for Policy Research, 1997.
20. Rawlins M. Background to NICE's Citizens Council. In: Littlejohns P, Rawlins M (eds). *Patients, the Public and Priorities in Healthcare*. Oxford: Radcliffe Publishing, 2009.
21. Littlejohns P. The Citizens Council's reports. In: Littlejohns P, Rawlins M (eds). *Patients, the Public and Priorities in Healthcare*. Oxford: Radcliffe Publishing, 2009.

22. Littlejohns P, Rawlins M. Social value judgements: implementing the Citizens Council reports. In: Littlejohns P, Rawlins M (eds). *Patients, the Public and Priorities in Healthcare*. Oxford: Radcliffe Publishing, 2009.

23. Pope C, Mays N. Reaching the parts that other methods cannot reach: an introduction to qualitative methods in health and health services research. *BMJ* 1995;**311**:42–5.

24. Giacomini MK, Cook DJ. Users' guide to the medical literature: XXIII. Qualitative research in health care. A: are the results of the study valid? *Journal of the American Medical Association* 2000;**284**:357–62.

25. Noyes J, Popay J, Pearson A, *et al*. Qualitative research and Cochrane reviews. In: Higgins JPT, Green S (eds). *Cochrane Handbook for Systematic Reviews of Interventions*. Chichester: John Wiley & Sons, 2008.

26. Centre for Reviews and Dissemination. *Systematic Reviews*. York: Centre for Reviews and Dissemination, 2009.

27. Campbell M, Fitzpatrick R, Haines A, *et al*. Framework for design and evaluation of complex interventions to improve health. *BMJ* 2000;**321**:694–6.

28. Lewin S, Glenton C, Oxman AD. Use of qualitative methods alongside randomized controlled trials of complex healthcare interventions: methodological study. *BMJ* 2009;**339**:b3496.

# SECTION 5
# Economic evaluation

# GENERAL PRINCIPLES

*A health economist is one who asks, not only if the treatment for dysentery is effective, but also the price of toilet paper.* Stephen Senn[1]

The details of the ways in which individual countries fund healthcare for their populations are almost as varied as the number of healthcare systems themselves. They are financed, to varying degrees, by four means:[2]

- private health insurance;
- social health insurance;
- taxation;
- out-of-pocket payments.

In *private health insurance*, as with other basic insurance models, individuals contract with insurance providers. The premiums are paid by individuals or, in part or in whole, by their employers as part of their salary packages. Health insurance may be supplied by for-profit or not-for-profit organizations. This form of provision is a major source of funding in the USA, but it is minimal in countries such as the UK.

*Social health insurance schemes* are based on the principal of social solidarity. In these schemes employees, employers and the government each make compulsory contributions to the financing of healthcare by paying premiums into a social insurance fund. Contributions for people who are unemployed or retired are made by the state, unemployment funds or pension funds. This arrangement finances the majority of healthcare in countries such as France, Germany and the Netherlands.

Funding for healthcare by *taxation* may cover either the entire or subsets of a population. It forms the main source of funding for healthcare in countries such as Italy, Spain, the UK and Scandinavian countries. Moreover, even in the USA, where private health insurance predominates, there is still a substantial (44 per cent) contribution from taxation through programmes such as Medicaid (for very poor people) and Medicare (for elderly people).[3]

Almost all healthcare systems include elements of *out-of-pocket payments*. In schemes funded by general taxation and social insurance schemes, these elements tend to be modest. In private health insurance schemes, however, they can be considerable.

## Background

Given the pluralism of funding it is perhaps surprising that, in general, a country's healthcare expenditure expressed per capita is closely related to its wealth as reflected by its *gross domestic product*. (For purists $r = 0.776$, $r^2 = 0.602$, $P < 0.01$.) As a consequence there is an eight- to tenfold difference in healthcare expenditure between member states of the Organisation for Economic Co-operation and Development (see Figure 5.1.1). It is obvious that a healthcare intervention that is affordable in countries such as Switzerland, Norway or the USA cannot necessarily be affordable in Mexico, Poland or the Slovak Republic.

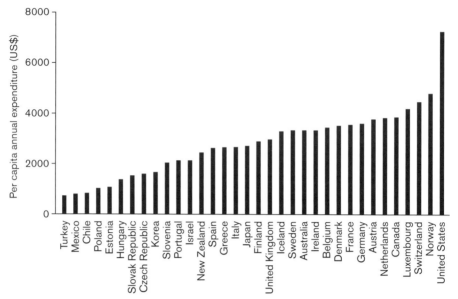

**Figure 5.1.1** Annual healthcare expenditure for 2007 of Organisation for Economic Co-operation and Development (OECD) member states.

Over the past 40 years expenditure on healthcare by most countries has risen faster than their gross domestic products.[4] Yet no healthcare system anywhere is able to provide for all the health needs or demands of its population. Because all healthcare systems have finite resources, economists attempt to compare the benefits that are expected to be gained from using a new intervention with the health benefits that will have to be displaced (or 'forgone') elsewhere in a healthcare system.

Section 5 is concerned with the economic evaluation of therapeutic interventions, but similar principles apply to the economic evaluation of new diagnostic procedures and the introduction of new services.

## Types of economic analysis

In the economic analysis of therapeutic interventions, the costs and benefits of one treatment are compared with the costs and benefits of another treatment for the same condition. Such an approach is therefore concerned with the marginal, or incremental, costs and benefits. There are five potential approaches to the economic evaluation of interventions:

- *Cost–benefit analysis:* in this form of analysis, both the costs of using an intervention and the additional benefits it brings are expressed in monetary terms. Although it is used in other areas of economic evaluation, it has not been popular in health economics, for two main reasons. First, there would be difficulties in expressing benefits in monetary terms, particularly those related to 'wellbeing'. Second, there is a view among health economists that physicians, patients and the public would find the concept of monetarizing benefits as distasteful. How much, for example, is a life worth?
- *Cost consequences analysis:* in this technique, the costs of a technology are set against the benefits in an itemized list. It can be regarded as representing part of the 'business case' for adopting a particular technology and is discussed further in Chapter 5.3.

- *Cost minimization:* this is used when two or more interventions produce the same (or almost the same) degree of therapeutic benefit. Its application depends on establishing therapeutic equivalence (see Chapter 5.2).
- *Cost-effectiveness analysis:* this involves estimating the additional costs in relationship to the additional benefits, as expressed in 'natural' units. Examples include the number of years of life gained with a treatment for cancer (cost per life-year gained), the fall in blood pressure with an antihypertensive agent (cost per mmHg fall), and increased height following treatment with growth hormone for children with growth hormone deficiency (cost per additional centimetre of height). This is discussed more fully in Chapter 5.2.
- *Cost–utility analysis:* in a cost–utility analysis the additional benefits are expressed in terms of 'usefulness' or 'utilities'. The most widely used unit of *utility* is the quality-adjusted life-year (QALY). The great virtue of cost–utility analysis is that it allows a comparison of the costs and benefits of treating one condition with those of treating another condition. This important method is considered in Chapter 5.2.

## Costs

In health economics, costs are often separated into 'direct' and 'indirect' costs; the direct costs are separated further into 'direct medical' and 'direct non-medical' costs:

- *Direct medical costs:* these include the acquisition cost of the intervention, the costs of any additional monitoring (such as extra blood tests or X-rays) and the cost of medical and nursing time. Direct costs also include what are sometimes called 'cost offsets' – the costs that will be avoided (i.e. the savings) by using an intervention. For example, the effective treatment of early breast cancer means that the cost of treating the advanced stages of the disease will be avoided. Similarly, the effective treatment of people with schizophrenia will avoid the cost of repeated admissions to hospital.
- *Direct non-medical costs:* these are the ancillary costs incurred by the use of a hospital's facilities (such as operating theatres) and for maintaining its physical infrastructure.
- *Indirect costs:* these are the costs of 'lost production', such as time off work or the need to hire temporary help at home. They may also include the cost to society more broadly in providing welfare services such as sickness or unemployment benefits. Whether such indirect costs are included depends on the *economic perspective* that has been adopted for the analysis.
- *Future costs and savings:* it has been suggested that future costs and savings should also be included in the analysis.[5] It is argued, for example, that if an intervention cures an otherwise fatal condition, then those benefiting will at some stage incur future healthcare (and other) costs for unrelated conditions. As pointed out by Moskowitz, however, 'this argument is inexhaustible and philosophically difficult to justify. If carried to the extreme it would lead us to abandon all medical care. This would be the ultimate cost effective strategy'.[6] Most would concur with this view, but a further argument against the inclusion of future costs is that they relate to specific programmes and treatments that should, of themselves, be the subject of future economic evaluation.

Examples of the costs that might be included or excluded, depending on the economic perspective, are shown in Table 5.1.1. Estimating costs can be difficult.[7] Clearly, the acquisition cost of an intervention can be obtained from a price list, although even this can prove awkward if variable discounts are available within a single healthcare system. Other costs may be derived from national tariffs, such as healthcare resource group data. Some costs may be aggregated from sample data, and others (such as simple blood tests costing very little) can sometimes be ignored.[7]

**Table 5.1.1** Inclusion and exclusion of costs in respect of the economic perspective[4]

| Costs | Economic perspective | |
|---|---|---|
| | **Healthcare system** | **Societal** |
| *Direct medical* | | |
| Physician time | + | + |
| Other clinical personnel (e.g. nursing) | + | + |
| Acquisition costs of the intervention | + | + |
| Special diagnostic tests | + | + |
| Special monitoring tests | + | + |
| Other costs of hospital attendance (e.g. food) | + | + |
| *Direct non-medical* | | |
| Administration | + | + |
| Physical facilities (e.g. hospital) | + | + |
| Utilities (hospital) | + | + |
| Patient's travelling costs for treatment | +/−* | + |
| *Indirect* | | |
| Patients travelling costs for treatment | +/−* | + |
| Time off work | − | + |
| Sickness benefit payments | − | + |
| Temporary household help | − | + |

* Dependent on whether patients are providing their own transport or whether they are travelling by ambulance, and, if the latter, who pays for it.

## Economic perspective

The costs and benefits of a therapeutic intervention depend on the economic perspective that is adopted. The perspective of individual patients and their families will differ from those of an entire healthcare system (both providers of services and those who pay the costs), the wider public sector, and the interests of society at large. Thus, where patients pay for their own healthcare, all the direct and indirect costs will fall on them. As discussed already, however, most (if not almost all) healthcare costs are borne by some form of private health insurance, by social health insurance schemes or by taxation. Such payers may be concerned only with medical and non-medical direct costs. The perspective from which a health economic evaluation is undertaken, therefore, is very important and needs to be determined in advance of any analysis.

Healthcare systems undertaking the economic evaluation of interventions vary in their approach to the perspective they take. For example, the perspectives in the UK and New Zealand are those of their healthcare systems, while Sweden and Portugal adopt societal perspectives.[8] Although a societal perspective may appear intuitively to be attractive, there are real difficulties. First, the definition of 'societal' is rarely clear. It might include the costs of sickness benefits and unemployment. But should it also, for example, take account of the economic benefits of a thriving national pharmaceutical industry that employs considerable numbers of people and generates substantial trade balances? And, if so, how? Second, a societal perspective will tend to benefit people who are economically active and, as a consequence, may disadvantage economically inactive people (especially those who are retired). Third, the methods for incorporating a wide societal perspective require very large assumptions to be made and increase both the complexity and the contestability of analyses.[8]

*Therapeutics, evidence and decision-making*

# Discounting

A key feature of economic theory is that individuals (and society) place greater value on benefits obtained in the present than in the future.[4] In other words, society will devote more resources to saving a life now than at some future time. To reflect this preference, both the resources spent and the benefits gained in the future are discounted when being compared with the costs and benefits in the present. The discounted values of the differences over time are described as the 'net present value'.

Although there is a consensus among economists about the merits of *discounting* costs, there is less agreement about discounting for benefits.[7] Discounting is normally annualized so that health benefits of less than a year are not discounted. Discounting for costs but not benefits for healthcare programmes lasting more than a year will have the effect of improving their cost-effectiveness. This will influence the relative cost-effectiveness of healthcare programmes with different time scales of benefit.

Nevertheless, most national guidelines for pharmacoeconomic research recommend that both costs and benefits should be discounted. The National Institute for Health and Clinical Excellence (NICE) uses a discount rate of 3.5 per cent per annum for both costs and benefits.[9] This reflects the discount rate used by the British government in its forecasts for the UK economy as a whole. Other discount rates, which may be different for costs and benefits, are used by other organizations.

# Modelling

There are two reasons why, in most economic analyses, analysts construct an economic model in order to simulate the conditions under which an intervention might be used.[2] First, any economic evaluation is inevitably based on multiple sources of data that have to be brought together. Second, there will be many sources of uncertainty about the quantitative data used in such economic evaluations, which will in turn yield uncertainties in the results. For both of these reasons, a formal model will provide the most reliable estimates of the expected values of alternative treatments. A good model will also help in identifying and understanding the inherent uncertainties in the data used to populate it. Two types of model are particularly used in health economic evaluation:

- decision trees;
- Markov models.

The brief descriptions that follow are intended only to provide an overview of each of these approaches. Fuller accounts are provided elsewhere.[2,7,10]

## Decision trees

Decision trees in the economic evaluation of therapeutic interventions are treatment pathways with decision points followed by the probabilities of success or failure for various possible consequences. An example is shown in Figure 5.1.2, which compares the use of surgery and antimicrobial treatment for acute appendicitis. The tree is made up of nodes, which represent the events, and branches connecting the nodes. The key features of a decision tree are as follows:[2]

- The square node denotes a decision point between two alternative treatments. In Figure 5.1.2, this is the choice between surgery or antibiotic therapy for the treatment of acute appendicitis.

- The pathways represent mutually exclusive events.
- The circles are chance or probability nodes indicating points at which two (or more) alternative events are possible. In Figure 5.1.2, for example, patients treated surgically may die either during the operation or in the postoperative period; they may recover uneventfully; or they may develop one or more complications such as postoperative wound infection. Similarly, patients treated with antibiotics may die (say) from overwhelming infection; they may recover uneventfully; or they may develop complications such as a recurrence of acute appendicitis.
- The probabilities, shown in parentheses in Figure 5.1.2, are the probabilities of each event. Apart from the first event, all the later events are conditional.
- The triangular nodes are the terminal nodes representing the final outcome associated with a particular pathway through the decision tree. Each of these will have a value assigned to it. In Figure 5.1.2 these are expressed as quality-adjusted life-years.

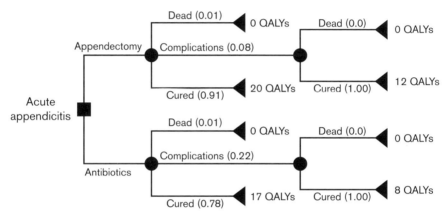

**Figure 5.1.2** Hypothetical example of a decision tree of surgery (appendectomy) versus antibiotic treatment (cefotaxime + metronidazole) for acute appendicitis.[11]

From the decision tree, working from right to left, it is possible to estimate the expected values for each of the events by multiplying the value of the event by the probability of the event occurring. Then, by peeling back, the effects of one treatment over another can be ascertained at each stage and ultimately allow an estimate to be made of the advantage (in this instance) of surgery versus antibiotic treatment for the treatment of acute appendicitis.

### Markov models

The decision tree shown in Figure 5.1.2 is a useful model for a condition that progresses with time.[11] This is often the case with acute medical or surgical conditions such as acute myocardial infarction or acute appendicitis. Such decision trees, however, are unsatisfactory for conditions such as many chronic diseases that evolve over time. In these circumstances health economists tend to use Markov models.[12] (Andrey Markov [1856–1922] was a Russian mathematician who famously refused to spy on his students for the Tsarist government. Equally famously, when Tolstoy was excommunicated from the Russian Orthodox Church, Markov formally asked to be excommunicated too. His request was granted.)

A simple depiction of a Markov model is shown in Figure 5.1.3. The model might, for example, reflect the progression of multiple sclerosis or ischaemic heart disease. The key features are as follows:

- The oval shapes depict the 'states'. The model in Figure 5.1.3 consists of only four states. The first state is 'asymptomatic'. From this state, patients may move directly to the dead state from an intercurrent, unrelated condition based on the all-cause mortality (taking account of age and gender). Alternatively, patients may move to progressive disease state 1, with the prospect of experiencing symptoms of the disease and a greater risk of death compared with the all-cause mortality rate.
- The arrows show possible transitions between states. The transitions are assumed to take place for each cycle of the model. An important limitation of the Markov model is that the probability of moving out of a state is independent of the states a patient may have experienced before entering that state. This is sometimes described as the 'memoryless' feature of Markov models (also referred to as the 'Markovian assumption').

The model in Figure 5.1.3 is one where there is progressive (stepwise) progression. Markov models, however, can accommodate improvements to a previous state when, as might occur in relapsing–remitting multiple sclerosis, patients become asymptomatic after an acute relapse.

Two different types of Markov model can be characterized by the form of the transition probabilities. In standard Markov chains, the transition probabilities are assumed to be constant over time. Although this has distinct analytical advantages, this approach may

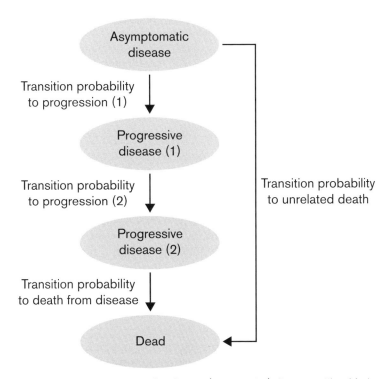

**Figure 5.1.3** Hypothetical depiction of a chronic (progressive) disease with a Markov model.[12]

be too restrictive. The more general Markov models, where transition probabilities can vary over time, are known as 'time-dependent Markov probabilities'.

In order to complete a Markov model it is necessary to attach 'weights' to the health outcomes. For health outcomes in each state, this involves weighting the length of time spent in each state by the quality of life experienced in that state. The calculation of costs over the lifetime of the model follows the same approach.

Two forms of adjustment to costs and outcomes are also likely to be incorporated in the model. First, discounting adjustments for costs and outcomes will be included. Second, rather than assuming that patients will move between states at the beginning or end of each cycle, a half-cycle correction may be employed. This is equivalent to the assumption that, on average, patients will move between states halfway through the cycle. The importance of half-cycle corrections will, however, depend on the cycle length chosen for the model: the longer the cycle length, the more important it will be to include a half-cycle correction.

# Time horizon

The time horizon for estimating clinical and cost-effectiveness will vary with the intervention and its use. Some interventions will have an impact over a patient's lifetime and especially in the treatment of chronic diseases. In such instances a lifetime horizon for clinical and cost-effectiveness is usually appropriate. A lifetime horizon is also appropriate for any mortality component in order to assess the implications of differential survival between one intervention and its comparator. For a lifetime horizon it will often be necessary to extrapolate beyond the results of clinical trials. In such circumstances, sensitivity analyses should be undertaken to assess the extent to which the assumptions about continuing benefits might contribute to the possible conclusions.

A time horizon that is shorter than lifetime is justified where there is no differential mortality between treatment options, and where the differences in costs and outcomes relate to a short time period. The treatments of acute infections and acute migraine are obvious examples.

# Sensitivity analysis

Uncertainties are inherent in all economic models. These may be due to the model itself or the data contained within it. Typically, a model consists of one or more equations. The quantities appearing in the equations are classified into *variables* and *parameters*. The distinction between these is not always clear and frequently depends on the context in which they appear. Usually a model is designed to explain the relationships that exist among quantities that can be measured independently in an experiment; these are the variables of the model. To formulate these relationships, however, one frequently introduces 'constants', which stand for inherent properties of nature (or of the materials and equipment used in a given experiment). These are the parameters.

Sensitivity analyses explore the impact of uncertainties in a model's parameters.

*One-way sensitivity analysis* involves examining the effects of changing one parameter at a time. It might, for example, involve changing the discount rate, the acquisition cost of an intervention, or the *incidence* of an intervention's adverse effects.

It is possible to vary more than one parameter at a time and examine the combined effects on the overall outcome. For example, it would be possible to examine the combined effects of varying the discount rate and the incidence of an intervention's adverse effects. In practice, such *multi-way sensitivity analyses* that involve more than two or three parameters can become unwieldy.

If the overall effects of a sensitivity analysis make little difference to the outcome, then a decision-maker can have reasonable confidence in drawing appropriate conclusions. If, however, the sensitivity analysis shows very different outcomes, then it may be necessary to decide reasonable upper and lower boundaries. This provides an estimate of the most plausible range for the particular parameter. The plausible ranges might be informed by expert opinion or by some other approach. It is also possible to undertake a statistically based sensitivity analysis that provides estimates of the confidence intervals for the outcome of interest.

# Thresholds

## *Incremental cost–effectiveness ratios*

Both cost–effectiveness and cost–utility analyses provide estimates of the additional (incremental) costs that must be paid to achieve some additional (incremental) benefits in comparison with an alternative intervention. The *incremental cost–effectiveness ratio* of the new intervention is derived thus:

$$\text{Incremental cost–effectiveness ratio} = \frac{(\text{cost}_{new} - \text{cost}_{existing})}{(\text{benefit}_{new} - \text{benefit}_{existing})}$$

Incremental cost-effectiveness is sometimes depicted as shown in Figure 5.1.4. In this figure, the differences in the costs of two interventions, and the differences in their benefits, are shown on the *y*- and *x*-axes, respectively. The figure shows four quadrants:

- *Quadrant A:* in this quadrant, the new intervention is more costly but less beneficial than the existing intervention. Choosing the new intervention would obviously be inappropriate.
- *Quadrant B:* in this quadrant, the new intervention is less costly but also less effective than the existing intervention. Whether it would be appropriate to choose the new intervention over the existing one would depend on the circumstances. In practice, however, it is an uncommon result.

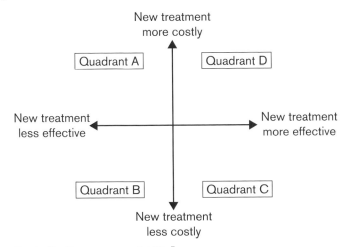

**Figure 5.1.4** Cost-effectiveness acceptability.[7]

- *Quadrant C:* this quadrant is a decision-maker's dream because the new intervention is more effective but less costly than the existing intervention. In health economic parlance, it is described as 'dominant'. It is a relatively uncommon situation.
- *Quadrant D:* in this quadrant, the new intervention is more effective but more costly than the existing intervention. This, for pharmaceuticals, is the most common result. Whether or not a decision-maker decides the incremental benefit is worth the additional cost depends on the threshold used.

## Cost-effectiveness thresholds

The level at which an incremental cost–effectiveness ratio can be regarded as a cost-effective or cost-ineffective use of healthcare resources – Quadrant D in Figure 5.1.4 – is one of the more vexed questions in health economics. Three approaches have been proposed:[13]

- setting the threshold to exhaust the healthcare budget;
- setting the threshold in order to determine the optimal budget;
- inferring thresholds from previous decisions.

### ■ Exhausting the healthcare budget

If all the interventions used in a healthcare system were to be ranked in increasing order of their incremental cost–effectiveness ratios, a point would come when the healthcare budget was exhausted. At this point, the incremental cost–effectiveness ratio could be used as the threshold between cost-effectiveness and cost-ineffectiveness.

League tables of incremental cost–effectiveness ratios have, indeed, been published.[2] In practice, most league tables are limited in scope, with typically only 10–20 interventions in each. Moreover, they have methodological limitations,[2] especially the inconsistent analytical approaches that were adopted in individual studies.

A more elaborate attempt in the late 1980s was made by the State of Oregon in attempting to decide what services should be provided under the Medicaid programme. (Medicaid is a publicly funded US healthcare programme intended to provide medically necessary care to poor people.) This involved assigning all possible treatments into 'condition–treatment pairs' and assessing each in terms of the cost per QALY gained. The 700 condition–treatment pairs were placed in rank order and were approved for funding down to the point at which the healthcare budget was exhausted. Apart from various technical and economic limitations,[2] the resulting list included many priorities that seemed counterintuitive.[14] For example, teeth whitening received a higher ranking than emergency surgery for ectopic pregnancy. The original list was never implemented.

### ■ Optimizing the healthcare budget

This approach is the reverse of exhausting a healthcare budget. It involves deciding a particular threshold and then making available all those interventions for which the incremental cost–effectiveness ratio was at or below this value.

One approach to deciding a threshold would be to determine society's willingness to pay for healthcare benefits. Although this method has been used in other areas of public expenditure, there is no consensus among health economists as to its appropriateness in a publicly funded healthcare system.

The late Alan Williams suggested that a 'common sense' value for the threshold would be to set it equal to the per capita gross domestic product.[15] The intuitive appeal of this proposal is that if every member of society were to be given a fair share of the nation's wealth, then they would each be eligible to receive the per capita gross domestic product.

Indeed, the World Health Organization's Commission on Macroeconomics and Health has made a similar proposal,[16] albeit based on disability-adjusted life-years (DALYs): interventions that avert 1 DALY for less than a country's per capita gross domestic product are considered very cost-effective; interventions that cost more than three times a country's per capita gross domestic product are not considered to be cost-effective.

Loomes has suggested that the threshold should be set at a level consistent with the value attached to life-years gained in other parts of the public sector.[17] Although again this seems intuitively reasonable, it assumes that the objectives of all public sector programmes that save lives are similar – but this may not necessarily be the case. For example, society may be prepared to spend more on preventing deaths from terrorist attacks than from disease.

### ■ Inferences from previous decisions

Inferences drawn from previous decisions based on the judgements of decision-makers may form the basis for deciding (or at least informing) an incremental cost–effectiveness ratio threshold.[18] There are two disadvantages to this approach.[2] First, it is not necessarily appropriate for current decisions to be constrained to the same decision criteria as those used previously. Second, it assumes that all factors relevant to previous decisions, and all evidence regarding each one, have been fully captured in the analysis.

An indirect approach to drawing inferences about thresholds based on previous decisions can be inferred from analyses of programme budgeting. Programme budgeting involves identifying the resources used by individual clinical services (such as mental health or cardiovascular disorders) either within a whole healthcare system or in individual units of the healthcare system. Programme budgeting is used internationally as a planning tool for resource allocation in the public sector. Using programme budgeting data from English primary care trusts and deriving the expenditure required to save a year of life, Martin and colleagues estimated the cost of an additional life-year saved for individual programmes.[19] Furthermore, after making a quality-of-life adjustment, they were able to estimate an approximate cost per QALY for individual programmes.

## Systematic reviews of economic analyses

The increasing use of economic evaluation in the appraisal of healthcare interventions has led to attempts to synthesize the results of multiple analyses that look at a single intervention.[20] The general principles underpinning the reviews of an intervention's effectiveness (see Chapter 1.6) apply equally to those reviewing cost-effectiveness. These include the need for a formal protocol, the question(s) that the review is expected to answer, the interventions, the types of data required for the evaluation of benefits and *harms*, and details of the study populations (including age and gender).

Systemic reviews of economic analyses will also need to encompass other data elements.[20] These include the type of model used, the economic perspective, the included costs, the discount rate, the currency and the time horizon. Where available (or when the information can be imputed from the data), the incremental cost–effectiveness ratio will also be captured. An evidence table including all these variables can then be prepared in an analogous fashion to the evidence table developed for other systematic reviews of the *effectiveness* of an intervention.

It is rarely possible, however, to undertake meta-analyses in systematic reviews of the economic evaluation of an intervention. Difficulties include the economic perspective that may be adopted, the *multiplicity* of models that may have been used, the variability in costs relevant to different healthcare systems, varying discount rates, and the time horizons. In a systematic review of screening for colorectal cancer by 10-yearly colonoscopy, the incremental cost–effectiveness ratio (expressed at US\$ 2000) varied from dominant (i.e. cost-saving) to US\$ 62 000 per QALY.[20]

## Discussion

The principles underpinning the economic evaluation of healthcare interventions are relatively straightforward. Some of the methodological details, however, require considerable expertise in both execution and interpretation. This applies particularly to the structure of the economic model that has been used and the inputs and assumptions that have been incorporated in it. Decision-makers therefore need considerable help from competent health economists before drawing conclusions.

The greatest challenge for decision-makers, however, is in determining whether an intervention should be regarded as cost-effective or cost-ineffective when it falls in Quadrant D in Figure 5.1.4. The most explicit approach is that adopted by NICE. NICE rejects the use of an absolute threshold for four reasons:[18]

- There is no empirical basis for deciding what level a threshold should be set at. As discussed, a number of approaches are available, but there is no consensus as to which should be adopted.
- There may be circumstances (see Section 6) when decision-makers want to ignore an absolute threshold for a variety of legitimate reasons.
- Such a threshold would imply that efficiency has an absolute priority over other objectives (particularly fairness).
- The manufacturers of many interventions are monopolies. An absolute threshold might therefore discourage price competition.

Rather than apply an absolute threshold, NICE makes its decisions on a case-by-case basis. This is shown stylistically in Figure 5.1.5. As the incremental cost–effectiveness ratio rises, the likelihood of rejection on grounds of cost-ineffectiveness increases. Interventions with incremental cost–effectiveness ratios to the left of A would generally be considered cost-effective. Interventions with incremental cost–effectiveness ratios

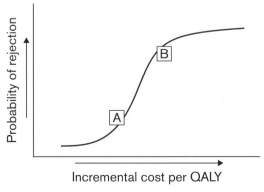

**Figure 5.1.5** Relationship between the likelihood that an intervention will be cost-ineffective and the incremental cost–effectiveness ratio.[18]

QALY, quality-adjusted life-year.

to the right of B would, if adopted, be increasingly likely to deny other patients (with different conditions) access to cost-effective care.

As discussed, there is no consensus among health economists as to what values should be assigned to A or B. NICE, however, has adopted the view that an incremental cost–effectiveness ratio of less than £20 000 per QALY should be regarded as cost-effective; above this, and especially above an incremental cost–effectiveness ratio of £30 000, special reasons would be required to conclude that an intervention represented good use of resources, taking account of the *opportunity costs* (i.e. the benefits 'forgone'). These 'threshold boundaries' were originally derived on the basis of 'judgement',[18] but they are nevertheless broadly compatible with the approaches discussed earlier in this chapter. The special circumstances that might be 'taken into account' when these threshold boundaries are to be ignored are discussed in Chapter 6.2.

# References

1. Senn S. *Statistical Issues in Drug Development*. Chichester: John Wiley & Sons, 1997.
2. Morris S, Devlin N, Parkin D. *Economic Analysis in Health Care*. Chichester: John Wiley & Sons, 2007.
3. World Health Organization. *Core Health Indicators*. Geneva: WHO Statistical Information Service, 2006.
4. Meltzer MI. Introduction to health economics for physicians. *Lancet* 2001;**358**:993–8.
5. Weinstein MC, Stason WB. Foundations of cost effectiveness evaluation for health and medical practice. *New England Journal of Medicine* 1977;**296**:716–21.
6. Moskowitz M. Costs of screening for breast cancer. *Radiologic Clinics of North America* 1987;**25**:1031–7.
7. Drummond MF, Sculpher MJ, Torrance GW, *et al*. *Methods for the Evaluation of Health Care Programmes*. Oxford: Oxford University Press, 2005.
8. Claxton K, Walker S, Palmer S, Sculpher M. *Appropriate Perspectives for Health Care Decisions*. CHE research paper 54. York: Centre for Health Economics, 2010.
9. National Institute for Health and Clinical Excellence. *Guide to the Methods of Technology Appraisal*. London: National Institute for Health and Clinical Excellence, 2008.
10. Briggs A, Claxton Karl, Sculpher M. *Decision Modelling for Health Economic Evaluation*. Oxford: Oxford University Press, 2006.
11. Hannson J, Körner U, Khorram-Manesh A, *et al*. Randomized clinical trial of antibiotic therapy versus appendectomy as primary treatment of acute appendicitis in unselected patients. *British Journal of Surgery* 2009;**96**:473–81.
12. Briggs A, Sculpher M. An introduction to Markov modelling for economic evaluation. *Pharmacoeconomics* 1998;**13**:397–409.
13. National Institute for Health and Clinical Excellence. *Briefing Paper for the Methods Working Party on the Cost Effectiveness Threshold*. London: National Institute for Health and Clinical Excellence, 2008.
14. Hadorn D. Setting health care priorities in Oregon: cost effectiveness meets the rule of rescue. *Journal of the American Medical Association* 1991;**265**:2218–25.
15. Williams, A. *What Could be Nicer than NICE?* London: Office of Health Economics, 2004.
16. WHO Commission on Macroeconomics and Health. *Macroeconomics and Health: Investing in Health for Economic Development. Report of the Commission on Macroeconomics and Health: Executive Summary*. Geneva: World Health Organization, 2001.

17. Loomes, G. Valuing life years and QALYs: transferability and convertibility of values across the UK Public Sector. In: Towse A, Pritchard C, Devlin N (eds). *Cost Effectiveness Thresholds: Economic and Ethical Issues*. London: King's Fund and Office of Health Economics, 2002.

18. Rawlins MD, Culyer AJ. National Institute for Health and Clinical Effectiveness and its social value judgements. *BMJ* 2004;**329**:224–7.

19. Martin S, Rice N, Smith PC. The link between health care spending and health outcomes for the new English primary care trusts. CHE research paper 42. York: Centre for Health Economics, 2008.

20. Pignone M, Saha S, Hoerger T, *et al*. Challenges in systematic reviews of economic analyses. *Annals of Internal Medicine* 2005;**142**:1073–9.

# COST-EFFECTIVENESS, COST–UTILITY AND COST-MINIMIZATION ANALYSES

Both cost-effectiveness and cost–utility analyses allow *incremental cost–effectiveness ratios* to be calculated (see Chapter 5.1). In both, the costs and savings are derived as outlined in Chapter 5.1, but the expressions of benefits differ between them. In a cost-effectiveness analysis the incremental benefits are expressed in so-called 'natural' units, while in a cost–utility analysis the benefits (and incremental benefits) are expressed as the gains in 'health utilities'. The third form of economic evaluation discussed in this chapter – cost minimization – can be used when two interventions have the same or very similar benefits, irrespective of whether these are expressed in natural units or as gains in health utilities.

## Cost-effectiveness analysis

The 'natural units' that can be used in cost-effectiveness analyses are numerous; some examples are shown in Table 5.2.1.[1–8] From the incremental costs and the incremental benefits expressed in these units, an incremental cost–effectiveness ratio can be estimated. Thus, for an intervention comparing the life-years gained (LYG) from two interventions (say, one new and one established), the incremental cost–effectiveness ratio would be calculated thus (see Chapter 5.1):

$$\text{Incremental cost–effectiveness ratio} = \frac{(\text{cost}_{new} - \text{cost}_{established})/}{(\text{LYG}_{new} - \text{LYG}_{established})}$$

**Table 5.2.1** Examples of effectiveness measures used in cost-effectiveness analyses[1]

| Clinical topic | Measure of effectiveness |
| --- | --- |
| Treatment of hypertension[2] | Reduction in blood pressure (mmHg) |
| Diagnosis of deep venous thrombosis[3] | Numbers of cases of deep venous thrombosis detected |
| Treatment of hypercholesterolaemia[4] | Reduction in serum cholesterol (mmol/L) |
| Asthma[5] | Episode-free days |
| Eradication of *Helicobacter pylori*[6] | Recurrence of duodenal ulceration |
| Family planning methods[7] | Pregnancies avoided per year |
| Secondary prevention of ischaemic heart disease with simvastatin[8] | Life-years saved |

An example of a cost-effectiveness analysis, based on the results of the Scandinavian Simvastatin Survival Study[9] (see Case study 1.4.1 in Chapter 1.4) is shown in Case study 5.2.1.[10] This shows the so-called 'base case' incremental cost–effectiveness ratio to be US$ 6768. The most significant assumptions used in reaching this estimate are indicated in the case study 5.2.1 but include:

- projecting life expectancy at the end of the trial (the mean follow-up in the trial was 5.4 years) to ten years;

- no additional costs for monitoring and office visits;
- the discount rate.

<table>
<tr><td colspan="2">Case study 5.2.1 Cost-effectiveness of simvastatin in the secondary prevention of coronary heart disease[8]</td></tr>
<tr><td>Background</td><td>The Scandinavian Simvastatin Survival Study (see Case study 1.4.1 in Chapter 1.4) showed a 30 per cent reduction in the relative risk of death (all causes) in the secondary prevention of myocardial infarction.[9] It also demonstrated a 26 per cent reduction in the rate of hospitalization for acute cardiovascular disease. These data were used to estimate the cost-effectiveness of simvastatin expressed as the cost (US$) per life-year gained.</td></tr>
<tr><td>Method</td><td>The following assumptions were used:<br><br>- The incremental cost of care was judged to be due solely to the drug, and it was assumed that all patients were under routine medical care.<br>- There were no differences in the trial in co-medications, and no extra costs for visits and tests were added.<br>- The costs of hospital admissions were calculated from the number of admissions by diagnostic group, and the standard cost of care in that group.<br>- Gain in life expectancy was calculated by addition of life-years saved during the trial to the difference in mortality at the end. The gain in life expectancy at the end of the trial of the trial was calculated assuming an average life expectancy of ten years.<br>- The expected total cost per patient for treatment with simvastatin was US$ 2532 over the study period.</td></tr>
<tr><td>Results</td><td>The total estimated gain in life expectancy was 0.054 years during the trial and 0.240 years after the trial. The 'base case' cost-effectiveness (cost per life-year saved) was US$ 6768. A sensitivity analysis for the assumptions used in the calculations were as follows:</td></tr>
</table>

|  | Incremental cost per life-year saved (US$) |
|---|---|
| Base case | 6768 |
| *Adjusting for life expectancy* |  |
| 8 years | 7692 |
| 12 years | 6132 |
| *Costs of initiating and monitoring* |  |
| Laboratory tests only | 8328 |
| Laboratory tests plus office visits | 11 532 |
| *Discount rate* |  |
| Costs at 10%, benefits at 10% | 9125 |
| Cost at 0%, benefits at 0% | 4740 |

<table>
<tr><td>Conclusions</td><td>By most standards, simvastatin appears to be cost-effective in the secondary prevention of coronary heart disease. This is achieved largely by assuming that its benefits are not immediately lost at the end of the trial. The adjustments for life expectancy do not make a substantial difference. Clearly, both the degree and the extent of monitoring, as well as assumptions about discount rates, can make a significant difference to the estimates of cost-effectiveness.</td></tr>
</table>

Several one-sided sensitivity analyses (see Chapter 5.1) were undertaken to assess the extent to which these assumptions might influence the results of the base case incremental cost–effectiveness ratio. It can be seen from Case study 5.2.1 that changing the projections of life expectancy to eight years or 12 years had only a modest impact. Including the estimated costs of laboratory monitoring tests and office visits, or changing the discount rates (for costs and benefits), however, had a much greater impact. Overall, the incremental cost–effectiveness ratio in Case study 5.2.1 ranged between US$ 4740 (£3078 at purchasing price parity or ppp) and US$ 11 532 (£7423 at ppp) per life-year gained, depending on the assumptions used in the economic model.

Two points are important from a scrutiny of these results. First, as is so often the case, the precise value of the incremental cost–effectiveness ratio is much less important than its range across the most plausible assumptions, as revealed by the sensitivity analyses. In this instance, although the range was more than twofold, the values are well within the threshold for cost-effectiveness of most developed countries. A decision-maker in these jurisdictions might reasonably conclude that simvastatin represents a good use of healthcare resources for the secondary prevention of myocardial infarction.

Second, if sensitivity analyses of the incremental cost–effectiveness ratios had indicated a very much wider range of, say, US$ 3000–60 000, then a decision-maker would have much greater difficulty in concluding that simvastatin is cost-effective. In such circumstances, the courses of action open to a decision-maker would include:

- seeking estimates of cost-effectiveness in specific patient subgroups, such as elderly people;
- obtaining, if possible, better estimates for the critical assumptions driving the incremental cost–effectiveness ratios at the extremes;
- deciding that simvastatin for this indication is cost-ineffective.

| **Case study 5.2.2** Cost-effectiveness of family planning methods[7,10] | |
|---|---|
| **Background** | Family planning services are one of the most highly utilized services in the British National Health Service. There have, however, been few empirical studies of the cost-effectiveness of various family planning methods. |
| **Methods** | The cost-effectiveness of different family planning methods was based on the cost per pregnancy avoided. The study compared the direct costs of provision with the number of pregnancies avoided relative to no method. |
| **Results** | The results (at 1991 prices) were as follows: |

| Contraception method | Cost per year (£) | Pregnancies avoided per year | Cost per pregnancy avoided (£) |
|---|---|---|---|
| Oral contraception | 111.43 | 0.82 | 135.89 |
| Diaphragm | 112.20 | 0.67 | 167.46 |
| Intrauterine device | 45.93* | 0.83 | 55.34 |
| Spermicide | 118.95 | 0.64 | 163.94 |
| Condom | 64.29 | 0.73 | 88.07 |
| Tubal ligation | 18.50** | 0.85 | 21.77 |
| Vasectomy | 15.51- | 0.85 | 18.25 |

*Discounted over 5 years.
**Discounted over lifetime of protection.

| **Discussion** | From the perspective of this study, family planning services are highly cost-effective. |
|---|---|

Case study 5.2.2 provides another example of the use of cost-effectiveness analysis in the evaluation of methods of family planning.[7,10] In this instance, however, the results were expressed as the cost per pregnancy avoided rather than as incremental cost–effectiveness ratios. It might appear, from a superficial examination of the results of this analysis, that the two irreversible methods of contraception (tubal ligation and vasectomy) should be preferred; this, however, would be erroneous.[10] If an individual's family-planning objective was to spread the intervals between successive pregnancies, then the irreversible methods would be irrelevant. Faced with the choice, however, an intrauterine device is clearly the most cost-effective form of reversible contraception and is what health economists describe as 'dominant'. For couples who have completed their families, tubal ligation for women and vasectomy for men are 'dominant'.

## Cost–utility analysis

In cost–utility analysis, the costs are derived in the same manner as in cost-effectiveness analysis. The benefits, however, are expressed as the gain in health reflected by improvement in the *health-related quality of life* multiplied by the time for which it is enjoyed. In cost–utility analysis the health-related quality of life is captured using a generic instrument with domains that are weighted in relation to preferences for particular health states.

A number of health-related quality-of-life instruments have been developed for cost–utility analyses,[1] but the one that has been used most widely is the EuroQol-5D (EQ-5D).[11] This provides a score ranging from 0 (dead) to 1 (perfect health) based on five dimensions – mobility, self-care, usual activities, pain/discomfort, and anxiety/depression (see Table 5.2.2). As can be seen from this table, each domain has three levels (no problems, some problems, major problems), making a total of 243 possible health states. Each of these 243 possible health states can be assigned a number or code. The number 12212 would mean that a particular respondent has:

■ no problems in walking about;

**Table 5.2.2** EuroQol-5D classification system

| Domain | Possible responses | Coefficients for tariff |
|---|---|---|
| Mobility | 1. No problems walking | |
| | 2. Some problems walking about | −0.069 |
| | 3. Confined to bed | −0.314 |
| Self-care | 1. No problems with self-care | |
| | 2. Some problems with washing or dressing self | −0.104 |
| | 3. Unable to wash or dress self | −0.214 |
| Usual activities | 1. No problems with performing usual activities (e.g. work, study, housework, family or leisure activities) | |
| | 2. Some problems with performing usual activities | −0.036 |
| | 3. Unable to perform usual activities | −0.094 |
| Pain/discomfort | 1. No pain or discomfort | |
| | 2. Moderate pain or discomfort | −0.123 |
| | 3. Extreme pain or discomfort | −0.386 |
| Anxiety/depression | 1. Not anxious or depressed | |
| | 2. Moderately anxious or depressed | −0.071 |
| | 3. Extremely anxious or depressed | −0.236 |

- some problems with washing or dressing themselves;
- some problems with performing their usual activities;
- no pain or discomfort;
- moderate anxiety or depression.

Such a number itself, however, would be meaningless as a single measure of a person's health state. If a person (as above) with the number 12212 changed as a result of the effects of an intervention to 21221, it would be uncertain as to whether this represented an improvement, no change or worsening: it would depend on the relative importance of switching from 'some problems with mobility' and 'no problems with self-care' to 'no problems with mobility' and 'some problems with self-care'.

Two approaches are available for converting this number into an index (from 0 to 1). The EuroQol visual analogue scale (EQ-VAS) asks respondents to mark their current state of health on a 100 mm vertical line with boundaries of 'worst imaginable health state' to 'best imaginable health state'. The difficulty with the EQ-VAS is that if a respondent marks the scale at 25 mm on one occasion and at 50 mm on another, are they now twice as healthy? Likewise, is moving from 0 mm to 25 mm the same as changing from 25 mm to 50 mm?

The alternative, and favoured, approach is to convert the EQ-5D profile into an index based on preferences. In this, the health states are weighted according to the preferences obtained from a random sample of around 3000 members of the UK adult population[12] using the *time trade-off* technique. These coefficients, or 'tariffs', are shown in Table 5.2.2. As can be seen from the table, the tariff for 'extreme pain or discomfort' is substantially greater than that for 'unable to perform usual activities'.

The calculation of an EQ-5D index or score is obtained by serially subtracting the relevant tariffs from 1 (see Table 5.2.3). For technical reasons, a respondent with *any* dysfunction attracts a reduction in the index of 0.081; and anyone with a level 3 response for one or more dimensions attracts an additional reduction of 0.269. Health state 12212 would therefore give rise to an EQ-5D index of 0.708. Multiplying the EQ-5D index by the number of years for which it is enjoyed provides the quality-adjusted life-years (QALYs) gained. The health-related quality of life as captured by the EQ-5D index may, of course, decline during the period for which it is enjoyed, but this can be incorporated in the calculation of the QALY gained. The QALY gained can, of course, also be discounted (see Chapter 5.1).

**Table 5.2.3** Calculation of the EuroQol-5D (EQ-5D) score for state 12212 by subtracting the relevant coefficients from 1.000

| Dimension | Coefficient for the tariff | Cumulative score |
|---|---|---|
| Perfect health | | 1.000 |
| Constant term for any dysfunctional state | −0.081 | 0.919 |
| Mobility: level 1 | 0 | 0.919 |
| Self–care: level 2 | −0.104 | 0.815 |
| Usual activities: level 2 | −0.036 | 0.779 |
| Pain or discomfort: level 1 | 0 | 0.779 |
| Anxiety of depression: level 2 | −0.071 | 0.708 |
| Level 3 in any one dimension | 0 | 0.708 |
| Score | | 0.708 |

From the estimate of the QALY gained, the incremental cost–effectiveness ratio, comparing one (new) intervention with another (established) intervention, can be calculated as discussed in Chapter 5.1:

$$\text{Incremental cost–effectiveness ratio} = \frac{(\text{cost}_{new} - \text{cost}_{established})/}{(\text{QALY gained}_{new} - \text{QALY gained}_{established})}$$

## Cost-minimization analysis

In some instances two interventions may be shown (or assumed to be) equally effective. Case study 5.2.3, which shows evidence of the therapeutic equivalence of intravenous and oral fludarabine, is an example.[13] In this instance, the only cost difference was related to the cost of administration. The preference for oral versus intravenous fludarabine is self-evident. In this study, however, it was assumed (based on expert evidence) that *adverse event* rates would be similar between the two treatments. A sensitivity analysis showed that the adverse event rate with oral fludarabine would have to be tenfold greater than with intravenous fludarabine in order for the conclusions about cost-effectiveness to change.

| **Case study 5.2.3** Comparison of intravenous and oral fludarabine in the treatment of B-cell chronic lymphatic leukaemia[13] | |
|---|---|
| **Background** | On aggregate, the available evidence suggests that intravenous fludarabine is effective in the second-line treatment of B-cell chronic lymphatic leukaemia. Oral fludarabine is bioequivalent to intravenous fludarabine and, in an uncontrolled study, produced response rates similar to those achieved with intravenous fludarabine in B-cell chronic lymphatic leukaemia. A cost-minimization analysis was therefore performed. |
| **Method** | Based on an average of 4.1 treatment cycles per patient, the direct medical costs were derived from a combination of data derived from the UK's healthcare resource groups, the results of previous clinical audits and expert opinion. |
| **Results** | The estimated costs (£) of treatment with intravenous and oral fludarabine were estimated to be as follows: |

|  | **Intravenous fludarabine** | **Oral fludarabine** |
|---|---|---|
| Drug acquisition | 2665 | 2665 |
| Administration | 2617 | 299 |
| Prophylaxis | 114 | 114 |
| Monitoring | 369 | 369 |
| Adverse events | 267 | 267 |
| Total | 6032 | 3714 |

| **Discussion** | On the basis that intravenous and oral fludarabine are clinically equivalent, use of the latter is to be preferred. |
|---|---|

# Discussion

The terminology used here in describing cost-effectiveness and cost-utility analyses is not uniformly applied. The nomenclature adopted in this chapter is used extensively in the UK literature, but in the USA the term 'cost–utility analysis' is, confusingly, sometimes included in the term 'cost-effectiveness analysis'.

Cost-effectiveness analysis, in the sense used in this book, has the advantage of simplicity, and the natural units are those that usually will have been derived from studies of an intervention's clinical *effectiveness*. Indeed, the primary outcome measure in the clinical studies is typically used (as in Case study 5.2.1) as the denominator in the estimation of the incremental cost–effectiveness ratio. Cost-effectiveness analysis, however, has four disadvantages:[1]

- The outcomes (apart from life-years gained) are specific to particular clinical programmes. Consequently, cost-effectiveness analysis cannot be used to compare the cost-effectiveness of two different interventions for two separate conditions.
- Decision-makers with finite resources not only have to determine whether a new intervention is cost-effective but also may have to determine where reductions can be made to free up resources. Cost-effectiveness analysis cannot typically address the issue of the *opportunity cost* of funding new programmes or interventions.
- With any one programme or intervention there is often more than one outcome of interest. Indeed, there are often a number of relevant outcomes, including extensions to life, health-related quality of life and potentially harmful (adverse) effects.
- Some outcomes are more important – or more valued – than others.

Cost–utility analysis was developed to overcome these limitations.[1] It provides a method through which a broad range of relevant outcomes can be incorporated into a single measure. This, in turn, allows broad comparisons to be made between different programmes and interventions. In addition, it weights outcomes so that those more highly prized are given greater prominence.

Cost–utility analysis, and particularly the use of the EQ-5D index, has been criticized:

- The EQ-5D may not necessarily capture all the components of health-related quality of life that are important to some patients with specific conditions. There is some truth in this. The EQ-5D probably fails to capture the lethargy that is common, although often ignored by clinicians, in conditions such as multiple sclerosis. Moreover, it is relatively insensitive at incorporating all the consequences of cognitive impairment, and it may fail to capture some of the health-related consequences of sensory impairment such as blindness and deafness. Because of these limitations, it is incumbent on decision-makers to assess the extent to which, in specific circumstances, the EQ-5D may have underestimated the decrement in a patient's quality of life and to use their judgement in accepting the findings at face value. This important issue is discussed further in Chapter 6.1.
- It has been pointed out that the use of the QALY is inherently utilitarian.[10] The EQ-5D gives equal weight to a change from 0.4 to 0.6 (a 50 per cent increase in health-related quality of life) as to a change from 0.7 to 0.9 (less than a 30 per cent increase in health-related quality of life). In other words, it is implicit in the approach that a QALY is a QALY is a QALY, irrespective as to who gains. Empirical evidence indicates that this is probably wrong. At least in a publicly funded healthcare system such as Britain's National Health Service, society appears to have a diminishing marginal valuation

for improvements in healthcare, and the social value is greater for those patients with worse lifetime health prospects.[12] It has been suggested that these difficulties might be resolved by weighting QALYs to take account of such societal preferences. This could, for example, be used to increase the QALY gained and hence reduce the incremental cost–effectiveness ratio for interventions that prolong life at the end of life. This would be particularly relevant to the economic evaluation of, for example, interventions for advanced malignant disease producing, say, an additional six months extra life. Such an approach could be adopted but the methods to develop reliable equity weightings have yet to emerge. Nevertheless, decision-makers may need to take some of these issues into account when deciding on whether a high-cost intervention should be made available. This is discussed further in Chapter 6.1.

- Some believe that the estimation of a cost per QALY gained is needlessly complicated. Others believe it to be too simplistic and have developed alternative, more complex metrics such as 'healthy-years equivalents' and 'disability-adjusted life-years'. These and other methods have, however, gained little traction among health economists internationally.

- It has been suggested that QALYs are inherently ageist and discriminate against elderly people. This might be theoretically possible in the case of an extremely expensive intervention, such as a procedure applied on one occasion with a lifelong beneficial effect.[14] In such circumstances it is possible that young people might enjoy these effects more than older people. In practice it is hard to identify such a single intervention that is so costly.[14] Many interventions, especially pharmaceuticals, are continued for the duration of their benefits. Indeed, because the *absolute risk reductions* (see Chapter 1.4) of many interventions are often so much greater in elderly people, older people are almost invariably advantaged by the use of QALYs gained.

- The EQ-5D and similar generic measures of health-related quality of life have been criticized because they take too narrow a view of the potential benefits of an intervention for patients and their families. This criticism, of course, is inherent in the debate about what *economic perspective* should be adopted in the economic evaluation of interventions (see Chapter 5.1) rather than any inherent flaw in cost–utility analysis.

Cost-minimization analysis is attractive to decision-makers because the results and conclusions are so obvious and uncontroversial. The difficulty in its application, however, is the assumption of therapeutic equivalence. Some economists regard the demonstration of equivalence as so challenging as to suggest that cost minimization is outmoded.[15] Although equivalence is, indeed, sometimes challenging to demonstrate, it is nonetheless possible (see Chapter 2.1). Decision-makers confronted by a cost-minimization analysis should examine its basis but not reject the approach out of hand.

The details of the methodologies underpinning both cost-effectiveness and cost–utility analysis can be complex and challenging. But, as has been argued by Sculpher and colleagues,[16] economic evaluation needs to focus on tackling the needs of decision-makers rather than the principles of welfare economics, and to become less concerned with economic evaluation but more involved with 'just evaluation for decision-making'. Decision-makers could hardly ask for more.

# References

1. Drummond MF, Sculpher MJ, Torrance GW, *et al. Methods for the Economic Evaluation of Health Care Programmes*, 3rd edn. Oxford: Oxford University Press, 2005.

*Therapeutics, evidence and decision-making*

2. Logan AG, Milne BJ, Achber C, *et al*. Cost effectiveness of a worksite hypertension treatment programme. *Hypertension* 1981;**3**:211–18.

3. Hull RD, Hirsh J, Sackett DL, Stoddart GL. Cost effectiveness of clinical diagnosis, venography and non-invasive testing in patients with symptomatic deep vein thrombosis. *New England Journal of Medicine* 1981;**304**:1561–7.

4. Schulman KA, Kinosian B, Jacobson JA, *et al*. Reducing high blood cholesterol level with drugs. *Journal of the American Medical Association* 1990;**264**:3025–33.

5. Sculpher MJ, Buxton MJ. The episode-free day as a composite measure of effectiveness. *Pharmacoeconomics* 1993;**4**:345–52.

6. O'Brien B, Goeree R, Mohamed AH, Hunt R. Cost effectiveness of *Helicobacter pylori* eradication for the long-term management of duodenal ulcer in Canada. *Archives of Internal Medicine* 1995;**155**:1958–64.

7. Hughes D, McGuire A. The cost effectiveness of family planning service provision. *Journal of Public Health Medicine* 1996;**18**:189–96.

8. Johannesson M, Jönsson B, Kjekshus J, *et al*. Cost effectiveness of simvastatin treatment to lower cholesterol levels in patients with coronary heart disease. *New England Journal of Medicine* 1997;**336**:332–6.

9. Scandinavian Simvastatin Survival Study Group. Randomized trial of cholesterol lowering in 4444 patients with coronary heart disease: the Scandinavian Simvastatin Survival Study (4S). *Lancet* 1994;**344**:1383–9.

10. Morris S, Devlin N, Parkin D. *Economic Analysis in Health Care*. Chichester: John Wiley & Sons, 2007.

11. Szende A, Oppe M, Devlin N. *EQ-5D Value Sets: Inventory, Comparative Review and User Guide*. Dordrecht: Springer, 2007.

12. Dolan P, Shaw R, Tsuchiya A, Williams A. QALY maximisation and peoples' preferences: a methodological review. *Health Economics* 2005;**14**:197–208.

13. National Institute for Health and Clinical Excellence. *Guidance on the Use of Fludarabine for B-Cell Chronic Lymphatic Leukaemia*. Technology appraisal guidance 29. London: National Institute for Health and Clinical Excellence, 2001.

14. Rawlins MD, Dillon A. NICE discrimination. *Journal of Medical Ethics*. 2005;**31**:373–5.

15. Briggs AH, O'Brien BJ. The death of cost minimisation? *Journal of Health Economics* 2001;**10**:179–84.

16. Sculpher MJ, Claxton K, Akehurst RL. It's just evaluation for decision making: recent developments in, and challenges for, cost-effectiveness research. In: Smith PC, Ginnelly L, Sculpher M (eds). *Health Policy and Economics: Opportunities and Challenges*. Milton Keynes: Open University Press, 2004.

# COST–CONSEQUENCES ANALYSIS

A cost–consequences analysis has been defined as an analysis 'in which costs and effects are calculated but not aggregated into quality-adjusted life-years or cost–effectiveness ratios'.[1] It comprises a listing of all the relevant costs and outcomes (i.e. consequences), which, depending on the *economic perspective*, may include (see Chapter 5.1):

■ direct medical and non-medical costs;
■ indirect costs;
■ clinical outcomes.

An example of a cost–consequences analysis is shown in Case study 5.3.1. In a randomized controlled trial comparing zidovudine alone with zidovudine plus lamivudine in patients with human immunodeficiency virus (HIV) infection, the combination convincingly reduced the rate of progression of the disease and improved survival.[2] During this trial, the investigators also captured the use of healthcare resources, and this formed the basis of a cost–consequences analysis.[3] The results summarized in Case study 5.3.1 showed reductions in disease progression, the number of HIV-related infections and mortality. There was also a reduction in the use of healthcare resources (including the number of admissions to hospital, additional out-patient visits and additional prescribed medication).

The estimated costs associated with these gains over one year ranged from an increase of US$ 371 to a saving of US$ 353. The uncertainty in this estimate was due to differences in estimates of the costs of the length of stay in hospital. At any event, even if the costs of combination therapy represent a modest increase compared with zidovudine alone, a decision-maker might reasonably conclude that the clinical benefits outweighed these additional, relatively modest costs. This is especially so given that the average annual costs at that time of treating a person with HIV ranged from US$ 6015 to US$ 29 000, depending on the stage of the disease.

## Discussion

Cost–consequences analysis is not popular among many health economists, and it is not mentioned in either of the two most popular textbooks on health economics.[4,5] This is probably because the approach is more akin to accounting than economics. Indeed, a cost–consequences analysis has sometimes been described as providing a 'business case' for health service managers.

Cost–consequences analysis has both advantages and disadvantages. For some health economists the outputs, in the form of a tabulation of costs and outcomes, fail to provide a secure basis for a fair comparison of two alternative treatments. Indeed, the method provides no *incremental cost–effectiveness ratio* and so is unable to make a formal examination of two competing courses of action; it also offers little to assist decision-makers in comparing different interventions for different conditions. Moreover, there is a tendency for cost–consequences analysis to lack clarity over the classification of

**Case study 5.3.1** Cost–consequences analysis of combining lamivudine with zidovudine in the treatment of human immunodeficiency virus (HIV) infection[3]

| | |
|---|---|
| **Background** | The CAESAR trial was a 1-year randomized controlled trial comparing the effects of adding lamivudine with zidovudine to zidovudine alone in the treatment of HIV infection.[2] The results showed the combination to be associated with a slower rate of progression (hazard ratio 0.42, 95% CI 0.32 to 0.57) and a significant survival benefit (hazard ratio 0.40, 95% CI 0.23 to 0.69). |

**Methods** As an integral part of the study, selected healthcare resource utilization was obtained. These related to the costs of:

- HIV-related illness;
- adverse events.

The health consequences for the trial period included:

- disease progression;
- new or recurrent HIV-related illness events.

The healthcare resource use consequences for the trial period included one or more:

- hospital stays (costs derived from various alternative sources);
- unscheduled outpatient visits;
- new prescribed medications.

**Results** The results expressed as the additional costs and consequences of managing 100 patients are shown below:

| | Placebo | Lamivudine | Difference |
|---|---|---|---|
| Total costs (US$ × 100) | 5312 to 6307 | 5683 to 5954 | −353 to +371 |
| In-patient costs | 4572 to 5566 | 2703 to 2975 | −1869 to −2591 |
| Out-patient costs | 56 | 42 | −14 |
| Medication costs | 564 | 525 | −39 |
| Lamivudine costs | 120* | 2413 | +2293 |
| *Rate of progression* | | | |
| Disease progression | 20 | 9 | −11 |
| No. of HIV-related events | 68 | 41 | −27 |
| Deaths | 6 | 3 | −3 |
| *Resource use (one or more)* | | | |
| Patient admissions | 11 | 6 | −5 |
| Extra out-patient visits | 15 | 10 | −5 |
| Prescribed medication | 43 | 30 | −13 |

*Some patients randomized to zidovudine alone were given lamivudine as rescue medication to treat HIV-related complications.

**Discussion** The authors claim the findings indicate that treatments that slow the progression of HIV infection have the potential to reduce the monthly costs associated with HIV-related illness and adverse events.

negative and positive costs and consequences. This may lead to inconsistencies with other forms of economic evaluation.[6]

Proponents claim, however, that the format is readily understandable and more easily applied.[7] By explicitly displaying and contrasting different options in tabular form, it is suggested that the approach allows decision-makers on behalf of society to impute their own values to these costs and consequences.[8] According to this view, cost–consequences analysis allows decision-makers to see clearly what has been included and omitted; where information is quantitative; where information is based on qualitative findings; and the implications for equity and need.[8]

A less polarized approach suggests that cost–consequences analysis can be useful in supplementing cost–utility analysis under two circumstances.[6] First, it may enable decisions to be better communicated to stakeholders and the public. Second, it may be able to provide a more easily understood reason for decisions rather than relying solely on an estimated cost per quality-adjusted life-year gained to a sceptical audience.

Cost–consequences analysis is simple and quick to perform. It has been adopted by the National Institute for Health and Clinical Excellence (NICE) in the assessment of new medical technologies (particularly devices and diagnostics) that appear to be therapeutically equivalent to comparators.[9]

In the assessment of interventions where the economic evaluation has been undertaken using cost–consequences analysis, decision-makers should exercise caution but not outright hostility.

## References

1. Russell LB, Gold MR, Siegel JE, *et al.* The role of cost effectiveness analysis in health care and medicine. *Journal of the American Medical Association* 1996;**276**:1172.
2. CAESAR Coordinating Committee. Randomised trial of lamivudine or lamivudine plus loviride to zidovudine-containing regimens for patients with HIV-1 infection: the CAESAR trial. *Lancet* 1997;**349**:1413–21.
3. Lacey L, Mauskopf J, Lindrooth R, *et al.* A prospective cost-consequences analysis of adding lamivudine to zidovudine-containing antiretroviral treatment regimens for HIV infection in the US. *Pharmacoeconomics* 1999;**15**(Suppl. 1):23–37.
4. Drummond MF, Sculpher MJ, Torrance GW, *et al. Methods for the Evaluation of Health Care Programmes.* Oxford: Oxford University Press, 2005.
5. Morris S, Devlin N, Parkin D. *Economic Analysis in Health Care.* Chichester: John Wiley & Sons, 2007.
6. Mauskopf JA, Paul JE, Grant DM, Stergachis A. The role of cost consequence analysis in healthcare decision-making. *Pharmacoeconomics* 1998;**13**:277–88.
7. Coast J. Is economic evaluation in touch with society's health values? *BMJ* 2004;**329**:1233–6.
8. National Institute for Health and Clinical Excellence. Evaluation pathway programme for medical technologies: methods guide. London: National Institute for Health and Clinical Excellence, 2010.
9. Chalkidou K, Culyer A, Naidoo B, Littlejohns P. Cost effective public health guidance: asking questions from the decision-maker's viewpoint. *Health Economics* 2008;**17**:441–8.

*Therapeutics, evidence and decision-making*

# SECTION 6
# Decision-making

# FOR INDIVIDUALS

*Nothing about me without me.* Delbanco *et al.*[1]

The principles of rational therapeutics were enshrined in the 1984 Nairobi Declaration.[2] Its cardinal features assert that the rational use of interventions involves providing the right patient the right intervention at the right dose (in the case of pharmaceuticals), at an affordable cost.

## The patient

The prerequisite for the effective use of any form of therapeutic intervention is a reliable diagnosis. An accurate diagnosis ensures that a patient is not offered unnecessarily an intervention that is ineffective or dangerous. There are, of course, circumstances when interventions are used in the absence of a clear diagnosis. Examples include the symptomatic treatment of severe pain and the initiation of 'blind' antimicrobial therapy in a person with suspected meningococcal meningitis.

In some instances a particular intervention is effective only in subgroups of individuals with a particular disorder. Targeting therapy in such a way is not new. Appropriate antimicrobial therapy has, for many years, been based wherever possible on the nature of the infectious agent and its sensitivity pattern. Advances in genomic medicine and molecular biology, however, are leading to redefinitions of disease and a more personalized approach to therapeutics.[3] Trastuzumab, for instance, is effective only in women with breast cancer whose tumour cells express the human epidermal growth factor 2 (Her2) receptor.[4] Similarly, the effects of cetuximab on overall survival in individuals with advanced colorectal cancer are dependent on the presence of the wild-type Kras epidermal growth factor receptor rather than the mutated form:[5] the *hazard ratio* for overall survival was 0.55 (95% confidence interval (CI) 0.41 to 0.74) in tumours expressing the wild-type Kras, compared with 0.98 (95% CI 0.70 to 1.37) in tumours expressing the mutated form.

## The intervention

There are three elements to offering the right intervention. First, there should be reasonable confidence that the intervention is likely to be effective in the particular circumstances. Second, the balance between the intervention's benefits and *harms* should be appropriate. Third, the decision should take account of the preferences of the patient and their families. The evidential base for clinical *effectiveness* has been discussed at length in previous chapters. Balancing benefits and harms, and the closely related issue of patient preference and choice, are, in some respects, more difficult.

### Clinical issues

For licensed (authorized) pharmaceutical products, the indications granted by the relevant drug regulatory authority provide a broad assessment of the balance between benefits **201** and harms. This is less so for devices because not only are the requirements for licensure less rigorous in some markets than others, but also the skill of the interventionalist may be important in determining success or failure. This latter consideration applies even more forcefully to interventional procedures where the technical competence of the operator plays an even larger role.

With pharmaceuticals in particular, other clinical factors may be important, even when their proposed usage falls within their licensed indications. These include, for example, the patient's age and the presence of comorbidities, both of which may impinge on the benefits or harms of an intervention.

For a few pharmaceutical products it is now possible to prevent type B adverse reactions (see Chapter 2.4) using genetic approaches. For example, abacavir, a reverse-transcriptase inhibitor used in the treatment of human immunodeficiency virus (HIV)/acquired immunodeficiency syndrome (AIDS), causes an acute multisystem hypersensitivity reaction in about five per cent of patients. Symptoms usually occur within six weeks of starting treatment and the reaction can be fatal.[6] There is now clear evidence of a close association between a genetic variation in the HLA-B region (HLA-B*5701) and the development of hypersensitivity to abacavir, with an *odds ratio* of 117 (95% CI 29 to 481).[7] Screening for the HLA-B*5701 haplotype substantially reduces the *incidence* of this reaction.[8] Routine prior testing is now recommended to be carried out before starting therapy with abacavir.[9]

## Patient choice

Patients generally want to be involved in decisions about the use of therapeutic interventions.[10] They have a right to know what treatment options are available, and the risks and benefits of each.[11] Autonomy overrides beneficence in all but exceptional circumstances. There is also increasing evidence that shared decision-making results in better outcomes.

There is evidence that there are differences in treatment preferences between patients and health professionals.[12] The magnitude and direction of these differences is, however, inconsistent across clinical conditions. Patients with malignant disease, for example, are much more willing than oncologists to accept intensive treatment with severe adverse effects for modest benefits.[13] By contrast, patients with hypertension seek greater benefits in relation to the cardiovascular events that are avoided than their family physicians.[14]

Shared decision-making has been defined as 'a process in which patients are involved as active partners with the clinician in clarifying acceptable medical options and in choosing a preferred course of action'.[15] Shared decision-making is particularly important when there is more than one reasonable course of action, including no treatment or supportive care, and where no single option is best for everyone.[16] It involves a two-way exchange between the patient and the healthcare professional. The healthcare professional provides expert information. The patient shares personal information about their social circumstances, their attitudes to illness and risk, and their values and preferences.[16]

Expert information can be verbal or supplemented from written or other sources. Decision aids that have been used include audiotapes, computer programs, videos, websites and structured interviews.[17,18] Systematic reviews indicate that such decision aids increase patients' knowledge of management choices without increasing anxiety or conflict. They also assist in promoting participatory decision-making.[17] In a randomized controlled trial of women with menorrhagia, the addition of a structured interview (as well as providing them with a booklet and videotape) reduced both hysterectomy rates and costs without any adverse effects on health status two years later.[19]

Not all patients, however, wish to take part in shared decision-making.[20–22] Although many patients wish to learn of the options available, there are also many patients who do not want to take active responsibility for the final decision. Factors associated with these preferences include age and the type of clinical problem. Older people are less likely to want to be involved in clinical decision-making. People with life-threatening events also tend to be more passive about making choices.

# The dose

For pharmaceuticals, appropriate drug dosages will usually have been determined during the original development programme. Drug doses and dosage regimens may be fixed or adjusted (titrated).

## Fixed dosage regimens

In adults, many pharmaceutical interventions can be prescribed at fixed dosages. Examples include aspirin for the secondary prevention of myocardial infarction, bendroflumethiazide for the treatment of hypertension and amoxicillin for uncomplicated lower urinary tract infection. The doses of many pharmaceutical products for the treatment of malignant disease are based on body size as reflected by a patient's surface area. In some instances, dose reductions may be necessary in patients with renal impairment (for products such as digoxin undergoing predominantly renal excretion) and for those with reduced hepatic function (for products eliminated mainly by liver metabolism). In children, fixed dosage regimens are generally adjusted in relation to body weight or age.

## Titrated dose regimens

For some pharmaceutical products there are wide interindividual differences in the response to any given dose. This may be due to differences in the rate of metabolism or differences in target organ sensitivity.

Traditionally, in these circumstances drug dosages have been titrated against the response as assessed clinically (such as the magnitude of the reduction in blood pressure in the treatment of hypertension) or symptomatically (such as the extent of pain relief with analgesics). For many drugs, a major cause of the variability in response is due to genetic differences in the rate of metabolism. In a few instances, dosages can be guided by monitoring plasma drug concentrations.

There is increasing interest, however, in predicting dose requirements using appropriate genetic tests before starting treatment, to maximize *efficacy* and minimize *toxicity*. At present this is available in only a few instances during routine clinical care, but many people anticipate that these techniques will become used more widely in the future. Indeed, a patient's thiopurine methyltransferase activity is now routinely measured before starting treatment with mercaptopurine or azathioprine.[23] A pharmacogenetic algorithm based on the genotypic variants of a specific cytochrome P450 (CYP2C9) and vitamin K epoxide reductase (VKORC1) has been developed to predict warfarin dose requirements.[24] Whether this approach to predicting warfarin dosage is cost-effective remains uncertain.[25]

# Affordable cost

In healthcare systems where the costs of an intervention fall largely on the patient, the price of its acquisition and administration will be a significant issue. High medication costs in the USA are strongly associated with the underuse of medication.[26] Indeed, in a US survey carried out in 2003, 25 per cent of older patients cited cost as a factor for not taking their medicines as prescribed,[27] and yet doctor–patient discussions about the out-of-pocket costs of medicines occur infrequently in the USA.[28,29] This is despite the fact that co-payments are substantially higher in the USA than in most other developed countries.

In countries where healthcare is funded from general taxation or by social insurance schemes, the acquisition costs of an intervention to an individual patient are less of an issue. Nevertheless, patients may still seek interventions that are not covered by their healthcare provider, either because they are regarded as too costly for the healthcare system in relation to the benefits they bring, or because they are considered to be inappropriate for reimbursement. In these circumstances shared decision-making needs to include discussions about costs as well as benefits and harms.

# Discussion

The current approach to decision-making for individual patients leaves much to be desired. The choice of intervention and, in the case of pharmaceuticals, the appropriate dose remains crude.

Over the next decade personalized medicine coupled with increasingly sophisticated electronic medical records holds great promise. The electronic medical record of the future will capture individuals' clinical data and will have the capacity to hold an individual's whole genome scan. This will promote better medical decision-making by patients and doctors and improve preventive care.

This approach will allow the use of knowledge that is currently available but impractical to adopt into routine clinical practice. For example, the *relative risk* of deep venous thrombosis in women receiving oral contraceptives is 3.8 (95% CI 2.4 to 6.0). In women with the factor V Leiden mutation, the relative risk of venous thrombosis (compared with women without the mutation and not taking oral contraceptives) is 34.7 (95% CI 7.8 to 154).[30] It might appear reasonable, therefore, for women to be screened for the factor V Leiden mutation before embarking on oral contraceptive treatment. A cost-effectiveness analysis[31] assuming that all women would be screened at the age of 20 years indicates that the cost per life-year saved would amount to an unaffordable US$4.8 million. Whole genome scans as part of a patient's electronic medical record will inevitably include information such as the existence of the factor V Leiden mutation. No additional screening tests would be necessary, and the identification of women at risk of developing venous thrombosis with oral contraceptives would be automatic.

A more complex situation exists with respect to resistance to antiplatelet drugs. Despite the unquestioned benefits of these interventions in the prevention of recurrent vascular events, some patients fail to respond to aspirin ('aspirin resistance') or to clopidogrel ('clopidogrel resistance').[32] It has been postulated that the heterogeneity of the therapeutic response to these agents may be determined by at least ten different genes.[32] Clearly, it would be impractical to screen routinely for each of these genes before embarking on treatment with one or other of these antiplatelet agents. However, the availability of whole genome scans within patients' electronic medical records will enable aspirin and clopidogrel resistance to be recognized automatically.

Although the medical record of the future has the potential to resolve many of the technical difficulties of individualizing the use of interventions, achieving shared decision-making will require a better dialogue between patients and healthcare professionals. There are unquestionable advantages in this shared approach to decision-making, but significant challenges persist in implementation. Some physicians may prefer to retain the imbalance of power between themselves and their patients. Patients may also be reluctant to ask questions or challenge their physicians.[33] Patients may believe that the physician is more knowledgeable and powerful and may be content to leave choices to doctors. Patients may also fear that the doctor will be angered by their questions and consider them as too challenging. Even those physicians who are sympathetic to the principles of shared decision-making may lack the skills to do it effectively. During their training, physicians are provided with little education about being interactive and inclusive with patients.[34]

Some patients do not wish to participate in shared decision-making. This is their privilege. They should not be bullied or cajoled into doing so against their will.[35] In this context it is disappointing that so many bodies regulating the health professions (including those in Australia, New Zealand, the USA and the UK) assert that 'a patient is not really acting rationally unless they share the ruling life-plan view of autonomy'.[35] There are, of course, occasional circumstances when a patient's autonomy cannot take precedence. One example would be the management of an acute psychotic episode. But autonomy should generally be respected, 'even when it means that a person has autonomously opted to delegate their autonomy to their physician or other health professional'.[35]

## References

1. Delbanco T, Berwick DM, Boufford MD, *et al.* Healthcare in a land called PeoplePower: nothing about me without me. *Health Expectations* 2001;**4**:144–50.
2. Rawlins M, Vale A. Drug therapy and poisoning. In: Kumar PJ, Clarke M (eds). *Clinical Medicine*. Edinburgh: Elsevier, 2005.
3. Bell JA. *Redefining Disease*. London: Royal College of Physicians, 2010.
4. Hudis CA. Trastuzumab: mechanism of action and use in clinical practice. *New England Journal of Medicine* 2007;**357**:39–51.
5. Karapetis CS, Khambata-Ford S, Jonker DJ, *et al. K-ras* mutations and benefit from cetuximab in advanced colorectal cancer. *New England Journal of Medicine* 2008;**359**:1757–65.
6. Hetherington S, McGuirk S, Powell G, *et al.* Hypersensitivity reactions during therapy with the nucleoside reverse transcriptase inhibitor abacavir. *Clinical Therapeutics* 2001;**23**:1603–14.
7. Mallal S, Nolan D, Witt C, *et al.* Association between the presence of HLA-B*5701, HLA-DR7 and HLA-DQ3 and hypersensitivity to HIV-1 reverse transcriptase inhibitor abacavir. *Lancet* 2002;**359**:727–32.
8. Mallal S, Phillips E, Carosi G, *et al.* HLA-B*5701 screening the hypersensitivity to abacavir. *New England Journal of Medicine* 2008;**358**:568–79.
9. Food and Drug Administration. Abacavir (marketed as Ziagen) and abacavir-containing medications. FDA Alert 24 July 2008.
10. Coulter A. Patients as decision-makers. In: Dixon A (eds). *Engaging Patients in their Health: How the NHS Needs to Change*. London: King's Fund, 2008.

11. Kravtiz RL, Melniokow J. Engaging patients in medical decision-making. *BMJ* 2001;**323**:584–5.

12. Montgomery AA, Fahey T. How do treatment preferences compare with those of clinicians? *Quality in Health Care* 2001;**10**:i39–43.

13. Slevin M, Stubbs L, Plant HJ, *et al*. Attitudes to chemotherapy: comparing views of patients with cancer with those of doctors, nurses and general public. *BMJ* 1990;**300**:1458–60.

14. McAlister F, O'Connor AM, Wells G, *et al*. When should hypertension be treated? The different perspectives of Canadian physicians and patients. *Canadian Medical Association Journal* 2000;**163**:403–8.

15. Sheridan SL, Harris RP, Woolf SH. Shared decision making about screening and chemoprevention: a suggested approach from the US Preventive Task Force. *American Journal of Preventive Medicine* 2004;**26**:56–66.

16. Askham J, Coulter A, Parsons S. Where are the patients in decision-making about their own care? Copenhagen: World Health Organization Regional Office for Europe, 2008.

17. O'Connor AM, Rostom A, Fiset V, *et al*. Decision aids for patients facing screening decisions: a systematic review. *BMJ* 1999;**319**:731–4.

18. Molenaar S, Sprangers MAG, Postma-Schuit FCE, *et al*. Interpretive review: feasibility and effects of decision aids. *Medical Decision Making* 2000;**20**:112–27.

19. Kennedy ADM, Sculpher MJ, Coulter A, *et al*. Effect of decision aids for menorrhagia on treatment choices, health outcomes and costs. *Journal of the American Medical Association* 2002;**288**:2701–8.

20. Robinson A, Thomson R. Variability in patient preferences for participating in decision making: implications for the use of decision support tools. *Quality in Health Care* 2001;**10**(Suppl. 1):i34–8.

21. Levinson W, Kao A, Kuby A, Thisted RA. Not all patients want to participate in decision making. *Journal of General and Internal Medicine* 2005;**20**:531–5.

22. Bastiaens H, van Royen P, Pavlic V, Baker R. Older people's preferences for involvement in their own care: a qualitative study in primary health care in 11 European countries. *Patient Education and Counseling* 2007;**68**:33–42.

23. Pirmohamed M. The applications of pharmacogenetics to prescribing: what is currently known? *Clinical Medicine* 2009;**9**:493–5.

24. International Warfarin Pharmacogenetics Consortium. Estimation of warfarin dose with clinical and pharmacogenetic data. *New England Journal of Medicine* 2009;**360**:753–64.

25. Verhoef TI, Redekop WK, Darba J, *et al*. A systematic review of cost effectiveness analyses of pharmacogenetic-guided dosing in treatment with coumarin derivatives. *Pharmacogenomics* 2010;**11**:989–1002.

26. Piette JD, Heisler M, Wagner TH. Cost-related medication underuse among chronically ill adults: the treatments people forgo, how often, and who is at risk. *American Journal of Public Health* 2004;**94**:1782–7.

27. Safran DG, Neuman P, Schoen C, *et al*. Prescription drug coverage and seniors: findings from a 2003 national survey. *Health Affairs* 2005;**Jan–Jun;Suppl. Web Exclusives**:W5-152–66.

28. Alexander GC, Casalino LP, Meltzer DO. Patient–physician communication about out-of-pocket costs. *Journal of the American Medical Association* 2003;**290**:953–8.

29. Tarn DM, Paterniti DA, Heritage J, *et al*. Physician communication about the cost and acquisition of newly prescribed medications. *American Journal of Managed Care* 2006;**12**:657–64.

30. Vandenbroucke JP, Koster T, Rosendaal FR, *et al.* Increased risk of venous thrombosis in oral contraceptive users who are carriers of factor V Leiden mutation. *Lancet* 1994;**344**:1453–7.
31. Creinin MD, Lisman R, Strickler RC. Screening for factor V Leiden mutation before prescribing combination oral contraceptives. *Fertility and Sterility* 1999;**72**:646–51.
32. Feher G, Feher A, Pusch G, *et al.* The genetics of antiplatelet resistance. *Clinical Genetics* 2009;**75**:1–18.
33. Say RE, Thomson R. The importance of patient preferences in treatment decisions: challenges for doctors. *BMJ* 2003;**327**:542–5.
34. Caldwell JG. Evaluating attitudes of first-year residents to shared decision making. *Medical Education Online* 2008;**13**:10.
35. Foster C. Autonomy should chair not rule. *Lancet* 2010;**375**:368–9.

In modern healthcare two types of trade-off have to be made in deciding about the appropriate use of therapeutic interventions in populations of patients. Decision-makers have to decide on the overall balance between an intervention's risks and benefits and the balance between its benefits and costs.

## Risk–benefit decisions

National drug regulatory authorities, such as the Food and Drug Administration (FDA) in the USA and the European Medicines Agency in the European Union (EU), make overall risk–benefit decisions about pharmaceutical products. Analogous decisions about the risks and benefits of devices are also made at a national level, although the detailed arrangements criteria vary. No country has established formal systems for undertaking risk–benefit assessments of new (or existing) interventional procedures, although there are voluntary systems in place in Australia and the UK.

There is a voluminous amount of literature on the scientific basis that should underpin risk–benefit decisions about therapeutic interventions, and much of this book is devoted to the subject. There is very little empirical evidence about how decision-makers in, for example, drug regulatory authorities reach their conclusions. The account that follows is, therefore, drawn heavily from personal experience[1] and by analogy with other fields.

In making risk–benefit decisions for populations, there are usually three possible conclusions that can be drawn. First, decision-makers may conclude that an intervention is safe and effective across the full range of clinical indications for which it is appropriate. Second, decision-makers may decide that an intervention should be used in more narrowly defined circumstances because it is only in identifiable subgroups of patients that the benefits outweigh the risks. Third, decision-makers may consider that there are no circumstances under which an intervention's benefits outweigh the risks and that it should be unavailable for general use. Such decisions can be based on one of three broad approaches:[2]

- formal analysis;
- comparative analysis;
- judgement.

### Formal analysis

Where there is clear evidence that an intervention produces harm, with no evidence of benefit, decision-making is straightforward, even if not always popular. The CAST study[3] (see Case study 2.4.1 in Chapter 2.4) is a clear example. In this trial there was an excess of deaths or cardiac arrests in patients randomized to a *class 1 antiarrhythmic agent* during the weeks and months after acute myocardial infarction, compared with controls randomized to placebo. Similarly, the Women's Health Initiative Trial of hormone replacement therapy[4] (see Case study 2.4.2 in Chapter 2.4) showed no benefits but showed significant *harms* (breast cancer).

In circumstances where there are indeed benefits but also harms, formal analysis may often be helpful to decision-makers. The administration of a thrombolytic agent for the treatment of acute myocardial infarction causes 1–2 haemorrhagic strokes per 1000 patients treated in the first few hours after administration but prevents 20–30 deaths per 1000 treated patients.[5] Even if the mortality rate for haemorrhagic stroke induced by thrombolytic treatment was 100 per cent (it is actually less than 50 per cent), the benefits clearly outweigh the small, albeit tragic, risk.

In many instances, however, the benefits and risks are less easily compared with such a simple type of analysis. This especially applies when the benefits and harms involve different types of health outcome. In a *meta-analysis* of published randomized controlled trials, the antiobesity agent rimonabant produced a mean reduction in weight of 4.7 kg (95% confidence interval (CI) 4.1 to 5.3) at one year compared with placebo.[6] The *odds ratio* for achieving a 10 per cent reduction in weight over this same time period was 5.1 (95% CI 3.2 to 7.3), with a *number needed to treat* of six (95% CI 4 to 8). This meta-analysis, however, also showed an overall increase in *adverse events* (odds ratio 1.35, 95% CI 1.13 to 1.60). Of particular concern were the number of patients withdrawn for anxiety (odds ratio 3.03, 95% CI 1.09 to 8.42) and depression (odds ratio 2.51, 95% CI 1.23 to 5.12). The *number needed to harm* for depression was 49 (95% CI 19 to 316) and for anxiety was 116 (95% CI 47 to 3,716). A later meta-analysis of the harms associated with rimonabant reached similar conclusions.[7]

In situations such as this, a formal analysis is hardly possible. Attempting to balance quantitatively the number needed to treat of six (for a ten per cent reduction in weight at one year) with the numbers needed to harm of 25 (all adverse events), 49 (depression), 59 (*serious adverse events*) and 116 (anxiety) makes no sense. In circumstances such as these, decision-makers have to exercise judgement about whether overall the benefits outweigh the harms. In this instance the European regulatory authority concluded that the benefits of rimonabant did not override its harmful effects and the product was withdrawn from the EU market in 2008.

Several suggestions have been made to develop better methods for undertaking formal analyses of risk–benefit decisions. The focus of interest has been concerned largely with attempting to measure patients' preferences for specific health states that include both the benefits and harms of an intervention. One approach, the Quality-Adjusted Time Without Symptoms of Disease and Toxicity of Treatment (Q-TWiST), compares interventions in terms of achieved survival and quality-of-life outcomes.[8] The Probability Trade-Off Technique (PTT) attempts to capture patients' subjective assessments of the *efficacy/toxicity* trade-off.[9] There has also been interest in using the technique of Multi-Criteria Decision Analysis (MCDA), which has been used widely in other fields, especially engineering. This approach seeks to take explicit account of multiple criteria in helping individuals or groups explore critical decisions. It provides an ordering of options from the most to the least preferred. It is based on models similar to the decision tree described in Chapter 5.1, with preferences and probabilities based on the values of either patients or decision-makers.[10]

Although these approaches have attractions, there are difficulties in their implementation. All would require assigning patients' preferences to the possible health states following the initiation of treatment. This itself is a formidable exercise and has not, as far as I am aware, been started. Whether the findings from such analytical approaches would have traction with patients, health professionals, politicians and the public is equally unknown.

## Comparative analysis

In some circumstances, comparing the harms of two or more interventions with similar *effectiveness* can provide a useful approach to decision-making. For example, the withdrawal from the market of a number of non-steroidal anti-inflammatory and antidepressant drugs during the 1980s and 1990s was based on such a principle.[11]

Comparative analysis played an important role in the withdrawal (in the EU) and severe restrictions on the use (in the US) of rosiglitazone. Rosiglitazone and pioglitazone, introduced in 1999 and 2000, respectively, are thiozolidinediones used for the treatment of type 2 diabetes. They reduce blood glucose by increasing insulin sensitivity in peripheral tissues to a similar extent. Both are associated with fluid retention and an increased risk of fractures.[12] In 2007, separate systematic reviews based on the results of randomized controlled trials on the cardiovascular *safety* of rosiglitazone and pioglitazone were published.[13,14] These suggested an increased risk of myocardial infarction with rosiglitazone (*odds ratio* 1.43, 95% CI 1.03 to 1.98) but not with pioglitazone (*hazard ratio* 0.81, 95% CI 0.64 to 1.02). These findings were largely replicated in two extensive observational studies comparing the cardiovascular risks of patients undergoing routine treatment with these products.[15,16]

In deciding what action should be taken in such circumstances, decision-makers, in this case drug regulatory authorities and their expert advisors, have to take various considerations into account. First, they have to decide whether the products are indeed therapeutically equivalent. Although equivalence may have been confirmed, or at least inferred, from the results of formal studies, there are sometimes lingering doubts as to whether there are individuals – unidentifiable from clinical trials – who gain greater benefit from one product than from another. Withdrawal from the market would be disadvantageous to them. Second, the strength of the evidence of greater harm with one product over another (in this case, rosiglitazone versus pioglitazone) has to be evaluated. In this instance there was apparent conflict between the results of the meta-analyses and observational studies on the one hand with the findings of a large ($n = 4447$) randomized controlled trial[17,18] comparing rosiglitazone with a combination of metformin and a sulfonylurea on the other hand. This trial, however, has itself been the subject of criticism.[19]

In this instance, the European Medicines Agency and the FDA made different decisions about the continuing availability of rosiglitazone. Both considered rosiglitazone to be more harmful than pioglitazone. The European Medicines Agency recommended that the marketing authorization (i.e. the licence) for rosiglitazone should be suspended in the EU.[20] On the other hand, the FDA decided that rosiglitazone should be prescribed only for patients who could not achieve control of their blood sugar with other medicines.[21]

In such circumstances where there is great complexity decision-makers have to draw conclusions based on their assessment of the evidence, the needs of patients, and the legal and cultural environment.

## Judgement

In all risk–benefit decisions, judgements must be made. Decision-makers will necessarily have to make scientific judgements about the nature and quality of the available evidence. In some circumstances, these judgements may lead, by formal or comparative analyses, to a clear-cut decision. In most circumstances, when the trade-off between benefit and risk cannot be formulated in such an analytical way, decision-makers have to exercise judgement in reaching their conclusions.

*Therapeutics, evidence and decision-making*

The judgemental approach necessarily has to take into account the nature and extent of the benefits and harms with a series of questions. For benefits, these questions include the nature, severity and prognosis of the condition(s) for which the intervention will be used. It will also include the extent, magnitude and duration of action of any (or all) the benefits that have been identified as attributable to the intervention under consideration, and the benefits provided by alternative interventions. For the risks, decision-makers will seek to consider the nature, severity and frequency of all associated adverse effects. Additionally, decision-makers will need to take into account the risks and benefits of alternative (if any) forms of treatment.

In weighing these factors, and making appropriate conclusions, decision-makers will draw upon cognitive processes that will encompass intuition and experience as well as their individual personal prejudices and biases. There are, in other words, strong subjective – as well as objective – elements to the conclusions that are reached. Individual decision-makers therefore need to be aware of how risk-averse or risk-tolerant they are. They need to appreciate their prejudices for and against particular forms of treatment, and they should try to imagine themselves being patients for whom the intervention might be used.

Judgemental decision-making is hard to learn and even harder to teach. The judgements of one group of decision-makers may differ from those of another, even when confronted with the same evidence. Judgements, moreover, can be difficult to explain or defend.

# Cost-effectiveness decisions

As discussed in Chapter 5.1, all healthcare systems are funded, to a greater or lesser extent, by a combination of public and private sources. All, and also to a greater or lesser extent, are financially constrained. In determining whether an intervention represents good or appropriate use of the available resources for healthcare, decision-makers have to make two types of value judgement:[22]

- scientific value judgements;
- social value judgements.

## Scientific value judgements

I have emphasized throughout this book that in evaluating the clinical effectiveness of therapeutic interventions, decision-makers must make scientific value judgements based on the totality of the available evidence of both clinical and cost-effectiveness. Relying on hierarchies of evidence is no substitute.

### ■ Clinical effectiveness

In practice, the evidence for an intervention's clinical *effectiveness* will usually be derived from a combination of experimental and observational studies. These may be pooled in a systematic review that incorporates one or more meta-analyses. Decision-makers will need, in particular, to make judgements about five components of the clinical evidence base:[23]

- *The strengths and limitations of the systematic review:* although systematic reviewing is based on accepted principles (see Chapter 1.6), judgements are needed in deciding which studies should be included and in the interpretation of the results. Different inclusion and exclusion criteria used in the review will lead to different conclusions.

- *The comparator:* in assessing the incremental benefits of an intervention in comparison with current standard practice, the comparator is critically important. Decision-makers therefore need to judge the relevance of the comparator used in the analysis. Moreover, because many studies of new products are compared with placebo rather than an active comparator used in current clinical care, the analysis often involves indirect or *mixed treatment comparisons* (see Chapter 1.5), which adds complexity.[24]
- *The endpoints used in the relevant studies:* the data for *effectiveness* often rely heavily on surrogate outcomes or other *biomarkers* (see Chapter 1.3). In only a minority of primary research studies is the *health-related quality of life* measured. Decision-makers will need to exercise judgement in assessing the relevance of endpoints based on biomarkers and in the way in which quality-of-life measures have been imputed.
- *The time scale of the studies:* clinical trials rarely last for more than 6–12 months, yet for chronic diseases the treatments usually continue throughout life.
- *The generalizability (external validity) of the available data:* despite the advantages of randomized controlled trials with respect to their *internal validity* (see Chapter 2.1), their relatively small scale and homogeneous patient populations can render the real impact of treatment uncertain (see Chapter 2.5). Observational data can assist the evaluation of generalizability but will be absent in the case of new products.

All of these considerations demand scientific value judgements to be made by decision-makers. These judgements will be informed by the science but are nevertheless judgements.

### ■ Cost-effectiveness

Most economic evaluations are based on economic models (see Chapter 5.1). Modelling requires judgements to be made by both modellers and decision-makers. The inputs to the model will be all those necessary to assess the incremental costs and benefits.

- *Incremental costs:* the cost differences between the intervention under consideration and standard care will include not only the price of acquiring the intervention itself but also other costs (see Chapter 5.1). These may include the requirements for hospital admission, the input from nursing and other clinical staff, the additional costs of monitoring the response to treatment, and the costs of treating any adverse effects. These costs may be subject to considerable uncertainty. For example, what is current best practice in the management of febrile neutropenia with anticancer drugs? And how much does it cost?
- *Incremental benefits:* the benefits may include increased overall survival for an intervention that extends life expectancy; enhanced quality of life, especially for interventions used in the treatment of chronic diseases; the time in different health states; and the valuation of these states on a *utility* scale for a cost–utility analysis.

In making judgements about these issues, decision-makers will often – rightly – draw on the advice of both experts in a particular field and patients with experience of the condition. This will enable the most plausible incremental cost–effectiveness ratio to be estimated.

### ■ Distributive justice

Once decision-makers have reached a conclusion about an intervention's most plausible incremental cost–effectiveness ratio, a decision must be made as to whether the increased benefits are worth the increased costs. In this, they are (or should be) influenced by the principles of distributive justice.

*Therapeutics, evidence and decision-making*

Distributive justice is the term used by moral and political philosophers in discussing what is right or just in the allocation of goods within society. Three moral theories of distributive justice – libertarianism, utilitarianism and egalitarianism – have a particular resonance for setting priorities in healthcare:[25]

- *Libertarianism* is based on the premise that individuals should be able and expected to finance their healthcare through their own efforts, and that market forces should enable them to do so at a reasonable price. This approach underpins much of the provision of healthcare in the USA, but most other developed nations attempt to provide healthcare to their citizens on the basis of social solidarity.[26] However, even in the USA, nearly 50 per cent of the population's healthcare is covered by public funds, including the Medicare, Medicaid and Veterans Administration programmes.
- *Utilitarianism* in its purist form considers distributive justice to be best served by maximizing social utility. Utilitarians expect healthcare expenditure to be distributed in a manner that maximizes the welfare of the population as a whole. The principle is often expressed as 'the greatest good for the greatest number' and has unquestionable attractions. It places a premium on efficiency. It asserts that using ineffective or costly interventions in one area of clinical practice will deprive other patients of cost-effective care. Utilitarianism, however, has disadvantages. It can allow the interests of minorities to be overridden by the majority. It has little to offer in eradicating health inequalities. And its emphasis on efficiency can have perverse solutions: for example, the original prioritized list of healthcare services in the original Oregon scheme based on efficiency produced a rank order that placed tooth-capping above emergency surgery for ectopic pregnancy and acute appendicitis![27]
- *Egalitarianism* seeks to distribute healthcare resources to allow each individual to have a fair share of the opportunities available. It allows an adequate but not necessarily maximum level of healthcare but raises questions as to what is fair and what is bad luck.

The tensions between utilitarianism and egalitarianism can be overstated. Many utilitarians accept that social values could (and should) be incorporated into their approach to distributive justice. *Qualified egalitarians* also accept the concept of *opportunity costs* with all its moral implications. There is, however, no formal synthesis of these two theories of distributive justice. Both clash at some point with the convictions of many people. Each approach articulates ideas that most would be reluctant to relinquish. Where one theory is weak, the other is strong.[25] Some middle way has to be found.

The middle way is *procedural justice*. Daniels and Sabin have proposed that in setting healthcare priorities, procedural justice requires four conditions to be met if decisions are to pass their test of 'accountability for reasonableness'.[28] They assert that if priority setting in healthcare is to gain broad acceptance and legitimacy, then the process must ensure *publicity*, *relevance*, *revision* and *regulation*. For 'publicity', Daniels and Sabin require that both the decisions themselves and the reasons for them are made public. 'Relevance' insists that the grounds for making decisions are those that fair-minded people would agree are relevant for meeting healthcare needs, especially where resources are constrained. 'Revision' refers to the premise that there must be opportunities for challenging decisions and mechanisms for resolving disputes. And 'regulation' requires that there should be some voluntary or statutory process to ensure that the first three conditions are met.

It is implicit in 'accountability for reasonableness' that decision-makers draw conclusions about clinical and cost-effectiveness on a case-by-case basis.[23] To set a **213** fixed and rigid incremental cost-effectiveness threshold would imply that efficiency has an absolute priority over other objectives such as fairness. The empirical basis for deciding the precise value at which such a threshold should be set still remains weak (see Chapter 5.1). Suppliers of interventions such as pharmaceuticals and devices are monopolists and a fixed threshold could be taken to imply a definite price that would discourage price competition. Finally, rigid adherence to an incremental cost-effectiveness threshold would create the impression that decision-makers had accepted all the related assumptions used in estimating the incremental cost-effectiveness ratio. It would therefore remove the discretion of decision-makers to assess costs and benefits when modelling had reached its limits.

There are special circumstances, based on social value judgements, when decision-makers should reflect, in drawing their conclusions, societal preferences in the allocation of resources. The UK's National Institute for Health and Clinical Excellence (NICE) has identified six 'special circumstances' to which it expects its decision-making bodies to give special weight when drawing conclusions about cost-effectiveness:[23]

- *Severity of the underlying illness:* although the relatively inexpensive relief of mild discomfort could give an equivalent incremental cost-effectiveness ratio to the expensive relief of a very serious condition, society would give priority to the latter. NICE therefore expects its decision-making bodies to give more generous consideration to the acceptability of an incremental cost–effectiveness ratio in serious conditions.
- *End-of-life treatments:* NICE recognizes that members of the public place special value on treatments that prolong life – even for a few months – at the end of life, provided that the extension of life is of reasonable quality and at least pain-free if not disability-free.
- *Patient advocacy:* patients and their advocates play an important role in shaping the views of NICE's decision-making bodies. Most particularly, they can explain from their own experience when their condition has been poorly reflected in the clinical trials because, for example, the most severely affected were not distinguished or were not included. Equally importantly, patients can describe the extent to which their symptoms have been reflected inadequately in the measurement of health-related quality of life. In a number of instances, as indicated in Table 6.2.1, patients and their advocates significantly influenced the acceptance of higher incremental cost-effectiveness ratios.
- *Significant innovation:* there may be circumstances where the advantages of an innovative intervention, defined as one that produces a demonstrable and distinct benefit of a substantial nature, may not have been captured adequately in the quality of life measure used.
- *Disadvantaged populations:* some healthcare systems, such as that in the UK, give priority to improving the health of the least advantaged members of the population, particularly poorer people and people from ethnic minorities.
- *Children:* NICE recognizes that assessing health-related quality of life in children is methodologically challenging. It understands that society would generally favour children being afforded 'the benefit of the doubt'. Consequently, NICE's advisory bodies tend to take a liberal approach in their assessment of products for use in children.

Examples of the application of these 'special factors' by NICE's decision-making bodies are shown in Table 6.2.1.

**Table 6.2.1** Special circumstances in the approval of some products with incremental cost-effectiveness ratios (ICER) over £30 000 per quality-adjusted life-year gained[23]

| Topic | ICER (£000s) | Severity | End of life | Patients and advocates | Significant innovation | Disadvantaged population | Children |
|---|---|---|---|---|---|---|---|
| Riluzole (motor neurone disease) | 38–42 | ✓ | ✓ | ✓ | | | |
| Trastuzumab (advanced breast cancer) | 37.5 | ✓ | | | ✓ | | |
| Imatinib (chronic myeloid leukaemia) | 36–65 | ✓ | | | ✓ | | |
| Pemetrexed (malignant mesothelioma) | 34.5 | ✓ | ✓ | | | ✓ | |
| Ranibizumab (macular degeneration) | >>30 | ✓ | | ✓ | ✓ | | |
| Omalizumab (severe asthma) | >30 | ✓ | | ✓ | ✓ | | |
| Sunitinib (advanced renal cancer) | 50 | ✓ | ✓ | ✓ | ✓ | | |
| Lenalidomide (multiple myeloma) | 43 | ✓ | ✓ | | ✓ | | |
| Somatotropin (growth hormone deficiency) | n/a* | | | ✓ | ✓ | | ✓ |
| Chronic insulin infusions (childhood type 1 diabetes) | n/a* | | | ✓ | | | ✓ |

n/a, not applicable.
*No ICER could be estimated.

# Discussion

Although they may appear to be different, decisions about balancing benefits and risks and cost and effectiveness have many features in common. In both types of decision-making there are five crucial elements:

- *Robustness:* decision-makers need to ensure that their conclusions are based on their assessment of the totality of the evidence base.
- *Transparency:* decision-makers should ensure that the process and methods by which their decisions are made are in the public domain. Moreover, the reasons for their decisions, and the evidence on which they are based, should also be available for public scrutiny.
- *Inclusiveness:* the decision-making process should enable all those with a legitimate interest in the intervention under scrutiny to be able to contribute to the review process. Those with legitimate interests include the relevant manufacturer(s), professional bodies, payers (in publicly funded healthcare systems) and patients' organizations. This requirement is not only predicated on fairness but also ensures that decision-makers have access to expert and other relevant opinion before reaching their conclusions.
- *Independence:* decision-makers must be independent of any inappropriate political, commercial or professional interests. Their decisions should not advantage or disadvantage them in any way.
- *Contestability:* except in emergencies, decision-makers should ensure that their decisions can be challenged by those with relevant interests. Decision-makers should also have the opportunity to review and revise their decisions in the light of significant new evidence.

These elements to decision-making are often difficult to fulfil. The evidence base is always imperfect and incomplete. Decision-makers will be tempted to demand additional or more robust data before reaching their conclusions. However, decisions have to be made on the information that is available. In balancing both risk and benefit and cost and effectiveness, decision-makers have to reach defensible conclusions on the evidence before them. Making no decision or maintaining the status quo is, in effect, a decision.

The requirement for transparency can cause two particular difficulties. First, where critical elements of the evidence base have been provided in confidence, decision-makers may find themselves in some difficulty in explaining their decisions to others. In these circumstances decision-makers should make every attempt to persuade those providing data in confidence to allow the essential information to be publicly available. Second, public confidence in the decision-making process is enhanced if decision-makers' deliberations are held in public. Some individual decision-makers are uncomfortable discussing data, expressing opinions and drawing conclusions in the presence of an audience. In my view, decision-makers who are not prepared to deliberate in public should not be involved in making decisions that have an impact on the public or on public health.

Even then, however, there may be limits. Some decisions have an impact on the share price of the manufacturer of an intervention, and limiting public disclosure of the decision only to those able to attend the meeting would breach stock exchange rules. Under such circumstances there are two potential solutions: either webcast the proceedings (as is the case with meetings of the FDA's advisory committees) or hold the discussion in public and leave the final decision-making to be made in private (as is the case with meetings of NICE's appraisal committees).

In ensuring transparency, giving all stakeholders the opportunity to provide evidence to decision-makers also has its challenges. Manufacturers generally have many opportunities to provide decision-makers with evidence. Experts, too, are generally given a platform that allows their views to be made known. The greatest problem is with providing patients and their families an opportunity to contribute effectively. Various attempts have been made, but none is entirely satisfactory. Patients and their families are able, at meetings of the FDA's advisory committees, to formally provide written and oral testimony. At meetings of NICE's appraisal committees, patients and the representatives of relevant patients' organizations are given the opportunity to express their opinions in writing and orally. No one has yet, however, used a process whereby the views of a representative group of relevant patients can be formally assessed and presented to decision-makers alongside the conventional evidence about risks and benefits or costs and effectiveness. Although this might be of a qualitative rather than quantitative nature, I believe that decision-making would be substantially improved by the development of appropriate methods.

Independence means not only ensuring that decision-makers will not gain any pecuniary rewards in relation to the decisions they make, but also that there are no reputational interests. Decision-makers who have made significant contributions to the evidence on which the decision is based can provide invaluable expert testimony. However, they may find it difficult, if not impossible, to form reliable judgements about the implications of the evidence base as a whole.

Finally, decision-makers should remember that their decisions will rarely be welcomed by all commentators. Irrespective of the conclusions they reach, some manufacturers, professional groups or patients' groups will feel disadvantaged. In all decisions about the balance between risk and benefit, or cost and benefit, there will be those who agree and those who do not. Decision-makers must therefore have courage. They should invariably draw their conclusions on what, overall, is best for patients and the public.

Decision-makers will never be loved but, in the long term, they should seek to earn respect. While politicians and legislators should, of course, set the overall boundaries for decisions, most lack the expertise to make appropriate expert judgements on the evidence. They are also inherently unable to avoid incorporating their electoral prospects in drawing conclusions.[28] For this reason, above all others, elected politicians cannot make decisions of this nature.

## References

1. Rawlins MD. Risk–benefit decisions in licensing changes. In: Walker SR, Asscher AW (eds). *Medicines and Risk/Benefit Decisions.* Lancaster: MTP Press, 1987.

2. Fischhoff B, Lichtenstein S, Slovic P, *et al. Acceptable risk.* Cambridge: Cambridge University Press, 1981.

3. Echt DS, Liebson PR, Mitchell LB, *et al.* Mortality and morbidity in patients receiving encainide, flecainide or placebo: the Cardiac Arrhythmia Suppression Trial. *New England Journal of Medicine* 1991;**324**:781–6.

4. Women's Health Initiative Investigators. Risks and benefits of estrogen plus progestogen in healthy postmenopausal women. *Journal of the American Medical Association* 2002;**288**:321–33.

5. Boland A, Dundar Y, Bagust A, *et al.* Early thrombolysis for the treatment of acute myocardial infarction: a systematic review and economic evaluation. *Health Technology Assessment* 2003;**7**:1–136.

6. Christensen R, Kristensen P, Bartels EM, *et al.* Efficacy and safety of the weight-loss drug rimonabant: a meta-analysis of randomised trials. *Lancet* 2007;**370**:1706–13.

7. Chavez-Tapia NC, Tellez-Avila FI, Bedogni G, *et al.* Systematic review and meta-analysis on the adverse effects of rimonabant treatment: considerations for its potential use in hepatology. *BMC Gastroenterology* 2009;**9**:75.

8. Gelber RD, Cole BF, Gelber S, Goldhirsch A. The Q-TwiST method. In: Spilker B (ed.). *Quality of Life and Pharmacoeconomics in Clinical Trials*. Philadelphia, PA: Lippencott-Raven, 1996.

9. Troche CJ, Paltiel AD, Makuch RW. Evaluation of therapeutic strategies: a new method for balancing benefit and risk. *Value in Health* 2000;**3**:12–22.

10. Mussen F, Salek S, Walker S. A quantitative approach to benefit–risk assessment of medicines: part 1. The development of a new model using multi-criteria decision analysis. *Pharmacoepidemiology and Drug Safety* 2007;**16**:S2–16.

11. Rawlins MD. Pharmacovigilance: paradise lost, regained or postponed? *Journal of the Royal College of Physicians* 1995;**29**:41–8.

12. National Prescribing Centre. More on glitazone safety: how do pioglitazone and rosiglitazone compare? MeReC Rapid Review. www.npci.org.uk/blog/?p=524.

13. Nissen SE, Wolski K. Effect of rosiglitazone on the risk of myocardial infarction and death from cardiovascular causes. *New England Journal of Medicine* 2007;**356**:2457–71.

14. Lincoff AM, Wolski K, Nicholls SJ, Nissen SE. Pioglitazone and risk of cardiovascular events in patients with type 2 diabetes: meta-analysis of randomized trials. *Journal of the American Medical Association* 2007;**298**:1180–88.

15. Juurlink DN, Gomes T, Lipscombe LL, *et al.* Adverse cardiovascular events during treatment with pioglitazone and rosiglitazone: population based cohort study. *BMJ* 2009;**339**:b2942.

16. Graham DJ, Oullet-Hellstrom, MaCurdy TE, *et al.* Risk of acute myocardial infarction, stroke, heart failure, and death in elderly Medicare patients treated with rosiglitazone or pioglitazone. *Journal of the American Medical Association* 2010;**304**:411–18.

17. Home PD, Pocock SJ, Beck-Nielsen H, *et al.* Rosiglitazone evaluated for cardiovascular outcomes: an interim analysis. *New England Journal of Medicine* 2007;**357**:28–38.

18. Home PD, Pocock SJ, Beck-Nielsen H, *et al.* Rosiglitazone evaluated for cardiovascular outcomes in oral agent combination therapy for type 2 diabetes (RECORD): a multicentre, randomised, open-label trial. *Lancet* 2009;**373**:2125–35.

19. DeAngelis CD, Fontanarosa PB. Ensuring integrity in industry-sponsored research: primum non nocere, revisited. *Journal of the American Medical Association* 2010;**303**:1196–8.

20. European Medicines Agency. European Medicines Agency recommends suspension of Avandia, Avandamet and Avaglim. www.ema.europa.eu/ema/index.jsp?curl=pages/medicines/human/public_health_alerts/2010/09/human_pha_detail_000020.jsp&murl=menus/medicines/medicines.jsp&mid=&jsenabled=true.

21. US Food and Drug Administration. Briefing on Avandia. www.fda.gov/Drugs/DrugSafety/PostmarketDrugSafetyInformationforPatientsandProviders/ucm227934.htm

22. Rawlins MD, Culyer AJ. National Institute for Health and Clinical Effectiveness and its social value judgements. *BMJ* 2004;**329**:224–7.

23. Rawlins MD, Barnett DB, Stevens A. Pharmacoeconomics: NICE's approach to decision-making. *British Journal of Clinical Pharmacology* 2010;**70**:346–9.

24. Sutton A, Ades A, Abrams K, Cooper N. Briefing paper for Methods Review Workshop on Evidence Synthesis (Indirect and Mixed Treatment Comparisons). London: National Institute for Health and Clinical Excellence, 2008.

25. Beachamp TL, Childress JF. *Principles of Biomedical Ethics*. Oxford: Oxford University Press, 2001.

26. Rawlins MD. Pharmacopolitics and deliberative democracy. *Clinical Medicine* 2005;**5**:471–5.

27. Haddorn DC. Setting health care priorities in Oregon: cost-effectiveness meets the rule of rescue. *Journal of the American Medical Association* 1991;**265**:2218–25.

28. Daniels N, Sabin JE. *Setting Limits Fairly: Can We Learn to Share Medical Resources?* Oxford: Oxford University Press, 2002.

29. Guttman A, Thompson D. *Democracy and Disagreement.* Cambridge, MA: The Beknal Press of the Harvard University Press, 1996.

30. Dashle T, Lambrew JM, Greenberger SS. *Critical: What We Can Do About the Health-Care Crisis.* New York: St Martin's Press, 2008.

FOR POPULATIONS

# Glossary

**Absolute risk**  The probability of an event or outcome among the participants in a clinical study.

**Absolute risk reduction**  The difference between the risk rates among participants receiving two interventions. Synonymous with attributable risk reduction and risk difference.

**Attributable risk reduction**  *See* Absolute risk reduction.

**Adverse drug reaction**  Any unwanted (harmful) event occurring after exposure to an intervention and that is caused by the intervention. The term 'harm(s)' is preferred by some.

**Adverse event**  Any unwanted (harmful) event occurring after exposure to an intervention. It may or may not be caused by the intervention.

**Bias**  Systematic (as opposed to random) deviation of the results of a study from the 'true' results.

**Biomarker**  An intermediate outcome of efficacy or safety used to assess whether an intervention appears to possess biological activity. Whether a biomarker is a harbinger of therapeutic benefit (or harm) may be less clear.

**Class 1 antiarrhythmic agent**  Interferes with the sodium channel, producing a membrane-stabilizing effect. Used particularly in the treatment of ventricular arrhythmias.

**Complex intervention**  Therapeutic or preventive intervention with a number of components, which may act both independently and interdependently. Examples include psychological treatments and physiotherapy.

**Confounding**  A distortion of the apparent effect of an intervention on an outcome when the outcome itself is influenced by an independent factor distributed unequally between treatment groups.

**Deductive inference**  Inferring, from a premise or a hypothesis, a prediction that can then be tested by empirical study.

**Direct comparison**  A head-to-head comparison of two or more interventions for the same indication.

**Discounting**  A procedure for reducing costs and benefits over time. It is based on the premise that costs and benefits are valued more highly today than in the future.

**Economic perspective**  The viewpoint from which an economic evaluation is undertaken, such as that of the individual, the healthcare system or wider society.

**Effectiveness**  The extent to which an intervention produces an overall health benefit when used in routine clinical care.

**Efficacy**  The extent to which an intervention produces a health benefit when studied under ideal circumstances.

**External validity**  The extent to which the results of a study are likely to hold true in normal clinical practice (synonymous with generalizability).

**Generalizability**  *See* External validity.

**Grey literature**  Written material that is not formally published in books or journals. It includes government reports, newspaper and magazine articles, manufacturers' literature and consumer brochures.

**Gross domestic product**  The total expenditure within an economy on domestically produced goods and services within a year.

**Harms**  Any unwanted (harmful) event occurring after exposure to an intervention and that is caused by the intervention.

**Hazard ratio**  The probability in a survival analysis that, if an event in question has not already occurred, then the event will happen in the next (short) time interval.

**Health-related quality of life**  The combination of a person's physical, mental and social wellbeing.

**Incidence**  The number of new cases of a condition during a specific time period.

**Incident cases**  Newly occurring cases of a disease (usually in relation to case–control studies).

**Inductive inference**  The construction of a premise or hypothesis on the basis of one or more observations.

**Incremental cost–effectiveness ratio**  The ratio of the difference between the mean costs of two alternative interventions and the mean difference in their benefits. Synonymous with marginal cost–effectiveness ratio.

**Indirect comparison**  A comparison of two interventions that have not been compared directly in a head-to-head trial. *See also* Direct comparison.

**Intermediate outcome (endpoint)**  Outcome that may be related to the outcome of interest but is more easily and quickly assessed. *See also* Biomarker and Surrogate outcome (endpoint).

**Internal validity**  The extent to which the results of a study approximate to the 'truth' for the participants recruited into the study. It is dependent on the integrity of the study's design.

**Log rank test**  A test in a survival analysis of the hypothesis of no difference between two populations in the time-specific probability of a particular event.

**Marginal cost–effectiveness ratio**  *See also* Incremental cost–effectiveness ratio.

**Meta-analysis**  A technique for combining (pooling) the results of a number of studies addressing the same question and reporting the same outcomes.

**Mixed treatment comparison**   An analysis that compares two or more interventions using a combination of direct and indirect comparisons. *See also* Direct comparison.

**Multiplicity**   In statistics, the problem of multiple statistical testing with the likelihood of obtaining one or more false positive results.

**Number needed to harm**   The number of patients needed to be treated with a particular intervention to produce one additional harmful outcome.

**Number needed to treat**   The number of patients needed to be treated with a particular intervention to produce one additional beneficial outcome.

**Odds**   The ratio of the number of people treated with an intervention who develop an outcome of interest to the number of people who do not develop the same outcome of interest.

**Odds ratio**   The ratio of the odds of a particular outcome of interest in two groups.

**Opportunity cost**   The cost of displacing one intervention by introducing another, more expensive one.

**Phase 1 study**   Initial pharmacological study, often in healthy volunteers, and usually involving fewer than 100 participants, of a new pharmaceutical product.

**Phase 2 study**   Early dose-ranging study of the safety and efficacy of a new product in patients for whom it might be indicated eventually. Efficacy may be inferred from changes in intermediate endpoints (i.e. relevant biomarkers or surrogate markers). Such studies are usually conducted in around 1000 participants.

**Phase 3 study**   Study designed to confirm the safety of a new pharmacological product over a longer period and in a more heterogeneous patient population. Efficacy is likely to be based on the effects on ultimate endpoints rather than intermediate endpoints. Studies may involve 2000 or more participants.

**Phase 4 study**   Further study of the efficacy and safety of a product after licensing (marketing authorization), usually against one or more active comparators.

**Phocomelia**   A congenital disorder arising from underdevelopment of the long bones in the arms and legs. It arose in babies whose mothers were prescribed thalidomide in the late 1950s. Most cases now are genetic (autosomal recessive) in origin.

**Prevalence**   The proportion of a population in which a particular medical condition prevails at a particular date (point prevalence) or over a period (period prevalence).

**Prevalent cases**   Existing cases of a disease (usually in relation to case–control studies).

**Rate ratio**   The ratio of the rates of a particular outcome in two groups.

**Relative risk**   The ratio of the risk rates of a particular outcome in two groups. Synonymous with risk ratio.

**Risk difference**   *See* Absolute risk reduction.

**Risk rate**   The ratio of the number of people treated with an intervention developing an outcome of interest to the total number exposed. *See also* Odds.

**Risk ratio**   *See* Relative risk.

**Safety**   Protection against the adverse effects of an intervention.

**Serious adverse event**   An adverse event that causes death, permanent disability or a prolongation of a hospital stay.

**Side effect**   Strictly defined, an adverse reaction to an intervention that inevitably accompanies the intervention's beneficial effects. In common usage, however, side effects are synonymous with adverse drug reactions.

**Standard mean difference**   A summary statistic used in meta-analyses when the same outcome is measured in more than one way. It is calculated from the mean difference of the outcomes in two groups divided by the standard deviation of the outcomes among participants. The method necessarily assumes that the differences in standard deviations among studies reflect differences in the measurement scales.

**Surrogate outcome (endpoint)**   Biomarker that is a reliable substitute for a clinically relevant final endpoint that measures directly how a patient feels, functions or survives.

**Survival analysis**   The analysis of a trial in terms of time to an outcome, such as death.

**Toxicity**   The extent to which a substance can damage an organism.

**Type I error**   Rejection of the null hypothesis when it is true (i.e. a false negative conclusion).

**Type II error**   Acceptance of the null hypothesis when it is false (i.e. a false positive conclusion).

**Time trade-off**   A method used in assigning utilities to health states. For chronic diseases, it involves asking participants how much time they are willing to sacrifice from a given lifespan in one health state for a shorter number of years in perfect health. For short-term illnesses, the choice is between the illness for a period of time and a worse health state for a shorter period of time. The utility value for both is found from the point at which participants are indifferent to the available options.

**Ultimate outcome (endpoint)**   The ultimate goal of treatment, such as survival or death from a potentially fatal condition; or success or failure in the relief of a symptom such as pain.

**Utility**   A measure of an individual's preference for a specific health state in relation to alternative health states. The utility scale assigns values on a scale of 0 (dead) to 1 (perfect health).

# Index

Notes
Glossary pages have not been indexed
Pages numbers in **bold** refer to tables
Pages numbers in *italics* refer to figures

*Therapeutics, evidence and decision-making*

*Therapeutics, evidence and decision-making*